P9-DNB-545

LEMMON

LEMMON

A BIOGRAPHY

DON WIDENER

Macmillan Publishing Co., Inc.
NEW YORK
Collier Macmillan Publishers
LONDON

For
*J*OHN *and M*ILLIE

Macmillan Publishing Co., Inc.
866 Third Avenue, New York, N.Y. 10022
Collier Macmillan Canada, Ltd.

Library of Congress Cataloging in Publication Data

Widener, Don.
Lemmon: a biography.

Includes index.
1. Lemmon, Jack.
PN2287.L42W5 791.43'028'0924 [B] 75-25712
ISBN 0-02-628200-3

SECOND PRINTING 1975

Printed in the United States of America

Foreword

AT THE CONCLUSION of *The Adventures of Huckleberry Finn*, Huck said: ". . . and so there ain't nothing more to write about, and I am rotten glad of it, because if I'd 'a' knowed what a trouble it was to make a book I wouldn't 'a' tackled it, and I ain't a-going to no more."

I've never known a writer who didn't have feelings similar to Huck's when his book was over and done with. This siege of depression is bad with a novel, worse when it's a biography—because you are forced to confess a supreme arrogance in assuming you could do justice to a man's life in the first place. And there is small consolation in knowing that it just isn't possible to capture it all; that no writer ever has.

The plus side of this discomfiting situation also belongs to the biographer. For me there was the delightful experience of spending hundreds of hours in conversation with Jack Lemmon; talks that spanned more than a year. Bright, summery days on the beach at Trancas, California, and long, rainy winter afternoons at his home in Beverly Hills. I'll miss the chats and those great

Havanas of his we shared—the kind writers are always planning to smoke when their book sells.

Because it's Lemmon you're writing about there are other moments to treasure, interviews with his friends—some of them living legends: James Cagney, sharp as ever, instantly diagnosing that I'm left-handed by the way I removed my raincoat; the fabled Henry Fonda, looking no older than when he was Mister Roberts, and asking if it was okay to be unshaven for the interview; marvelous Robert Mitchum offering me a drink of something "deadly, really deadly," and then adding, comfortingly, "but it's expensive as hell!" And gracious Fred Astaire, making me feel important by asking my opinion of a new song he's written. There's this thing you learn about superstars; they really are super.

One more note. Whatever else it may be, this is an honest try at an honest book. From the beginning that's the way Jack wanted it. If a key was left unturned, a door unopened, it was an oversight by the writer. There was not a single question asked that Lemmon did not answer, and willingly.

There. It's finished. I suppose the best attitude to adopt is that of the corporal who faced the unenviable task of teaching radar to a roomful of generals. Said he: "There are probably two hundred guys in the country who know more about this subject than I do. But, since I don't see any of them here today, I will begin."

DON WIDENER
Northridge, Calif.
June 17, 1975

Acknowledgments

It would not be practical to list the many people who gave a helping hand to the *Lemmon* project. Some of them were interviewed and their names appear elsewhere in this book. I am indebted to Richard and Ruth Carter for their kindness, encouragement, and sharp insight; to Macmillan senior editor Ray Roberts for his expert advice; and to copy editor Lorraine Steurer, who did an outstanding job; to Victoria Brooks, always cheerfully interrupting her work to help with mine; to Charles Parker for many favors; and to Milton Farber for the solution to my "chemical" problem; to Reva Frederick for her assistance; and finally, to my beautiful wife Veda Rose, who critiqued every line with merciless candor.

Chapter I

"My, look at the little yellow Lemmon."
—*Nurse, Newton, Massachusetts*

IT'S NOT NICE to fool Mother Nature. If you try, she rains on you. Then how does it come to pass that one John Uhler Lemmon III slipped her a tub of oleo and came up roses? For the record, if Jack had been born a cat he would have been on the way to the river in burlap within the hour.

Study the man and you come away consumed with the suspicion that, somewhere up there, a saintly Neil Simon in the sky is roughing in a script that Lemmon but follows. It's all there in the neat formula plotting; in the way incidents always pay off and pat situations abound. It's even money that when all the subplots have been worked in and the conflicts resolved, they'll go with a two-shot happy ending.

Take the opening, which is unlikely. Lemmon was born February 8, 1925—in an elevator at Newton-Wellesley Hospital in Newton, Massachusetts, a suburb of Boston. The elevator scene needed a little extra something, so Jack came in with acute jaundice and one testicle that refused to drop. A nurse supplied the comic relief with: "My, look at the little yellow Lemmon."

The parents were a piece of inspired casting. They had to be, to provide believability for the son who was to develop. Mildred

LaRue Noel Lemmon, "Millie" to all who knew her, was a pretty brunette, extroverted, bright, and witty. She was a woman who straight-armed reality with one-liners and perfectly mixed martinis; the sort of lady who would laugh away physical messages of impending birth in order to dally at a bridge party. She would and she did, thus setting up the elevator delivery scene.

John Uhler Lemmon, Jr. was the perfect mate for Millie. Dignified, charming, and successful, he was a man admired by virtually everyone who ever knew him. He had an uncanny sense of timing and salesmanship—valuable inputs for John Uhler Lemmon III.

Millie was one of nine children in the Noel family, old-line Maryland and sternly Baptist. The family head, Jack's Grandfather Noel, was president of the Noel Construction Company, a prestigious Baltimore firm that served as principal contractor on many government projects, including the U.S. Naval Academy. The Noels were wealthy and lived in a 28-room mansion on Mount Royal Terrace with a phalanx of servants.

Jack's uncle E. M. ("Bud") Noel, now a semiretired manufacturer of bakery machinery living in Newton, is a younger brother of Millie. Later in life she was to insist on introducing him as "my older brother," in a determined campaign against old age—a battle she waged until her death.

Bud remembers that the strict Baptist life led by the Noels often made things difficult for a boy. "Every Sunday I had to parade around in a stiff collar with my hair in curls, for crissakes!"

For all their starchiness, the Noels now and then exhibited a streak of defiance to Gospel morality. An example shows up in the family Bible, one of those massive volumes common to families a generation ago. One page, gilt and red with a border of foliage and entertwined serpents, is missing. Wording on the page thundered about the evils of Demon Rum and contained a temperance pledge, with a place for the proposed teetotaler to sign up for salvation.

"Well, one of us signed that thing," said Bud. "We always suspected it was our Uncle Billy Chuning, who was on my father's side of the family. They were Virginians. Anyway, that page got torn out in a hurry. He was sort of excommunicated." The Noels apparently believed an occasional nip was reasonably godly and a palatable barrier to grippe, the vapors, and divers other afflictions of the day.

Uncle Billy did not languish alone in exile. Bud's mother, Sadie

Noel, once conducted an expensive survey of the family genealogy and turned up an encouraging array of dukes and earls. These were dutifully and happily added to the list in the Bible—with certain exceptions. These unfortunate individuals, the record showed, had been evicted from the French province of Noailles (whence the family name, Noel) in the sixteenth century. They migrated to England, there to ply a new vocation as highwaymen. The British, no more liberal than their former countrymen, promptly hanged them all.

At least one absentee was expunged for earthier habits. "My grandmother refused to even discuss him," Jack says. "This fellow came over here a long time ago and hooked up with a barmaid—a Black Irish, as they called them—and I think he knocked her up, is what he did, and then made good on it. You'd think that doing the honorable thing would have saved him, but he was—well, the whole page was removed. Come to think of it, the girl might have been Jewish—and you simply didn't discuss *that*.

"At about the same time they discovered we had a descendant who was the Earl of Gainsborough or some such thing, and they thought that was terrific. They went right out and had a crest made up, the coat of arms and all that crap."

Grandfather Noel died at age forty-nine from a heart attack, leaving a widow, nine children, six servants, and Bud suspects, a crooked lawyer. In time, the servants were dismissed, the mansion was converted to apartments to afford Mrs. Noel an income, and the family moved to respectable but more modest accommodations in Mount Washington near Pimlico Racetrack.

It was to this dwelling that John U. Lemmon was drawn one evening in the early 1920s for the suspenseful purpose of a blind date with the fetching Millie. John was a former naval officer, one of World War I's "90-day-wonder" products of Annapolis. He prospered, becoming a lieutenant and being selected as a member of the team attending ceremonies at the surrender of the German fleet at Scapa Flow in the Orkney Islands off northern Scotland.

Millie was at once enthralled by the debonair Lemmon who, Bud remembers, dominated any room he entered, "Not with a loud voice or anything he said or did—just his presence." Standing over six feet and straight as a mainmast, he was gracious, charming, and handsome.

John was no less taken with the scintillating Millie, and it was apparent to everyone that they were a perfect match. "I knew at once there would be a wedding," said Bud. "He was made for her. Millie was gay, constantly active, and loved partying. John was patient and always courteous. I doubt if he ever had an enemy in the world; I know I never heard of any. I never saw him angry for more than a minute, except when he was driving a car. Then everybody else on the road was a damned fool."

The dapper Lemmon loved his car, a sporty Lexington touring sedan with a folding seat that extended *outside* the vehicle. "He loved to cruise around in that car wearing a derby hat," said Bud. "He put me in that damned outdoor seat for a little spin one day and all I can remember is wind and dust."

On the day of the wedding, the much-in-love Lemmon lost his carefully maintained reserve in a fit of prenuptial panic and rammed the Lexington into a telephone pole—the *only* such pole between his house and Millie's. "I don't see how he managed that," said Bud. "You'd almost have to plan to bash into that pole, the way it was situated. But he was on the way to pick up Millie and I suppose his mind was somewhere else. She never let him forget that."

The newlyweds moved to Boston in 1924 when John was promoted to the job of New England sales manager for the Read Machinery Company, a bakery equipment manufacturer based in York, Pennsylvania. It was here that he began to exhibit exceptional business acumen—an intelligence that was to show up in his son.

With perfect timing, John resigned from Read to accept a position as vice-president in charge of engineering for Hathaway Bakery Company, at the precise moment Hathaway was embarking on a major program of expansion and acquisition. It mattered not a whit to John that he knew little about engineering. "Never sell your product," he would later advise son Jack, "sell yourself."

At a point when Hathaway seemed to be enjoying an endless boom, the alert Lemmon detected a shift in the wind. When approached by the Doughnut Corporation of America, which was searching for a new vice-president of sales, he abruptly resigned from Hathaway and took the job. One year later the roof fell in on Hathaway's building program.

"Those perfectly timed moves are good examples of how really bright the man was," Bud explained. "As the years went by he quite literally made the Doughnut Corporation into a major company. He did this primarily by his actions during World War Two. At the time you couldn't get sugar or any of the supplies that a prepared mix needs. Those materials were either in short supply or for export only. He managed to get that stuff for

Doughnut Corporation, and even convinced the government to build DCA a plant to produce powdered eggs for the military service."

At war's end, he was assigned a new and difficult task—the introduction and popularization of doughnuts in Europe and England. The company had already launched several attacks on the market, plowing in large sums to no avail, especially in England, where the American pastry was viewed with haughty disdain.

Establishing a beachhead at military posts in Frankfurt, Germany, the engaging Lemmon shortly had Rhinelanders munching sinkers by the peck. Soon other neighboring countries fell meekly in line, adopting the raised and glazed as their own. In time, England, the last holdout, succumbed. The victory was total, and today the common doughnut is a staple in Europe.

The birth of "little Jackie" a year after the Lemmons settled in Boston was to have a profound and lasting effect on the fun-loving Millie, to whom the inconvenience and discomfort of pregnancy had been durance vile, squared. The last-minute race to the hospital and the spectacle in the elevator were appalling to her and a resolution already half-formed was solidified: this would be an only child.

A few years later, Jackie sought a reason for the absence of brothers and sisters. "She just looked at me and said, 'Are you kidding?' then gave me a shot as only she could do—with that up-and-down look, the head tilted, and the eyes going zunk! and said: 'Never again. I'm damned glad you came out all right, but I vowed never again.'

"Believe me, she meant it. I guess the whole thing was horrendous for her. I was premature; we were late getting to the hospital and it was in the middle of the night. They had to lay her down in the elevator and it jammed or something. With my luck it was probably going *down*. At any rate, she sure didn't like it even a little bit and wasn't about to go back for seconds."

If there was abhorrence in the contemplation of a second child, there was no lack of love for the first. Millie and John adored Jackie, as did everyone on both sides of the family. "It was," according to Bud, "damn near impossible not to love the child. He was always kind and polite—you enjoyed him. Because of this there was a tendency to spoil him. I worried about that a lot and had a hard time keeping my mouth shut around his parents because they gave him practically anything he wanted. If his father didn't, Millie would.

"If you'd known him at the time, you'd have considered him a spoiled brat because he had everything. He had doting parents. But Jack wouldn't accept it; he just never became spoiled and he had every reason to be.

"Part of the problem was that the boy was alone much of the time. His father was on the road a great deal in his business and Millie was restless and always on the go. She even had trouble sitting in a chair and holding a conversation for very long; always had to be on the move. Then, too, Jackie was sick a lot. Millie used to say he 'popped in and out of hospitals like a cork.' So these things weighed on the parents and I expect they were trying to make up by giving the kid things—doing for him, even when he didn't really want them to."

Today Jack remembers the illnesses with a wince. "Physically, I know you can go through things as a kid that would kill you later in life. I had every conceivable childhood disease. You name it, I had it—this fever, that fever, rheumatic fever, scarlet fever—I think I had that for awhile, plus the measles and mumps and five major operations before I was ten years old.

"I've undergone three mastoid operations—and they removed my tonsils three times. Adenoids? They yanked them *five* times. Later, when I entered the navy, those doctors took one look and said, 'Those tonsils have got to go' and I said, 'No way, baby. I've had 'em out and out and out *again* and they're back and they're gonna stay back!' I've got adenoids and tonsils today. I don't know what it's like to breathe out of both sides of my nose at the same time.

"In those days there was no penicillin, which kills mastoiditis, so it was a big deal. That was terribly traumatic for me, no mistake about it, because I can remember every minute of it—the pain and that wick they inserted in my head behind my ear to soak up the pus. Every day I would see this goggle-eyed doctor with a mustache who would pull that wick out of my head and put in another one. He was a marvelous doctor, the best my father could find, but I hated him at the time. The mastoid trouble came on when I was six, again at seven, and again at nine. I remember I used to get earaches and try to hide the fact by going to my room alone and crying. I didn't want anyone to know because it might mean another operation.

"Once, in the hospital, the principal of my school came to see me; short, dumpy broad—very sweet, very nice, but she had made a mistake at school one day. She was a disciplinarian and I had pushed into line ahead of somebody else or something. Anyway, she began shaking me and my head was hitting a wall with every shake and she kept saying, 'Answer me!' and I was being knocked out. I had headaches for a year after that.

"Anyway, at the hospital I remember her trying to touch me and I—I pulled back. I pulled back from anybody who wanted to touch me—anybody."

Early on, Jack began to discern differences between his parents—friction points that would abrade the marriage through the years. Jack was Catholic because "Dad was a Catholic," while Millie's approach to organized religion was one of mild indifference. After the marriage she shed her rigid Baptist teachings as one removes an itchy sweater.

The sharply differing attitudes toward matters theological was a continuing source of puzzlement to young Jack, who each Sunday was exposed alone, or in the company of his father, to the eucharistic mysteries of the mass, while his mother remained at home. One winter morning he decided to pose the question to Millie, still abed.

"Mom, why don't you ever go to Communion with me?"

No answer.

"Mom!" A little louder.

A mumble. "Because I'm not a Catholic."

"But if you're not a Catholic, what are you?"

Millie rolled over, pondered this for a moment, then opened one sleepy eye. "I'm a Baptist—I think."

Summer for Jack meant camp, another of those mixed blessings that are the certain lot of an only child in a prosperous family. John and Millie packed their son off to the woods for all the reasons why other parents do the same thing, reasons notarized to be good and sound by adults. Generally, it works to the advantage of both child and parents. In the case of Jack it was a paradox, like having lockjaw in an ice-cream parlor. A problem which would surface again at a later time in another place plagued him now. He couldn't fit in.

It was not that he did not take to the wilderness environment. One of his favorite spots was a field strategically located between his home in Newton and his school, half a mile away. He remembers that it was ". . . beautiful and I liked it. You could lie on your back and make pictures from the clouds, or read Big Little Books and Dick Tracy, or whatever. Life was marvelous."

What made Camp Mitigwa, an otherwise lovely spot in the Rangely Lakes region of Maine, *not* so marvelous was that Jack was a chronic bed wetter. The social acceptability of a bed wetter in a boys' camp roughly parallels that of the man toting the flame-thrower in an assault force. Even though consumed by his own embarrassment, Jack had empathy for the fellow in the bunk below him. "It wasn't like a little dribble here and there. I was a fountain!"

Mitigwa was under the iron control of Chief Gray, a big man with a penchant for feathered headwear and corporal discipline. Bed-wetting was high on the list of punishable crimes tacked on a tree at the camp, and in the chief's mind it was more an infraction than a human malfunction. He devised a sentence to inhibit the crime. Each morning those quartered in Jack's hut—eight to ten kids—would line up following inspection (and the inevitable discovery of wet sheets) and spread their legs. Jack was obliged to crawl through this tunnel, affording each boy a chance to spank him as he passed.

"Naturally," said Jack, "the more they did this—and it was almost daily—the worse I got. I don't know what the hell made me do it, or hide behind doors. I did that, too. Maybe a psychiatrist could explain it; I can't. I know I don't actually blame anybody for those things because I don't need to blame anybody for anything. When I do blame someone or I don't like somebody, you can bet your sweet ass I've got a real reason."

Jack recalls that along with the regular doses of humiliation, Camp Mitigwa offered some great fun and good times. The campfire pow-wows were a big item. Chief Gray would wear his biggest and most colorful feathers and squat cross-legged. "He'd lift his head and go, 'Oh-ha, oh-ha, hiya-ooyah' and we'd give it back to him, 'Ha-pa-wah, wah-wah' and somebody would flog hell out of a drum. It was great."

Occasionally, the chief would gear up for a hunt and unleash the children to go crashing through the forest in search of game—a slothful possum, a squirrel—anything injudicious enough to linger in the vicinity. Being a mountain man, the chief recognized that the possibility of his charges returning with anything more than a case of poison ivy was blessedly remote. However, in their trampings they would sample nature's unsullied wonders, improve their physical condition, and diminish their often vexing surplus of energy.

It was on one of these forays that Jack stumbled, panting and sweaty, into some bushes—and stopped in disbelief. There it was—something! An animal, already dead. "I couldn't believe it,"

Jack said. "I guess it was a fox or something, because it had a bushy tail. I grabbed it and dragged it back to camp. The chief just looked at it and said, 'Oh, my God!' The kids started jumping around and crying, 'He did it! He got it!' After that the spankings stopped. The guys said they wouldn't do that anymore because I'd caught an animal, and you didn't put a guy through the mill who'd done that."

Physical punishment from his parents was unknown to Jack. Millie couldn't bear the thought of it and his father was a master of the feint-and-fall-back. The one time John finally determined to do the deed, he faltered and became the butt of a family joke. Says Jack: "I don't recall what I'd done, but Dad came into my room looking very stern, and closed the door. Mom was standing just outside, listening. Instead of spanking me, he started yelling and stomping around and banging on furniture—I swear he did everything but drop golf balls. After awhile he stopped and hollered, 'There, is that enough?' I said, 'Yes, I think that ought to do it.' He just couldn't bring himself to lay a hand on me."

Although Jack was never in jeopardy of a thrashing, and knew it, he nevertheless feared his father. "There was the innate tension from trying as a young man to come up to what your father is or was. I don't think he tried to instil this; the reaction was within me."

As fathers go, there's no doubt that John Lemmon was a very tough act to follow. Not only was he tall, good-looking, disarming, and intelligent, but he could dance and he could act. "He'd dance at the drop of a hat," says Jack. "Throw a little sand down and he'd do a shuffle at the slightest invitation. Once when Bill Robinson was in Boston doing *The Hot Mikado,* Dad got up and they danced together for twenty minutes, doing the old soft shoe. He was terrific."

Many who knew him believe that John, beneath all that dignity, was a born showman, just as others are convinced Millie's gregariousness was merely camouflage for hiding from the world a rather introverted, puritanical lady.

John was a storyteller of the first magnitude who had the ability, Jack swears, to "stare you right in the eye and tell the damndest yarns you ever heard" and leave one permanently wondering if any of the tales were supported by one grain of fact. The suspicion ever lurked in his audiences that they were being outrageously conned, and as some protection they gave him the nickname of "Lilac" because "Nobody can lie like Lemmon."

According to Jack, his father once worked for George Washington Hill, the prototype for the Sidney Greenstreet character in *The Huckster*. "He told a lot of lies about that, I'm sure. Remember Planter's Mr. Peanut? The figure with the arms and legs and the hat and such? Well, Dad claimed that was his idea. He also swore he invented the Bayer Aspirin box—and he said *that* was taken from him. I don't know what to believe, because he was so successful and respected. I wouldn't doubt he did—on the other hand, he told me he once ran away from home, jumped a banana boat, and ended up in China!

"Whatever, I know that my feelings about my father were an important drive in my life—a good drive, I think. I always loved him very much but it's difficult to differentiate, when you're young, between real love and duty and respect, a feeling of obligation. For me it was a peculiar combination, trying to be 'on' and prove, and also being reticent and afraid I could never—you know —satisfy my father or satisfy other people that I could be on a level with him. I guess the only thing that's important is that he *was* my father. He was some guy, my Dad was. Some guy."

Chapter

II

"Jackass! You—*jackass!*"
—*John Uhler Lemmon, Jr.*

STUDY A PICTURE of young Jack (see photo section) and it becomes clear why he so easily ensnared the hearts of those around him. He looks like a cross between the Little Prince and Emmett Kelly. His countenance is one of utter innocence, of sad sweetness seen only in those who have suffered more than their due or who are about to be ingested by a lion for religious wrong turns.

He has a handsome face, running slightly to cute—the kind of face that makes grandmothers imprudent when dispensing cookies. Jack's physiognomy created in adults a feeling of benevolent trust. The mask was readily penetrated by his youthful colleagues, however, who were working the same ploy with varying degrees of success. Within Jack were Huck and Tom elements sufficient to balance the Sid, as his elders would discover in time.

From the beginning, Jack had talent; everyone said so. By the age of four he had appeared on stage with his parents in a local charity production, *Gold in Them Thar Hills.* It was a speaking role ("Hark. A pistol shot!") but not a featured part. Still, there was something he hadn't experienced before: applause. He liked the sound of that, and he still does.

Here and there one excavates other clues to the makeup of this boy who was to become one of the celebrated actors of our time. It has been said of genius that it is often marked by disorganization. If that's true, one glance at Jack's room would have tipped off any authority that here was a mind to be reckoned with. His room was—untidy. It was, in fact, Jack recalls, "a total claptrap. I had an old four-poster bed and over that I hung everything imaginable: spaceships, airplanes, pennants. And on the wall I tacked pictures I'd drawn. Every corner was stuffed full of gimcracks. I would read *Popular Mechanics* and then send off for this and that—erector sets and the like. I was always building and doing. Inside the closet there was this little door, about two feet by one foot, through which you could get into the plumbing for the john—and I had that space crammed with junk. It was a firetrap, that room. I never threw anything away. I kept it all. You know, old whoopee bags, rubber bands, marbles, twine, and kite parts, pots and pans, Big Little Books and enough Good Humor sticks to roof a pagoda! I'm telling you, the Collier brothers were monks compared to me."

The more exotic items in Jack's room were smuggled in from Daddy Jack's Joke Shop in Boston, an outlet for everything from exploding cigars to gorilla masks. A specialty of the house was firecrackers big enough to blow up a quarry. The store had an array of goodies to delight the eye of any boy, and it was only a nickel trolley ride from Newton.

It was contraband from Daddy Jack's that was to bring about what Jack remembers as perhaps "the worst day of my life," a fine autumn afternoon when John Lemmon decided to give his son a lesson in football.

The Lemmon home in Newton was located on Ivanhoe Street, in a pleasant, tree-shaded, upper-middle-class neighborhood. Situated on a corner lot, the house was so constructed that the garage was a basement affair with the driveway slanting downward to a point ten feet below street level at the garage door.

After a few minutes of basics, the elder Lemmon set about to instruct Jack in the requirements for the long pass. "You must lead the receiver," he said, "and you have to really put it out there. You have the runner out here, see, and you have to get the ball over him. He's looking over his shoulder and the ball has got to be in front of him."

Young Jack surveyed the field of play, the front yard, and commented that there was a problem with the driveway, which prevented any really mammoth "bomb."

"Don't worry about it," said John, impatiently trotting out to receive the pass. "Just lay it out here."

The first pass was inadequate. "Come on," yelled John. "Is that the best you can do? Put something on it!"

"Well," Jack remembers, "I had to show Pop that he had a human slingshot for a son, that I could really heave it. He started running and hollered, 'Throw it,' and I let go with everything I had. And at that awful point everything became overcranked, as they say in the movie business. It went into slow motion. Those seconds seemed like an eternity. I couldn't speak, because I didn't really believe what was about to happen."

Racing out for the pass, a spiraling thing of beauty, John was looking over his shoulder at the ball and yelling, "Wow!" Both the great distance of the pass and the proximity of the driveway had been seriously miscalculated by the delighted flanker. Football and father sailed majestically beyond earth to a point midway over the driveway and then disappeared from Jack's horrified view.

"I was frozen," said Jack. "Dad was going hell-bent for leather and I couldn't say 'Stop' or 'Look out' or anything until he went out of sight in a swan dive, going ten feet down and at top speed, to go crash! on the gravel. Just as his heels were vanishing over the edge I finally, very weakly, said, 'Watch out for the driveway.'

"Well, I slowly walked to the driveway and he was sitting down there, cut and bruised. He thought he had broken his back, his arms, his neck, his legs—everything. And he was in a state of shock. I kept looking down at him and saying, 'I'm sorry.' He looked up at me; he was purple, sputtering and fuming, but not wanting to swear at me. Finally he screamed: 'Jackass! You—*jackass!* Why didn't you holler; why didn't you?' "

Lacerated, bleeding, and benumbed, John staggered into the house trailed by a subdued son who at this moment was considering his own diminishing chances of survival. Inside, a shocked Millie did a take and blurted: "My God in heaven! What happened? Were you run over by a car?"

A shaky John didn't answer. His attention was on Jack. "You get your ass upstairs," he croaked. "If I ever recover, I'm going to give you the spanking of your life!"

In the now-fragile redoubt of his bedroom, Jack awaited the certain Armageddon. Below, he could hear his father cataloguing contusions and calling loudly for balms to ease his suffering. There were no ointments, and a trip to the drugstore would be necessary.

Stationed at his open window, Jack watched as his father dragged his battered frame toward the family car. "At that moment," recalls Jack in horror, "I remember! I have placed, as a small and harmless lark, one of Daddy Jack's best under the hood of our automobile! A six-inch whistling firecracker! I could hear my father swearing as he tried to get into the car and he couldn't bend and he couldn't sit because of the pain. I wanted to yell, 'Don't do it—wait a minute!' so I could come down and disconnect the bomb, but once again I was tongue-tied.

"Well, I want to tell you, when he turned over that motor, nothing happened for about four seconds, then—WHEE-E-E-E-E-E-E, this enormous siren started going and I heard him hollering 'Wha—ha—who—hoah—ah-h-h-h!' and then PAH-WOW! Never in my life have I heard such an explosion. I think it was a small hunk of dynamite. It took the whole hood off the car—wack! just like that—and shook it loose.

"Well, Dad catapulted out of the car and fell down again! Jesus! There is one, and only one, reason why I am alive today, and that is because of Mom. Dad came into the house, worse off than ever, and looked at my mother and said: 'For crissakes—my car just blew up!' Well, you have to have known my mom to understand that there was only one reaction you are gonna get. She had hysterics. The idea that he was cut all over his body and bleeding, and his muscles were sore and he wasn't sure he hadn't busted something—and then his car blew up right on top of it—was just too much. She started to laugh and couldn't stop. Finally, Dad had to laugh, too. But he didn't speak to me for a month."

Weeks passed, and as John made the long march back from infirmity there was a corresponding return of civility toward Jack. Détente, however, was to be short-lived because of a certain proposal set forth by a peer of Jack's named Brooks Slocum—a suggestion eagerly seized upon by Jack, especially since the firecrackers to be used in this operation were the limited-warfare one-inchers useful only for frightening girls and elevating the decibel level on unreasonably quiet days.

"Brooks would do anything," Jack said. "As a matter of fact, I believe he was the one who induced me to do the Mafia hookup on my old man's car. He was a ripper, that kid. Anyway, Brooks and I were sitting on my upstairs porch and we were lighting these firecrackers and throwing them. Well, one of them landed on an awning that was partially rolled up—and the 'cracker stayed there. It didn't go off or anything, so we figured it was a dud and threw another one over."

After awhile, this activity began to pall and the boys left the porch, only to meet Jack's father coming up the staircase. This jolted Jack, who had forgotten that it was the weekend and John would be home. It was a narrow escape; they had been casually sauntering around in the parental minefield. "I remember," said Jack, "thinking, 'My God, I didn't know he was home or I wouldn't have been tossing those things!' "

About thirty minutes after this near-miss, while at Brooks' house next door, Jack heard a "commotion you wouldn't believe going on at our house. I ran over. Fire engines were screaming up the street; my mom was in hysterics on the telephone, calling still more firemen; and my Dad was out there on the porch yelling and screaming and wrestling with an extinguisher." What chilled Jack's blood was the source of the flames—the awning! The firecrackers had done their work and "the whole friggin' house was about to go up."

Jack watched the scene with the fascination that the condemned find in witnessing a gallows being constructed. "That was the closest I have ever come," recalled Jack, "to wanting to just pack it up and quit this life, because as I stood there the whole bloody awning—fire, ashes, the works—came right down on top of my father. I mean, forget it! This was going to do it for good!"

Inexplicably, Jack's father went unscathed and the crime undetected. Since few things in life are more seductive than illicit success, Jack was malleable when the next opportunity for transgression arose. It came in the form of an old Victorian house which lay conveniently at hand between Ivanhoe Street and Ward school, which Jack attended. In disrepair and long empty, the house nevertheless presented an irresistible array of fine, old, stained-glass windows—all mockingly intact—to Jack, Brooks, and two other boys who were with them.

Jack remembers with surprising clarity that the idea was not his and was "more likely George Spelvin's." At any rate, someone suggested a course of action so simple, so logical, that his three comrades marveled aloud that they had not thought of it first themselves. "I know what," said he, "why don't we bust out the windows?" There being little need for a caucus, the boys set to work with stones.

"We broke out every one of those beautiful old windows," said Jack. "What we didn't know was that there apparently was a caretaker who followed us and saw where a couple of us lived and contacted our parents. God, my father was mad! He didn't spank me, but we had to pay to have all those windows replaced and I was grounded for about a month: no bike, nothing—period. A stay-in-your-room kind of thing. Then I had to pay my father back for the windows at the rate of a nickel a week out of the fifteen-cent allowance I got, for I don't know how many years, to make up about twenty dollars. He was really furious and made me aware that this wasn't a bit funny. It was somebody else's property and this wasn't simple mischief—it was bad."

Jack did not arrive at this state of prepubescent dissoluteness all at once. There were earlier capers. At age seven, Jack came up missing for most of an afternoon, spawning a house-to-house search. Eventually he was discovered—in the garage of a neighboring home. With him were three comely damsels, all in minimal attire and awaiting examination by "Doctor" Jackie. For loosing this most ancient of male stratagems on the girls, Jack, according to Bud, "really caught hell."

From his earliest memories, only matters pertaining to the arts could capture Jack's attention for very long. The "solid" subjects at school—mathematics, history, science, civics, and geography—were mammoth bores, chores to be endured. His grades reflected this through Andover and Harvard, except in courses such as art, which he enjoyed and in which he scored an A. "The best description of the academic Lemmon," says Jack, "came from my Latin teacher, Mr. Pointer, who scared hell out of me. He once said to my father: 'I'm convinced your son has brains; but they are scattered all over Andover Hill.' "

Bud, who spent more time with Jack during his first years than anyone other than John and Millie, was impressed with Jack's intelligence. "He was an extraordinarily bright child. Sure, he got poor grades in school, but it was because he just wasn't interested. Jack could easily have gotten an A in any subject if he'd cared. All he really loved was music and acting. Make no mistake about it—Jack is extremely intelligent and sensitive. He may not show it, but he's usually way ahead of you—several jumps. But if he let you know that, then he might in some way embarrass or hurt you, and *that* he will never do. He's much too kind, gracious, courteous. He was always like that, even as a little kid. He always will be." (Says Jack: "I think he's related to me.")

Good grades or no, John and Millie were determined to expose their son to the best they could afford; and that was very good, indeed. John strove mightily to follow the old American dream of providing the child with all that the father and his father before him had not had. The schools for Jack were the finest: the exclusive Rivers Country Day School, Andover Academy, and finally, Harvard.

John tried to set an impeccable example of all that a father should be, in word and deed. Sometimes, it worked; occasionally it flopped spectacularly. An example of the latter was John's insistence that Jack have his own pony, an important "image" item in the late 1920s.

Having decided on the pony, John purchased one from Hathaway Bakery, which at the time still employed horse-drawn wagons to deliver its products. The animal was called Pepper, a name given it by its former owners on the basis of considerable experience.

"Dad was always trying to do good things for me," explained Jack, "and one of those things was Pepper. I didn't want any part of it but my father figured every boy would like a pony. He was determined to get a snapshot of me sitting on Pepper, and every Sunday for weeks we went through the same ritual.

"Pepper was a mean little cuss. He didn't mind pulling a wagon, apparently, but he hated like hell to have anyone on his back—and I didn't like it up there anymore than he did. Anyway, every Sunday Dad would go to Watertown several miles away, and that man would *walk* that beast all the way back. Then he would put me in the saddle and back away with the camera. At that point the same thing always happened—the moment that shutter clicked Pepper would take off like a shot and I would go plop! down on the grass. I never did ride that pony; I would just fall off and cry.

"Well," Jack recalls, "Pop would take off screaming and swearing down Waverly Avenue, the main drag in Newton, chasing Pepper. About a mile and a half away there lived a chauffeur, who always caught Pepper and brought him back. The first time this happened, the poor guy was all scraped and bleeding because he'd been dragged half a block, so Dad gave him five bucks. After a while, the chauffeur got wise and stationed himself there every Sunday, even if he had to stay home from his job. It was good steady work, I'll tell you. After about five Sundays of this my old man finally gave up and sold the pony back to Hathaway, and the chauffeur went back to work."

As most kids do, Jack had an early go at the free enterprise system in the high hope of salting away a bundle of coin and impressing his parents. Two such projects, both conducted before the age of ten, were failures. The first collapsed because of a parental ruling that First Amendment rights do not necessarily extend to offspring; and the latter, because of poor location.

Jack aligned himself in the initial venture with his neighboring buddies, Billy Tyler and Brooks. They formed a newspaper, primarily because Billy owned a partially functioning printing machine. "It was mostly the gossip-type thing," Jack recalls. "You know, the stuff we'd overheard our parents say. What time they got home at night, what they had to say about the neighbors, and so forth. The printing machine had this horrible red ink, and you could hardly make out what was written, anyway. But I guess our parents made out enough because as soon as they read it we were shut down, freedom of the press be damned. We had been going house-to-house selling our paper for a penny, and in the two editions we got out before the axe fell, we made ourselves twenty cents or so."

The second, more professional undertaking, was a stamp store. Jack and Billy Tyler had been avid philatelists for quite a while. Brooks had only a nodding acquaintance with stamps, but a wholesome interest in money, so the combination worked admirably. The store was set up and "it was terrific," said Jack. "We got this sheet of glass and had all the stamps spread out under it with a piece of paper describing what each one was, the works. There was only one minor flaw in the whole operation. Our headquarters were in Brooks' basement, which wasn't exactly Fifth Avenue. It ended up with just the three of us down there looking at the stamps and each other. No customers."

Bedeviled by continuing illness, Jack suffered a new and strange malady at seven years—a malaise mystifying except in the retrospect of maturity.

"Strangely," said Jack, "I cannot even remember her name. She was my teacher before I started to attend Rivers Country Day School. I can remember her vividly from the neck down. I was—I remember how it happened. I was at school one morning and she got up to the blackboard and when she pushed her boobs out to face the flag—I'm telling you, I don't know what it was, but wah-h-h-ow!

"I just sat paralyzed all day looking at her. I could not work, I could not remember anything, or do anything. It's a blank period in my life for about a year. I was absolutely crushed when I discovered she was married. Her husband would come to pick her up from school and I would just stand and watch him. She'd get in the car and he'd give her a little kiss and they'd drive off. It tore my heart out. I hated him." Jack was not to undergo the ethereal anguish of love again until his middle teens.

When Jack was nine years old, he was enrolled in Rivers Country Day School, a private institution in Brookline, Massachusetts. It was here that he was thrust into his first real theatrical role. "If there was one thing that kicked me off in this business it was that school play," says Jack.

It was a sudden introduction, reminiscent of an old MGM musical plot. One of the kids became ill and Jack was given the part literally the day before the play was to open. Recognizing that it was impossible for Jack to learn the lines overnight, his teacher told him not to worry: "Anytime you can't remember a line, I'll be right over here at the side of the stage behind the curtain and you can just walk over and I'll whisper it to you."

Outfitted with a cape and a black cowboy hat, Jack was ready when the curtain rose. "What I did," he said, "was very simple. I came out in the middle of that stage with this idiotic costume—the hat fit the other guy but came down over my eyes—I strolled out there and laid the first line on them, which was the only one I knew. Then I casually walked over to the wings and listened, and the teacher whispered the next line. Back I went to the middle of the stage and mouthed the new information, after which I wheeled and wandered back to the wings for another supply of words. Well, after about four or five trips to the well the place was in bedlam. I didn't know at the time what the hell was so funny, but I loved it!"

Later, because of his good reviews in the play, Jack was tagged for the part of a pitchman at the school carnival, selling with a technique copied from a medicine-show hustler he'd seen in the movies. From that performance Jack expanded and polished his repertoire, adding an incredible variety of *snores.* "I had about twenty-five, as I recall. One was like a train. I worked up a complete routine. Mom and Dad, of course, were not averse to putting me on, you know, when we had company. So I built up a whole act. I had the snoring, and I added imitations of Mae West and W. C. Fields, and later on I started telling jokes. Not jokes, really, but long stories where the humor depended on the telling, not just the punchline.

"All this was leading toward the performer, and I think I did it because I found that I could do it well and get attention. I felt secure in it, it was the only thing I could do, that and music. I don't know—I've often wondered about the drive to act. It's a combination of a lot of things. I'm not sure this applies to me, but I think some people become actors basically because they want to be somebody else.

"They are," Jack went on, "usually very good character actors who are a bundle of neuroses and they never come alive except when they are performing. It's a great breath of relief to them when they are someone else and they can forget their own problems. A light comes into their eyes and they come alive—until the curtain drops. Then they crawl back into their own little shells—and become someone else—themselves."

Chapter

III

". . . the grace to make a fool of himself."
—Fred Jordan

ILLNESS, Jack's ancient enemy, began to weaken in the late rounds at Rivers Country Day School, but climbing through the ropes was a potentially greater menace, this one psychological. Millie and John had begun to sleep in separate bedrooms.

There had been confrontations for several years; not the slam-bang physical kind, but the civilized not-in-front-of-Jackie verbal bouts. The "wounds" were internal, leaving no telltale surface scars, but they were wounds nevertheless, and they did not escape the notice of the sensitive boy.

"They didn't have a lot of quarrels," said Jack, "but I do remember that as a small child the arguments that I did hear fascinated me—I was absorbed with them. Once, a kid named Sykes sat with me outside their bedroom door and we just listened. What they were saying upset me terribly, because Mom was threatening to move out and live at the Ritz-Carlton Hotel. I guess I must have been about seven years old at the time."

With the move to separate rooms, Millie tried to cover up by assuring the child that his father was sleeping apart from her because he snored and kept her awake nights. By the time Jack was thirteen and preparing to enter Andover Academy the marriage was beginning to unravel and the worried son could not (and still can't) diagnose the underlying reason(s).

"I don't know what was wrong. I guess the bloom wore off; they just kind of drifted apart. The physical part of their relationship—I don't know how good that was, although I think it was okay when I was very young.

"I know they were trying to hold the marriage together for my sake, in the belief that it was best for their child; but it wasn't, really. They probably would have been much happier if they hadn't; I knew the situation wasn't good. I could feel it. Very often well-meaning people will remain together solely for the sake of their children, and I don't think that helps, because the kids do sense that things aren't right and they suffer the strain.

Andover Academy. The prospect of attending the school filled Jack with feelings akin to those of a Kamikaze pilot whose motor catches on the first turn and runs perfectly. He realized he was going to have to do this thing, but he had no zest for it, none whatever. The safe haven that had been Rivers Country Day School was now lost somewhere in his dim boyhood past, replaced by this sprawling campus that looked like a college with its imposing buildings and hundreds of students.

Jack was adrift, and with the exception of the brief summer-camp outings, completely alone for the first time, severed from the cocoonlike security of home and parents. "Some kids, I guess, are better off not going away to school at a young age," he said. "Others take to it immediately. I suppose I was sort of in-between, because I loved it later on; but it was pure hell at first. I never told my father that, because it was his dream that I would go to a top school and get the kind of education he could never have."

To the thirteen-year-old Jack this new society seemed alien, a world in which he did not fit and would never be accepted. "I don't know why I felt that way," he said, "but I did. And the first thing I did was study those guys that everyone seemed to think were the big men on campus and try to copy them. I didn't want to lead, to be myself—I just wanted to be accepted. If one of the kids thought to be a big wheel at Andover wore white socks and shoes and turned up the cuffs on his gray flannels, then Lemmon was sure to follow suit."

First-year students at Andover were called juniors, not freshmen, with subsequent gradations known as lower middle, upper middle, and senior, in that order. For some reason, seemingly rooted more in ivied tradition than in pure logic, junior classmen were segregated in the manner of lettuce heads—by size. Those of lofty stature were quartered in a building known as Rockwell Hall. Shorties drew Williams Hall, and since Jack was not to "stretch out" until his upper-middle days, he became a Williams man.

The thinnest of mutualities will bond the friendless and shipwrecked, and so it was with Jack and another of the Williams diminutives, Fred (Freddie) Jordan, who was to become a lifelong friend and who is today owner and operator of Producers Studio in Hollywood. Both were small, lonely, and shared a common love (but ineptitude) for the piano.

Williams Hall was equipped with its own dining hall, which included a recreation room outfitted with a pool table, a small library, and a piano. Here it was customary for students to gather for a few minutes prior to their meals.

"One of three guys," said Freddie, "would always be at that piano. Charley Arnold was the best, and when he played, everyone would gather around. When he wasn't playing, one of two other fellows would play—Jack or myself. Well, we'd clear the room. We were, you know, just bad. Of course, I knew how it felt to have everybody walk out on you, so I would hang around when Jack played and he would do me the courtesy of standing by when I was performing." (Says Lemmon: "I wasn't that polite—I was just waiting for him to finish, so I could play.")

It was not Jack's introduction to the piano. He'd had a few lessons earlier in life, but showed little patience with the running of scales. When not under the direct gaze of his teacher, he would decamp from the scene or pick out tunes of his own choosing by ear. In desperation, Bud Noel tried bribery, providing a new baseball in return for diligence at the keyboard. This measure had little lasting value and the lessons were eventually dropped.

Freddie says Jack "ruined" him as a piano player. "In my second year at Andover I discovered this piano in the waiters' dining hall, where I waited tables to help earn my way through the school. Well, that was great because I could go up there and be alone and practice with nobody around to hear my mistakes or laugh at me. After a few weeks I began to have an attack of conscience about hoarding my find, and I thought I'd better tell my friend Jack. After that I had to share it with him.

"About six weeks later it dawned on me that I was learning about the piano from him, but he wasn't getting anything from *me.* Whatever he was learning was coming from inside *his* head somewhere. It was during that year that Jack became a very decent piano player, and by the time we'd graduated he was better than any of the guys who were taking lessons and who could read music.

"I can still sit down and play 'Embraceable You' or 'The Man I Love' because Jack showed me where to put my fingers and I simply memorized the chords. But they are Lemmon's versions, not mine."

After a year and a half at Andover, Jack noticed he had suddenly become well known. "I don't know what it was; the piano-playing probably helped, along with the athletics I was involved in—especially track, because by this time I could run like a rabbit, well enough to break a couple of New England high school records."

Jack had started running while attending Rivers Country Day School. "They would dismiss me from class every afternoon on doctor's orders," said Jack, "and take me to the Athletic Association in Boston for physical workouts because I was really a ninety-pound weakling. I began to run, and hell, by the time I was twelve I was covering a three-mile cross-country course and making the first mile in less than five minutes.

"I was good, I know that, but I was beginning to burn myself out. At sixteen I started to lose interest in track. You've got to be a madman anyhow to run around a course until your lungs are searing hot, just to get back to where you started."

Part of Lemmon's problem with track may have been his cross-country coach, a man for whom Jack harbored a lively dislike. This feeling, he says, was shared by a number of the runners. They found especially harrowing the coach's habit of driving his car behind the team, nudging them to greater effort with the bumper while cuddling a girlfriend.

"He'd set that car in first gear," remembers Jack, "and say, 'Run!' He damn near killed us! I was sure he'd start looking at the girl and run right over us."

Jack's dwindling interest in track carried over to one of the big sporting events of the year, the annual Andover–Exeter Meet, and resulted in a crushing personal defeat. The event was the half-mile run, which would close out the meet, then tied.

"Exeter," said Jack, "had a couple of guys named King and Hall who were one-two in the country. I don't remember their times, but they were just sensational. I was beaten long before that race ever came up; psyched right out of it. I had the pole, and when the race started I set the slowest pace you ever saw. I had talked myself into being totally tied up, and I don't even remember when they went by me. I couldn't run at all; I was just plodding along back there. By the time I reached the finish line I had to keep yelling for officials to clear the track, which was full of people congratulating Exeter.

"I knew I'd given up, never even tried, and it almost killed me. I was very disappointed in myself. I didn't stop, just went straight on to the gym. I remember a couple of guys saying, 'Too bad, Jack,' but I never answered them—I couldn't talk. I don't think I could have beaten King and Hall anyway, but I'd never even given it a shot."

In even the worst of potboiler scripts, the hero must not be allowed to disappear in the mire of gloom and defeat. A way out must be found that will buoy his spirits, return him to robust health, and bring a new appreciation of life's wonders. In Jack's case, these showed up in the form of (1) fish, and (2) girls—and in that order.

In his junior year at Andover, Jack's father purchased a summer home on Lake Winnepesaukee in Wolfboro, New Hampshire, "The oldest summer resort in America." Jack recalls that the house wasn't finished and a local man was hired to put up paneling and paint the interior. "It had been owned by a young moneyed guy," said Jack, "who sort of lay around all day and drank bottle after bottle of seltzer. The rumor is that's what did him in—it was like taking fifty aspirins a day."

The home sat on a lake lot which sloped down to the water's edge. Back of the house was a small shack, which John ordered renovated so that Jack would "have his own little place." The bungalow, situated about twenty feet from the main dwelling, was equipped with a heater and plumbing and was a delight to Jack. "It was terrific," he said, "like having a treehouse or something, just a ball. It had double-decker beds, the whole works—just what every boy dreams about."

It was here that Lemmon developed a passion for fishing. John bought him a boat, "a wide little thing with a one-lung motor that would push me along at about four knots or something. It was simply marvelous."

To support his fishing, Jack teamed with a boy named Petey Lyon in a fund-raising venture—one that finally succeeded. The two would rise before dawn and bicycle four miles to Moody's ice pond, which was owned, not surprisingly, by Mr. Moody, the ice-man for Wolfboro. Mr. Moody, an obliging man, knew the boys and had given them permission to borrow his boat to gather lilies which grew on the pond in profusion during summer months. Sometimes they were diverted from their commercial task. "There were some pretty good pickerel in there," explained Jack.

By the time they had picked the lilies and bicycled into town it would be eight-thirty in the morning, with the town just awakening and women coming to do their shopping. The product, "great, big, open gorgeous pond lilies," would be sold two for a nickel. When they had exhausted their supply of shoppers, the boys would canvass the summer homes along Sewell Street, Wolfboro's main thoroughfare.

"We'd end up with thirty-five to forty cents apiece," said Jack, "and by nine o'clock we'd be sold out and could go buy crawfish and hellgramites for bait. Worms we could get ourselves on the golf course at night with flashlights. They would all come up—big beauties that I kept in our basement. That was okay until they died and then, God, what a stink!

"Anyway, we'd be off fishing by ten o'clock. God, those were the days—marvelous!"

The fishing became such a joy that Jack entertained the idea of becoming a fish and game warden, the only occupational plan that ever competed seriously, even for a moment, with his determination to become "another George Gershwin or the world's greatest actor."

Teenagers are what scientists call an "unstable element," and before the second summer had passed in Wolfboro, the fishing was being threatened by a pretty young girl living four houses down the block—a girl who was to become Oscar-winning actress Estelle Parsons.

"Estelle," Jack said with a sigh, "was my first big crush. She was terrific, really *it* for me. I mean, she had me walking around talking to myself. Estelle came perilously close to beating out the fish—and I want to tell you I love fishing."

So great was his love, Lemmon became obsessed with the idea that he might be rejected. This hoary affliction of the young male was so strong he could not bring himself to risk a kiss. "I was so slow you wouldn't believe it. We'd go out in the car for a soda and talk with the other kids, then come back to the house to dance—put on the Dorsey records and turn out all the lights, the whole bit.

"Even so," Jack said with a pained expression, "nobody ever kissed anybody because I was afraid to. Talk about hiding behind doors! I would literally dance her behind a door and we'd stand there! She wasn't resisting or anything, she'd just stand there and I would stand there, but I wouldn't kiss her. I'd hold her a lot, and there was a little squeezing going on, but nothing else."

Another time Jack tried a time-honored maneuver that works consistently despite there being no known case where a girl was fooled by it. "I stalled the car and I gave her the big number, like, 'Well, isn't that funny? Wonder what happened? We're not out of gas.' And then we sat and we talked and I worked my head right next to hers and—I couldn't kiss her. When I got her home I gave her a quick peck at the door, and ran!"

Jack's wretched state of self-inflicted celibacy was the very thing that caused the ancients to complain that "innocence is but a poor substitute for experience.." As weeks passed, it became plain that a fix was needed for this impasse. There was a mountain here that had to be climbed.

A neat set of crampons showed up at this feverish point in the form of Dolly, a new girl in town who possessed sovereign credentials. "Dolly," said Jack emphatically, "was zoftig. She had all the accoutrements. She was about fifteen and looked nineteen, and had a couple of adorable lung warts—a set of cupcakes that had a chance and took it!

"I finally got her down by the old wishing well, as I called it, because I was wishing I would 'get' her down by the well. (I remember saying that to myself and going ha, ha, ha.) The well must have been two miles from my house on Sewell Road, in a big empty field. It was a night for bold doings, with a big moon and a zillion stars. Well, we're walking along and talking and this time I played it subtle. I said: 'Let's go down by the well.'

"That worked fine and soon we're sitting against the well and I have my arm around her and then suddenly, in one incredibly swift movement, I lunged, grabbed, and did it! I kissed her! Only I missed her mouth by about three inches, and almost broke her cheekbone. I cut my lip and my two front teeth were loose for a month. But the wonderful thing was, while she was saying, 'My God, my cheek!' I realized where my hand was! I may have missed the kiss, but I got a cupcake!

"Of course, it didn't occur to me until much later that I had broken into Tiffany's and stolen a Timex.

"The thing so marvelous about youth is the mystery of that

unexplored territory. Inside, those juices are going and it's unimportant what it *ought* to be like. The only thing that counts is *doing* it. The kiss was terrible, and touching the girl's breast didn't mean anything, but that didn't matter. You've done it! You've conquered Everest!"

Most who knew Lemmon at Andover saw him as a popular guy, gracious and kind to everyone and always cheerful, always ready with an upbeat line or story. Freddie Jordan, his constant companion, saw another side. "If you were close to Jack, you could sense a sadness about him. I spent a lot of time with his parents and I could feel that something was not right, not totally fulfilling between them. I think that hurt Jack, hurt him terribly.

"I've never talked to him about this but I believe he was affected by it. To use an overused word, he was a sensitive guy; not in the sense that he would pout or go off in a corner; it never went in that direction. He wasn't given to anger—he was just like he is today—nice and sweet to everyone.

"He developed a façade of fun and games that exists to this day. Jack is a deep person, and although he's more open today, very few people get through to him. I keep remembering those early parties where he would just go off in the corner and play the piano. That piano was his security blanket."

Jordan admires the Lemmon who, somewhere along the line at Andover, learned to "have the grace to make a fool of himself. At a party, we might be asked to imitate an elephant. Now I know I can't imitate an elephant, so I wouldn't try. But Jack, even if he knew he couldn't do it, either, would still try just to keep the game going."

Jack took little interest in dramatics at Andover, but not because of a disinterest in the craft of acting, as Jordan discovered when Lemmon asked him to go along on a visit to the Old Howard, a burlesque theater. "It was the thing at the time for boys at Andover to go there to see the girls. It was supposed to make you a man, like smoking a cigarette. Jack said he wanted to watch the comics, which I thought was one of those things a boy says when he means something else and needs an acceptable reason for doing it. I thought he wanted to go see the girls take their clothes off. That's why *I* wanted to go."

They visited the Old Howard several times and Jack, according to Freddie, actually did go to see the comics work. "He was studying those guys' routines and I couldn't help remembering what his father had said: 'Everyone has talent, and it comes out of one of three places—your feet, your hands, or your mouth.' I remember thinking that I knew where Jack's was—in his hands. I never envisioned him as an actor. His thing was music at Andover."

Whether it was a psychological buffer or an exceptional talent beginning to break through, Jack, in his senior year, had become Andover's leading "entertainment" figure. He was chosen Class Poet, and when the school decided to substitute a musical production for regular exercises on Class Day, it was Lemmon who was charged with writing the songs. Craig Gilbert, who was to become another close friend, wrote and directed the production.

"At this point in our senior year," said Jack, "we were all going off to the army or navy, so the show reflected the times. For one of our big songs we stepped forward all in a row and sang the corniest, most god-awful number you ever heard. It went like this:

> I'm in the U.S. Army,
> and if Hitler ever sawr-me
> he'd never, never dare to harm-me
> now . . .

"Well, we got that far and nobody heard anything beyond that. The audience was hysterical, because it was so bad it was funny."

In his senior year, Lemmon was, by admission, "a big muck" on campus. He was not a muck in the classroom, where his grades hovered consistently just above the failing mark of 60. Freddie remembers that the dean said to him on graduation day: "Jordan, you and Lemmon are the greatest sixty-shooters in the history of Andover."

With graduation, the Andover class of '43 scattered wildly, some to war, others to college. Freddie Jordan enrolled at Yale; Jack was accepted for the U.S. Navy's accelerated ROTC program at Harvard, but would not begin his training until the fall term because of overfilled classes. Yet with a long summer ahead before entering college there was no desire for vacation, for play. The bright, halcyon memories of Wolfboro and the lake were now only snapshots in an album. John and Millie had finally and permanently separated.

As previously mentioned, the parting of Jack's parents remains an enigma to him and to the couple's friends and relatives. The consensus theory holds that John's success in business took him away on long and frequent trips, especially during the war years.

Millie was active and, as Bud Noel emphasized, "a woman who loved a party." She began making daily visits to the bar at the Ritz-Carlton Hotel in Boston during John's absence. There she would laugh away the afternoons with comrades of like bent. Those who knew her well say that Millie drank too much for her own good then and later, and that John, in the waning years of the marriage, took a dim view of both the booze and the parties.

Little more is known of problems that may have existed. Religious differences seemingly played a minor role, if at all. Bud, who spent a great deal of time with John, described him as "not a strong, church-going Catholic in later life, although when he was young he used to tip his hat when we passed the church."

Mrs. Marge Wickersham, an old friend of the Lemmons, believes little could have been known about any conflicts that might have brought about the breakup. "As far as I know, they never talked about each other to anyone," she said, "and they remained the best of friends."

The separation was entirely amicable and John moved quietly to an apartment at the Sheraton Hotel in Boston. There never was a divorce, not even a written agreement, according to Bud: "Just an oral understanding. I don't know what the arrangements were; they didn't volunteer any information and I never asked. I do know that John was good to her always and so was Jack. If we must pinpoint one central problem that Millie had, it was loneliness. She missed her son and she never stopped loving John—deeply."

Jack stayed in Boston that summer and managed to catch on as an apprentice with the Marblehead Players, a top theatrical stock company. Also joining the Players was an old friend from Wolfboro, Estelle Parsons. "I suppose I had something to do with Estelle becoming an actress," said Jack. "She wasn't there because we were going together or anything; we never did, really, but we were attracted to each other."

With customary confidence, Jack backed up, took a run at the acting profession—and flunked his first two tryouts, failing to get even a second reading for either role. "The parts only had a few lines," said Jack, "but not being able to cut it hurt all the same."

Usually the Players would import a star for the lead role and fill in lesser parts with resident members of the stock company. Were an apprentice right for one of the parts, he could have a chance at it.

The third production that Jack tried out for was *Burlesque*, starring Bert Lahr, who was breaking in the show in summer stock before taking it to New York, where it was to become a smash hit.

"Bert was playing the part of a broken-down vaudevillian on the skids, a semidrunk whose wife was leaving him for another man. He had Eileen Heckart with him, and God, she was brilliant!" Jack said.

Lemmon got a part and was delighted. The role was that of a young, drunken piano player and featured a long scene in the second act where he would accompany Lahr in the star's big number, "Here Comes the Bride."

"I was playing the song by ear and Lahr was just dippy about me," Jack said. "I couldn't read a note, never could and still can't; but Bert didn't know that because I had the music sitting right there in front of me."

Somehow, on the fourth day of rehearsals, Lahr discovered Jack's deception and demanded that he be replaced with an actor who could read music. "We gotta get someone else in here," said Lahr. "We can't have a guy doing it by ear."

"Why?" the director protested, "It's perfect the way it is now."

"Yeah," said Lahr, unconvinced, "But the kid might forget and we have to have the music there. Something might go wrong."

Jack was crushed—and annoyed. "Bert was an incredible worry-wart, fussing over every little thing. Fact is, if you're playing by ear you *can't* forget; it's only when you *have* to have the notes that you can get into trouble. At any rate, Bert said, 'Out,' and that was that, and I was given the gate again. Still, I knew it wasn't me this time; it was just Bert and his worrying."

Later, Lahr tried to give Jack twenty dollars to make up for his disappointment but Lemmon turned him down. Bert then said: "Listen, kid, you're the smartest one here. You're the smartest. Stick around out front and tell me if I'm breaking Helen Hayes' record."

Jack was amused. "Here he trusts me to count the house and tell him how things are going, yet he's scared to let me play the part."

Lemmon was not the sole sufferer from Lahr's anxiety. An apprentice playing the part of a bellhop was given the treatment over a small scene in which he was to deliver a bottle of liquor to Bert's hotel room. The bellhop was to say, "Here you are, sir," accept the payment and big tip, then exit with a bow and a "Thank you, sir, and if you need anything else my number is two seventeen."

In rehearsal, Lahr stopped him. "Where'd you get that line?" he demanded.

"It's in the script," said the youth.

"Never mind the line," snapped Lahr. "It's too much. Just bow and say, 'Thank you.' "

With each rehearsal, Lahr chipped away, reducing the bellhop's part, until on opening night the tyro was down to a mute nod. "I was working the curtain," said Jack, "and this kid was there with his prop, waiting for his cue that was coming up in three or four minutes. Lahr came up to make an entrance and just before he walked on stage he turned and said: 'Hey, kid, ya better start practicing that *bow*.'

"I don't believe that Bert was trying to be mean. He was just one of those guys that worries himself silly over everything."

With the end of the play came the end of the summer—and the beginning of maturity. Harvard.

Chapter
IV

"My boy, I don't see how you will ever amount to anything."

—*Dean, Harvard University, 1946*

THE LEMMON who entered Harvard in the fall of 1943 bore scant resemblance to the frail, insecure lad who had quailed before the gates of Andover. Taller now, and handsome, Jack exuded a confidence that in one less affable might have been taken for arrogance. He felt at ease, altogether prepared for the great university. It is at least questionable, in retrospect, whether the reverse was true.

Instead of sorting students by size, as was the quaint custom at Andover, Harvard's navy preferred lumping them together in alphabetical order. Lemmon, therefore, found himself quartered in a wing of Eliot House with a throng of young men, most of whom bore surnames beginning with L.

As were all ROTC cadets, Jack was outfitted with a no-nonsense navy curriculum notable for its dearth of elective subjects. Harvard itself offered not a single course or instructor in the field of theater arts, the sole study likely to germinate the faintest interest in Lemmon, whose soul yearned for the wicked stage.

Harvard's attitude toward the boards was long-standing. From the autumn of 1636, when the General Court of the Colony of Massachusetts voted $2,000 to establish "a schoale or colledge," the university had been manufacturing a consistently superior breed of lawyer, doctor, politician, and such. Several old grads went on to attain the presidency of the United States. The school had never felt compelled to gear up for the production of actors. Anyway, the theater had about it the faint indecency of saddle oxfords with tails. The matter was relegated to the extracurricular along with bonfires, sex, and drinking.

Two creative conduits did exist for fledgling thespians: the Harvard Dramatic Club, which produced perhaps three plays each year, depending on available time and funding; and the historic Hasty Pudding Club. An undergraduate dramatic club founded in 1795, the Pudding took its name from a cornmeal mush served at the club in its formative years. It had produced an annual show since 1844, except during the years of World War II.

These outlets, limited as they were, proved sufficient to siphon virtually a hundred percent of Jack's time and attention from his assigned studies. Lemmon's interest beyond the theater and music lay in two areas, psychology and law; the former because it explored human motivation and was therefore useful to the actor, and the latter because lawyers, after all, were *performing* up there before the bench.

While the military's pedagogues mounted a generally futile assault on Jack's mind, a cadre of chief petty officers labored earnestly to bring his character and body into line with applicable government specifications.

"The chiefs," recalls Jack, "were not the sort of men you'd send to sea. They were big, burly guys like former football linemen and some of them weren't the world's brightest fellows."

The chiefs operated under a GI canon essentially unaltered since Rollo the Northman. It is a triumph over logic that requires anything motionless to be excavated, disinfected, or given calisthenics. It was so at Eliot House, where each day at first light the ROTC cadets were rallied to the courtyard in shorts and sneakers regardless of the weather.

Formed in ranks and counted, they were then dispatched at a gallop into the countryside, only to be ordered out again upon their return. For the artistic Lemmon it was treatment transcending indignity all the way to cruel and unusual punishment. He soon became possessed with the notion that a swindle could be executed, one that would short-circuit the senseless and often frigid sprints.

A survey of the course—which led over a bridge, along the

Charles River, and back over another bridge to the courtyard—produced a suitable place of concealment: a six-foot clump of bushes just beyond the first bridge. The next morning Jack defected to the brambles, there to lie in smug comfort "while those other chumps beat their brains out." Rejoining the panting pack at the end of its second lap Lemmon trotted in with them, having traversed but one quarter of the required real estate.

Within a month the thicket complement had tripled, two other goldbrickers having spotted Jack's "good thing." At this point the chief in charge of the group sensed something irregular—a mysterious first-lap thinning. Within a week he had devised a countermeasure, and one morning when snow was in the air he blew his squad whistle and abruptly recalled his troops after a single lap.

Lounging cold but superior in their coppice, the lawless trio reacted with justifiable panic at the far-off sound of the whistle. Bolting from cover they dashed for Eliot House. Too late. The gate was locked. Led by Lemmon they scaled the fence. "The chief knew—he knew," said Jack, "but he didn't say anything. Climbing that fence was punishment enough and he knew that. Damned near killed ourselves and used five times more energy than if we'd run the course in the first place. No one ever had the guts to try it again."

Near the end of his first year at Harvard, Jack was nominated and subsequently accepted as a member of the Delphic Club, one of several social organizations on campus. Normally, one could anticipate nomination as a by-product of family wealth or social position, exceptional personal popularity, or well-placed contacts within the club. In Jack's case, consideration was brought about by his lifelong proclivity for favoring copse or alleyway over civilized latrines.

He continues this rustic ritual even today, defending the practice as "a need, a drive to return to nature." The need is, apparently, more acute when he is on a golf course, where it has the added benefit of throwing his partners off their game.

At Harvard it was Jack's habit to visit an alley outside a beer joint adjacent to Eliot House. He frequented the pub not only for the beer, but to study the barkeep who "was an artist at watering drinks. A master; and fascinating to watch. Anyway, I would never wait the extra twenty seconds until I could get to my room. I'd go in that alley; I sort of liked to let it all hang out.

"There was another fellow who went pretty good in that alley, too. He was always a couple of seconds behind me—which was about two seconds before we were supposed to be in our rooms. One night, he commented that he'd never seen me when I wasn't going someplace, but never in a conventional bathroom. He felt that this marked me as one apart from the crowd and that, therefore, I rightfully belonged in the Gas House—the Delphic Club. He nominated me and that's how I got in. (I never told him, I practiced at Camp Mitigwa.)"

Lemmon loved the Gas. There was good fellowship, food, and best of all, a piano on which he could practice endlessly. A short time later he was accepted as a member of the Dramatic Club and the Pudding. Joyously occupied with the clubs and his music, he devoted ever-smaller increments of attention to his studies. As a result his grades began to hover in perilous proximity to failing. He was placed on academic probation, a status which became more or less permanent.

Despite his dismal record in class, he did leave a literary legacy at Harvard. It would be petty to dwell on the fact that this occurred more by chance than design. Working in a small room upstairs at the Gas, Jack happened upon some yellowed writings in an old desk. Studying the notes, scribbled in longhand in brown ink, he recognized a familiar style—that of Thomas Wolfe, whose play, *Mannerhouse*, he was reading at the time.

"The writing was very dim," said Jack, "and the corner of each page was torn. At the bottom there was a comment by George Santayana, the great Spanish poet who graduated from Harvard in the late 1800s and then returned to teach there until about 1910 or so. Wolfe would sit up all night writing at the Gas and then comment on his own work by jotting bawdy jokes in the margins. The writings were authenticated and I turned them over to the university."

Ever alert to the possibility of escaping the drudgery of physical education class, Jack sniffed out the promising fact that he could escape an enormous number of push-ups and side-straddle hops by joining the Harvard Band, whose members were excused from calisthenics. His conscience was unruffled by the fact that he still could read not one note of music and hadn't the slightest intention of learning.

"I selected as my instrument that thing you carry that sticks up and you bang on it.* I picked out a song, listened to it and worked

* Author's note: Apparently a glockenspiel, a percussion musical instrument consisting of a series of graduated metal bars tuned to the chromatic scale and played with two hammers; in this case, indifferently.

until I could fake it well enough to pass the test. They put me in the band and things were fine until half time of the first game. I wasn't worried because I had forty horns around me; and since I myself could hardly hear this thing I was beating on, I was sure nobody else would notice me. We began marching around and they started playing some march. I didn't like that so I started playing "Deep Purple"—in tempo, of course. Well, what I didn't know was that this instrument of mine made a sound that could pierce pig iron! In the stands you could hear it above every other thing in the band. It was back to phys-ed for Lemmon."

While the classroom was depressing, Jack enjoyed his free time immensely. His circle of friends included the sons of some of New England's wealthiest families. "I was not a social climber," said Jack. "I never have cared about how much money someone had or his station in life; but somehow I fell in with people of considerable means—families like the Gardners, the Humphreys, the Cochrans, and Sears. They lived in and around Boston and had marvelous country homes. They were hardly average, and they certainly didn't have an ordinary lifestyle, but they were wonderful, open people, not snooty at all."

Among Jack's group were Robert Gardner, Richard ("Rick") Humphrey, and John Knowles. "Bobby Gardner's family owned these magnificent estates and we'd flop around in his lily pond. A butler would take a tray with a big rim and push it out to us. We'd just pick a drink off as it floated by. It was *not* a rough war."

Though it was not a rough war, it was a perplexing one. "We were in the ROTC and wore uniforms," said Jack, "but the war was remote to us. We really weren't affected because we'd never gone to sea, never been in combat, and we approached college in much the same way we would have in peacetime. We had too good a time, I guess. Maybe we should have been more aware, although I don't see how we could have done anything about the situation. There was a certain lack of pressure on us and perhaps a consequent failure to recognize the hell that was going on overseas. In a sense we were the one group left untouched. We were naive—and lucky. Very lucky."

Humphrey voiced similar feelings. "It was a funny time. We thought we'd soon be in the war and it seemed more important to be together and have a good time than to be serious about school. None of us worked at our studies; we did what we had to in order to get by, and we spent a lot of time trying to get drunk; drank ten times more than we should have.

"We thought of ourselves as wild, but I guess we really weren't—not by today's standards. As far as girls were concerned, Jack was about like everybody else. In fact, would you believe there was a time when he might have been satisfied with my cast-offs! Jack had the normal relationships; by that I mean he wasn't out every night trying to get laid. None of us were."

Now a prominent advertising executive in Boston, Humphrey occupied a room near Lemmon at Harvard, and remembers that Jack came in for a lot of ribbing because "he was sloppy as hell. We used to accuse him of never doing his laundry! But he was bright and witty, always great fun."

Today, Humphrey shakes his head at some of the "fun" he and Jack had with their friends. "My God, I remember four of us in two cars going down the road at eighty miles an hour and passing a bottle back and forth from one car to the other."

Such goings-on probably were known or suspected by their parents, which may have prompted a statement by Humphrey's father, who called him aside one day and said: "Son, I sometimes wonder about your sense of discrimination. You have two friends that I bet will never amount to a hill of beans. One is Jack Lemmon and the other one is John Knowles."

Knowles became Dr. John Knowles, director of the Massachusetts General Hospital. He was later nominated for the office of Surgeon General of the United States and is now president of the Rockefeller Foundation.

"Lemmon and Knowles," Humphrey said with a grin, "are probably the two most outstanding guys that I know from my generation."

Knowles and Lemmon were not scions of the very wealthy and socially elite, and they had one other thing in common—a passion for the piano. It was this that brought them together. Humphrey insists that they needed each other. "John is left-handed; and Jack, right; and they would play the piano together endlessly. Knowles had a very strong left hand and bass and, although he doesn't like to admit it, not a hell of a lot on the right. Lemmon had a very frothy, melodic right but not much on the left, and no basic understanding of music. Neither of them could, or can, read music; but together they were extraordinary."

Knowles remembers that he and Jack used to perform four-handed piano renditions each morning from six to seven o'clock over the Harvard radio network. There were, he said, two reasons for the dawn recitals. "In the first place, we both enjoyed playing the piano; and in the second place, neither of us wanted to run around the river with the ROTC."

Music, as Jack was soon to discover, could provide other pleasant and quite undreamed-of benefits. Such a bonus materialized in the form of a young lady who, as luck and any good Hollywood script would have it, resided just across the alley from the Gas House. The girl adored music and it was her custom to listen each afternoon as young Lemmon practiced at the piano.

One afternoon when leaving the Gas, Jack chanced to glance over at her window in which a placard was displayed. On it was scrawled in neat feminine script the provocative plea: PLAY SWANEE RIVER.

"I had seen her before," said Jack. "She worked at the bookstore in the Circle at Cambridge. After I saw the sign we got acquainted and would talk across the alley and I would play songs for her. One thing led to another and I finally invited her to the Hasty Pudding one Saturday night when I had weekend liberty. She was older, like twenty-two, had red hair and—wow!"

Smarting yet from romantic indignities visited upon him during the summers at Wolfboro, Jack was determined that on this trip to the love lists he would be girded with faultless suavity and employ an invincible artifice. He would get her drunk.

"So here I am," said Jack, "buying her booze, booze, and more booze until it finally becomes obvious that we are going to make it! Now I'm not about to tell her I've never done a thing like this before and, as a matter of fact, I'm not sure what it is you *do*. It's like the parody on the old song: 'This is my first affair-r-r-r, so won't you tell me what goes where?'

"Anyway, I finally suggest that we go find a car and I must have put out enough loot to get her blind because she says, 'Sure!' So we leave the Pudding and wander down the street to this parking lot, where I spot a little car in the back row where there aren't so many lights.

"It's an old Model-A Ford coupe, the kind with the rumble seat. It has a canvas top held up by these rickety wooden cross members and the top has rips and holes in it. We climb in and immediately I can see there's no way. Houdini couldn't make it in this car. The gearshift—I still have bruises.

"Just the same, we're in there and trying. I can feel it coming up! Now it's going down and she keeps whispering, 'Why are you sweating?' I answer, 'I don't know—you excite me!' And it's up again and then it's down—and then it's a noodle. Anyway, I finally get the damned thirteen buttons loose and my flap down and now—finally—I'm in! At least I *think* I'm in; I'm not sure. In the meantime I've gotten cramps because one leg is sticking straight up and my foot goes right through one of the rips in the top and gets stuck in those wooden things.

"Now I'm frantic to get my leg down, so I'm squirming around like crazy and she says, 'Wow, you're terrific!' and she starts really going like an old-fashioned washing machine, yelling, 'Oh-o-o-o-o-h-h!' and telling me I'm the greatest thing that ever happened, and all I know is the roof is being ripped to hell and the car belongs to someone else.

"Then all of a sudden some guy starts waving a flashlight and yells, 'Who's there? What's going on?'

"Well, my heart stops, but *she* doesn't stop; she's still going, 'O-o-o-o-a-a-h-a-a-,' and I say, 'My God, somebody's coming!' And so help me, she hollers, 'Not yet!'

"I didn't go near another girl for at least nine months. There was no desire—nothing. It was an absolute disaster. I was exhausted, and up to that point it was the worst single experience of my life."

As a consequence of that episode, says Jack, the girl chased him for a year, convinced that she had chanced upon possibly history's greatest lover. "I never did tell her the truth about my foot being caught, and it was years before I mentioned the incident to anyone else. I had to get a lot older before it became funny to me."

For a time after his confrontation with the redhead Jack sought less traumatic ways in which to deplete his youthful energy. Boxing seemed a likely avenue; but the first time he put the gloves on, a neighbor at Eliot House flattened him with one left jab. As soon as he arose from the canvas Lemmon left the fight game and turned to wrestling, a sport he'd enjoyed at Andover.

In his second year, sports, girls, and classroom work paled to insignificance as he buried himself in activities at the Dramatic Club and the Pudding.

When the Dramatic Club decided to stage J. M. Synge's *The Playboy of the Western World*, Jack tried out for and got the part of Old Mahon, an Irish squatter and father of Christopher Mahon, played by a close friend, Ted Allegretti. The play, which tells the story of a timid boy who becomes something of a hero by apparently killing his father, was directed by Mrs. Maude DeWolfe Howe, formerly associated with the Abbey Players.

The part was a challenge to Lemmon who, not yet twenty, was

asked to portray an aged and scraggly man. "Mrs. Howe was a fine director," said Jack, "and it was great fun playing the part—but tough, because I had nothing to work with at that age, no lines in the face or anything. Also, I had to fight a tendency to be too athletic for an old man."

Lemmon's performance was an eyebrow-raiser to theatergoers, who saw flashes of brilliance that a few years later in New York would startle more than one veteran professional actor. Even so, his execution was not without characteristic Lemmonesque moments.

"As part of my makeup," said Jack, "I had blacked out two front teeth with wax. In my first entrance I was supposed to have just been belted over the head by my son. I crawled onstage and hissed something or other. With the first sentence, those wax teeth shot out and nailed some old gal in the front row right in the puss. That was the end of the teeth but it got the biggest laugh in the play."

In 1945 Jack was elected president of the Hasty Pudding, an honor he insists was the result of his name. "There was another fellow named Appel, and everyone thought it would be a great idea if 'Lemon' ran against 'Apple.' I think I beat him out by two votes."

At the urging of members and friends, the Pudding decided to stage its first production since 1941. The show, *Proof of the Pudding*, was written by Lemmon, William Scudder, Hugh Sharpe, and H. Allen Dingwall. The cast included, along with Jack, friends John Knowles and Rick Humphrey, who appeared as a debutante adorned in "a snappy blue gown."

Reviews were mixed, with the music (by Sharpe with lyrics by Scudder) and a piano interlude by Lemmon, singled out for acclaim. *Boston Herald* critic Rudolph Elie, Jr. concluded that the show "isn't much, but the old spirit is there, and this one happens to have the liveliest music in years. If you have any sentimental attachment at all, you'll think it was great."

In his third year at Harvard, Jack had entrenched himself as one of the best-known, most popular figures on campus. He was president of the Hasty Pudding, vice-president of the Dramatic and Delphic clubs, was recognized as one of Harvard's leading actors, and his prowess at the piano made him the center of attraction at social gatherings.

This rosy picture was not without a darkling border. Jack's academic standing was such that it prompted comment from one of the university deans, who declared that he had never before seen anyone so capable as Lemmon for managing to hang on and do nothing, scraping by with just a "spurt here and a spurt there." The dean capped this dour assessment with a prediction: "My boy, I don't see how you will ever amount to anything."

Eventually, the situation deteriorated to the point where Jack was forced to engage in subterfuge in order to appear in a play. He changed his name to Timothy Orange, a maneuver dictated by a Harvard rule that forbade those on probation (as Jack now was) to participate in extracurricular activities. Jack admits the camouflage probably fooled no one but it made his appearance "technically okay."

Lemmon's survival of final examinations to emerge with passing grades and a commission in the U.S. Navy has about it a preternatural similarity to the throwing-away of crutches at Lourdes. Certainly the event must remain somewhat of a mystery to both Harvard and the ROTC. There are those who do not dismiss lightly the theory of divine intervention. The more cynical simply attribute it to Lemmon's faithful companion—incredible good luck.

Chapter

V

"My God, you're fast, boy. You are fast!"
—*Capt. Logan C. Ramsey*

LEMMON TOOK to the ROTC like a mallard to an oil spill. The corps, to its credit, survived the episode and presumably learned and gained from the experience. War Service Science was the catchy title of Jack's study course. Wherever Lemmon's talents lay at the time, it is now generally agreed by most military observers that they were not in the area of war, the armed service, or any known branch of science.

From the first day at Harvard, Jack displayed a massive and widespread disinterest in chemistry, physics, mathematics, and nearly every subject not having direct and immediate application in the fields of acting or music. It is probably no stain on the navy that it was unable to captivate Lemmon. The army would have suffered defeat as well. The navy's only profitable out might have been to revive *H.M.S. Pinafore* as a seafarers' benefit and toss Jack the lead—but it never thought of that.

The piper's bill became due and payable with the onset of final examinations, an event faced with profound dread. "I was nervous, worried sick," Lemmon recalls, "especially about physics. I was rotten at that and chemistry. They were subjects I cared absolutely nothing about, but I knew I had to make a passing grade or that was *it*—I was out. And that thought terrified me.

"Somehow—I don't know how—I got through up to the physics examination, but I was a total wreck. I'll never forget that test. They gave us two hours to solve ten problems. Well, it went okay for a few minutes. I wrote out the first answer, solved it right up. Then I took my time and finished off the second one beautifully. Then—nothing! I couldn't do one thing with the other eight questions."

For a while Jack sat there staring at the clock, miserable. Finally, he began what may well be the greatest acting job of his career. "I don't know how I did it," he said, "but I began to work on myself. It took about fifteen minutes and I began to feel the perspiration pouring off me. I took a couple of more minutes, then did it. Threw up! Right in front of the instructor."

They rushed him to the infirmary. Said Jack: "My temperature was a hundred and one degrees. I was certified sick and popped into bed. I slept all day and night, and the next morning I was fine and went on back to the dorm."

In one of those mysterious moves peculiar to the military, Lemmon was never asked to take the physics exam over. "I guess they looked at those first two answers and thought I knew the rest. Anyway, they passed me and that was that."

Jack remembers that the ROTC captain congratulated him, but with a marked lack of zeal. "I swear he had the look of a guy who suspected he might be aiding and abetting the enemy by making me an officer," Jack said. "He just walked up and said, 'Congratulations, Lemmon. You have the lowest marks of any officer ever commissioned by the ROTC!"

That parting salvo, however, could not dim Jack's exhilaration at not having failed. Now, with great earnest and logic, he set about to convince the navy that he was ill-suited for any warlike duty with the old flotilla. He had not shone in all those classes on medieval rock-throwing, and war flags of the world. Instead of employing him with shot and shell, how much better it would be to make him an entertainment officer—maybe putting together shows and the like, boosting the morale of our boys in uniform so far from home. That sort of thing!

The United States Navy took this petition under advisement—and assigned him as a straight line officer. Orders were cut directing him to report aboard the aircraft carrier U.S.S. *Lake Champlain*, lying at anchor in Norfolk, Virginia.

The Pulverian ensign might have worked up another useful trauma had he known that his new commanding officer would be World War II hero Capt. Logan C. Ramsey, a tough, efficient, altogether uncompromising officer. Captain Ramsey had gained fame in 1937 by authoring an article "Aerial Attacks on Fleets at Anchor," an essay that Adm. Chester W. Nimitz later called a "prophecy of Pearl Harbor." In fact, it was Ramsey who flashed the first word of the eventual Japanese attack with this terse message: AIR RAID. PEARL HARBOR. THIS IS NO DRILL. He was, in short, not the sort likely to accept the ability to play Gershwin by ear as a fitting substitute for gunnery prowess.

After dallying a few days in New York, Jack journeyed to Norfolk, arriving late one misty evening. He was driven to the dock in a jeep for his introduction to the 888-foot, 24,000-ton *Lake Champlain*, which materialized from the gloom like some ectoplasmic resurrection of the *Titanic*.

"This sailor dumped me and my gear out," Jack said, "and just tootled off, leaving me standing there boggled at the biggest ship I'd ever seen. It looked for all the world like the Empire State Building turned on its side. And lights! I had the feeling I was peering down Fifth Avenue.

"I was near a gangplank, so I grabbed my gear and trudged to the top, where I saw this petty officer. Now I knew you were supposed to salute the flag and whoever greets you, whether he's an officer or not. So I saluted, but this old guy never moved a muscle. Just stared at me."

"I'll tell you, kid," growled the chief, "you've come up the wrong gangplank. So pick up your crap and go up the right one."

The next gangplank turned up an officer who registered no more interest in the new arrival than had the chief; but he did ask: "Where you from?"

"Harvard—sir!"

"Harvard, huh?" (A sigh.) "Well, then you must be the new communications officer. C'mon, I'll take you to the exec."

Communications officer? Even the sound of it was ominous. "I knew they had to be making a terrible mistake, but I didn't say anything. If they were running anything this big they must know what they're doing. We found the executive officer asleep and had to awaken him. He looked up through the hair in his eyes and said the same thing: 'Harvard, eh? Okay, you're the new communications officer.'

"Now, I'm really worried," Jack said. "I was sure communications officers were supposed to be commanders or at least full lieutenants. I guess the word 'Harvard' threw them, because it had a big communications school. I didn't know what to do. I couldn't read lights or flags, and I would've been pressed to get off an SOS from a Western Union office! But I was communications officer, and that was that!"

Fortunately for the *Lake Champlain*, the war effort, the American Way of Life—and John Uhler Lemmon III—the big ship had no plans for setting out to sea. She was in the process of deactivation, having completed her duty as a temporary transport bringing American troops home from the European theater of operations as part of the post V-E Day "Magic Carpet" fleet. She had already been stripped of her firepower. Gone were the twelve 5-inchers, the 38-caliber dual-purpose weapons, and the eighteen quadruple 40mm cannons.

The opportunistic Lemmon saw in this back-to-the-plowshare activity a possible hole in the fence, a means of hastening his departure back to home and Harvard. "They were logging material ashore like crazy," Jack remembers, "so I decided to clear the ship of everything assigned to communications. Maybe I could get the hell off with the rest of the hardware. The decoding machines went first, then the flags—you never saw so many damned flags—and finally the lights. All of them. At last it was done, and baby, she was clean as a hound's tooth. If they were going to signal anybody now it would be smoke puffs and tom-toms."

This inspired export program was carried out on Lemmon's "own recognizance," as the military would phrase it, his chief petty officer being away on leave at the time. It was one of those functions of command that, upon reasoned reflection, would have been far better unexercised. It also was in flagrant violation of a primary survival code that all servicemen since Scipio have held inviolate: never volunteer anything. A rider to this code stipulates that the gods of war will avenge any profaning of the ordinance by having very large trouble fall on your head.

The logging-out of the last brace of lights corresponded nicely with the return of the chief petty officer and orders dispatching the *Lake Champlain* to Newport News, Virginia. Not a real sea voyage, to be sure, but still a hazardous hour and twenty-two-minute trip up a crowded channel. A trip, the chief screamed in horror, without so much as a bullhorn for communications.

"Well," Jack recalls sweatily, "I was beginning to panic just a little, but the chief was undergoing apoplexy. He wasn't an officer, but he ate my ass out mercilessly. Of course, I wasn't about to put him on report—and he knew it. I was scared to death of him. He looked about a hundred years old and I swear he must have had fifty-two hash marks."

As the carrier got underway, Jack and the chief took up positions directly below the captain's bridge. For the first few minutes, all was well and Jack's spirits were beginning to improve. Perhaps nobody would have to wave any flags or blink any lights. Presently he chanced to glance up and was immediately sorry. People were stirring around Captain Ramsey, who was staring down questioningly.

"It was about ten seconds later," Jack recalled, "that the exec came roaring down, yelling about where in the hell was the breakdown flag or some such thing. It seems that when a ship starts moving it's supposed to run up a certain flag. I could see Captain Ramsey up there waiting. He was a fearsome sight; a big man, maybe three hundred pounds, and tough-looking.

"By this time the exec was making a big scene about the flag not flying and I said, 'Good heavens! Didn't they do that?' Well, I knew damn well all the flags were on shore, but I made a big thing of running over to the flag locker and looking in. Can you believe it?—over in one corner was a solitary flag, one we'd missed somehow. It was furled and I didn't know whether it was the right one. Hell, it could have been a Jolly Roger and I wouldn't have cared!

"I turned to the exec and said, 'Here we are, sir!' He said, 'Right,' and went back up toward the bridge. I handed that thing to a sailor and said, 'Here, run this up, sailor,' and he did. It was the right one."

No sooner had the flag flap subsided than a new and more formidable crisis arose. As the *Lake Champlain* rounded a bend, she found herself confronting a tanker bearing down on a collision course and yawing badly.

Jack stared in disbelief, transfixed by the certainty of the impending calamity. "Instead of cutting straight through the water, that ship was skittering toward us cockeyed, almost sideways," said Jack. "Sirens were going, bells and horns sounding, lights flashing, and more pennants flying than a used-car lot; in short, all hell was breaking loose and I was sure we were going to collide; they appeared to be right on top of us."

Jack recalls that his chief was no help at all. He was plastered against a bulkhead, eyes rolled to heaven, pouring sweat and muttering curses directed at ensigns in general and at Lemmon with some specificity. "I heard a lot of 'Oh, Christ; oh, Christ,' and his swearing that his career was going down the tubes."

At that point, Jack heard Captain Ramsey scream down from the bridge: "What the hell's wrong with that ship? What are they flying?"

Jack answered, "Working on it, sir!" A last beseeching glance at the chief was fruitless. "He was out of it, and I didn't know what the hell to do. But I had to do something, even if it was wrong. With all that racket going on, it didn't take a genius to figure out that that ship was in trouble. It couldn't have been more than five seconds when for some reason I yelled up: 'Their right screw is out, Captain. They've lost control—and they have the right-of-way.'"

Snapping orders, Captain Ramsey maneuvered the big carrier up against the bank and into the mud; the tanker eased by, *under* the flight deck overhang. "As the other ship went by under there," Jack continued, "I heard one of its crew shout, 'Thank you, Captain—our right rear screw—we lost it.' Well, nobody was more surprised than me."

Moments later, the executive officer came bounding down from the bridge. "Captain wants to see you—on the double."

"Yessir."

It was a nervous Lemmon who mounted the bridge and faced Captain Ramsey. What in God's name could happen next? The captain stared at Jack from his perch atop a swivel chair. "What's your name, boy?"

"Lemmon, sir. Ensign Lemmon, sir."

The captain looked away for a moment and shook his head. "My God, you're fast, boy. You are fast! Giving you a four-0 on your report, boy—a four-0."

Four-0. Perfect. A hundred percent performance rating from the demanding Captain Ramsey. "That flossy rating," said Jack, "got me a cushy job in Washington in some kind of decoding section where all the navy messages came and were filed. All I did was count numbers all day."

After a couple of weeks, the newly confident Lemmon requested a transfer to Boston. The four-0 rating worked its wonders and he was reassigned at once to the Fargo Building, where he was placed in full charge of the motor pool, a position he enjoyed until he had accumulated enough points for discharge.

"It took the navy awhile, but it finally found a job I could handle," laughed Jack. "I had this list of vehicles and I would just check them out until they were all gone. Three and a half years at Harvard it took to get ready for that kind of responsibility—picking up the phone and saying: 'Ensign Lemmon—jeeps and trucks!' "

Chapter

VI

"Thank God for a British boy!"
—*Roddy McDowall's mother*

IN THE SUMMER of 1946 Ensign Jack Lemmon and the United States Navy parted company with a sigh of wary relief, like opposing enemy soldiers who have run out of ammunition at the same time with no damage done. The navy went about its business of preparing for the enemy, real and imagined, and Lemmon went back to what, in reality, he had never left: the theater.

With an entire summer at hand prior to his reentry to Harvard, Jack joined the North Shore Players, a Beverly Massachusetts stock company gearing for its fourth season after having been dark during the war years. He signed on as an assistant carpenter, with the assurance he would get a tryout for three plays then in the works.

His first chance to drop the clawhammer came with the staging of Patrick Hamilton's *Angel Street*, starring Francis Lederer, Bramwell Fletcher, and Helen Shields. Jack was awarded the part of a policeman—a nonspeaking role requiring only that he rush on stage in the final act and apprehend Lederer, the heavy, who at that point would be taking flight. Small though it was, the part was to teach young Lemmon a rudimentary lesson: Always inspect the wardrobe.

Jack zipped through the rehearsals flawlessly, nabbing Francis with the goods on cue. The bit was so simple he didn't bother trying on his full costume until opening night. "Everything seemed to fit, so I didn't waste time checking out the hat. Schmuck! I was standing in the wings enjoying the whole thing, when suddenly there's my cue! I grabbed the hat, slapped it on and bolted onstage where Francis was already starting to run. Well, the hat was miles too big and fell down over my nose and caught there. I couldn't see a damned thing and I didn't know where I was.

"Of course," said Jack, grinning, "Francis saw what was happening and he covered by sort of grabbing me. But I felt so ridiculous I think I ducked him afterwards."

Lederer feels the incident went largely unnoticed by the audience. "We had a magnificent set and it was darkly lit," said Francis. "I'm just surprised Jack remembers that situation at all. I had forgotten it until he reminded me of it recently at a function here in California."

His embarrassment soon forgotten, Jack confronted a new challenge. Tryouts were being held for *Young Woodley*, John Van Druten's tale of an English schoolboy's first love, which was to star Roddy McDowall. The part of Milner, third largest role in the play, was up for grabs, and although Jack felt his chances of landing it were remote at best, he decided to have a go at it—as did every other young actor for miles around, plus a flock of pros from New York.

"It seemed like five thousand kids were up for the part," Jack said. "This was an important opportunity—a chance to work with Roddy, who was a big kid star at fourteen, and one hell of an actor. Roddy's mother was there and she could be really tough, as I'm sure Roddy would agree, but if she liked you, she was terrific. She was up there in the first row of the balcony and as each kid came out to read, he would only get through about four lines when she would stand up and yell: 'He's not *British*. He won't do!'

"Well, most of them were British, and I watched eight guys in a row go down the tubes before my turn came. I was petrified. But I walked out on the stage, waited until Roddy threw me my cue, and started talking in an English accent. Three lines into it, up pops his mother, and I couldn't believe my ears. 'Thank God for a British boy!' she said, and I got the part."

It was a turning point for Lemmon, who checked in with a first-rate performance. "I was good in the part and I knew it," said Jack. "It gave me confidence and I think for the first time I realized that perhaps I wasn't just whistling Dixie about this acting thing."

In the fall of 1946, America was trying to readjust to peace and millions of returning GI's. Harvard, like college campuses all across the land, was in tumult. Acne-troubled teeny-boppers were mixing with crusty combat veterans while perplexed school officials wrestled with courses and codes woefully out of sync with the times.

One of Harvard's returning warriors was Andrew McCullough, a handsome and talented young man aiming at a career in the theater. Andy did, in fact, become a highly respected director, and today is busily writing his first novel while selling California real estate to support that venture. He remembers clearly the hectic postwar days, especially his introduction to another returning veteran—a brash young fellow named Jack Lemmon.

"It was kind of a crazy time," said Andy. "The war was over, a lot of the people you had known were now dead, you were back to get your degree, you were broke and way behind. We were all twenty-one or twenty-two and thought we were ruined, that we would never amount to anything. Classes were all jumbled and there were new people you'd never seen. So my roommate, Dick McCarthy, and I gave a cocktail party in our suite to find out what the hell was going on. About fifty or sixty people showed up."

During the party, while chatting with a friend, Andy happened to glance across the room where, on a couch, an altogether unsettling event was transpiring. "There on the sofa was this young guy kissing my girl! I watched for a minute, and it went on and on and *on*. I finally went over and pushed him off and said, 'That's my girl!' He looked up and said 'Delighted you brought her!'—and he kissed her again! Well, I thought, 'Son of a bitch,' and started to swing at him, but my roommate intervened."

"What are you doing?" demanded McCarthy.

"That son of a bitch is kissing my—"

"Aw, forget it. He's a terrific guy, marvelous guy. He's in the Gas with me. You'll love him."

"I *don't* love him," snapped Andy. "Get him the fuck outta here!"

After McCarthy pulled Lemmon away from the girl, Andy recalls that he cooled off and had some conversation with Jack. "He was as fresh as paint. You know, everybody today thinks of

Lemmon as having been like a young Jimmy Stewart when he actually was more like a young Jimmy Cagney."

A few weeks after the cocktail party, McCullough was casting a play he was directing for the Harvard Dramatic Club and was having trouble finding anyone to fill a small but showy part—that of a Cockney. During a conversation with Ted Allegretti, Andy mentioned the role.

"I know a guy," said Allegretti, "who does a great Cockney. Lemmon—Jack Lemmon. I just saw him; he's back from the navy and he would be fantastic. In fact, I just left him over at St. Clair's."

The pair walked directly to St. Clair's, a coffee house, script in hand. "I hadn't caught Lemmon's name at the party," said McCullough, "so I was stunned when we walked in and there was this same guy—and with my girlfriend again—*ex*-girlfriend. I said, as icily as I could—which made no dent on Jack at all—'I understand you do a Cockney?' "

"I do the best Cockney in the world," Jack said airily, "in the world! Absolutely the best Cockney accent you will ever hear."

McCullough was almost nauseous. "I thought, 'Jesus Christ!' but I finally said, 'Would you like to look over the part? I have a copy of the script here.' "

"I'll read it right now," Jack said. "Best reading you will ever hear in your life. If Lemmon says he can do it, he can do it!"

Incredulous, Andy asked, "You don't need any time to understand the play? What it's all about?"

"Absolutely not," Jack said, grabbing the script. "Let's see, now, how does the line go? Scatty-vatty-voo, da-de-da . . ."

"He gave the reading," Andy said with a laugh, "and he was marvelous, but I thought to myself, 'I *can't* cast him, he is the worst prick I have ever met in my life.' Yet, he was certainly the best actor.

"We started rehearsals and it was marvelous working with him. I think anyone who has ever worked with Jack on any level will tell you that; he's excited, he's involved, and he isn't theoretical—doesn't like to talk about it, he loves to *do it.*"

The play was *Adam the Creator*, a satiric fantasy in seven scenes by Karel and Joseph Capek. McCullough, who not only directed but played the role of the Voice of God, staged the production in Cambridge at the Sanders, a replica of an Elizabethan theater.

Lemmon remembers the play vividly because of one hysterical

moment which occurred before a third-night packed house. "In that marvelous old theater, above the proscenium, there was a little hidden pulpitlike affair. The theater was so beautifully designed that anything spoken from there would seem to come from everywhere. As the Voice of God, Andy read all his lines from there. He had one line he was crazy about and he'd read it in these rolling stentorian tones. It was: 'Adam, what *have* you done?'

"The play was very avant-garde for its day, all about the bomb and destruction of the world and whatnot. Well, I was Oddly-Come-Short, the little Cockney, and Teddy Allegretti was Adam. This particular night, Ted was wailin' away—he was a damn good actor—and I was waiting in my cave to make my entrance.

"In moving and looking around, Ted turned his back to the audience and bent over. At that point, unfortunately, he involuntarily broke wind! Well, it was such a thundergust that I don't think I have ever in my life heard the equal of it—a veritable cannonade, so incredibly loud and long. Ted was frozen and the audience was in a state of shock. But not McCullough—he saved the day by blasting out his favorite line: 'ADAM, WHAT *HAVE* YOU DONE?'

"Well, that did it! I want to tell you I have never heard a louder, longer laugh. It must've lasted five full minutes. People were getting up, stomping on the floor, the whole play was stopped. I had the common sense to delay my entrance, but that left poor Teddy out there, wandering around the stage ad-libbing, until things quieted down."

Working together on the play, Andy and Jack became friends and began writing songs together. "Out of all this," said McCullough, "I met his mother, who had an apartment in Boston. I got to know Millie very well. She wasn't like most of the middle-class gray-haired mothers I had met; she was kind of cafe society, a platinum blonde, very slinky, who always seemed to be on the way out to the Copa or Ritz Bar.

"As it happened, Jack graduated from Harvard in mid-year, while I had to stay on for another six months; so I didn't see him again until the summer of 1947 because he had gone on down to New York."

Although the subject had not been seriously discussed, John and Millie knew of Jack's determination to go to New York and make a life on the stage. His parents were worried about him—especially John, who had hoped his son would follow him in the bakery business. Later John was to confide to friends that he hated the thought of Jack running around with "God knows who" down in New York. Still, when Jack approached him with his decision and a request for a $300 loan, his father was typically gracious.

"You're sure you want to be an actor?"

"Yes," answered Jack.

"Do you love it?"

"Yes."

"Then," said his father, "you have to do it. I have always said that when the time comes that I don't find romance in a loaf of bread I'll quit the business."

Jack got the $300 and his parents' blessing.

He took the train to New York, standing up most of the way, hanging on between two cars and "grinning like a horse's ass because I was so thrilled, so filled with excitement. I was going to be the next Gershwin, because the country was sorely in need of someone of his caliber, and I was going to save the American theater! It was only much later that I found out they wouldn't let me do that, for some peculiar reason."

Lemmon's introduction to Gotham was more or less predictable for that city, which the cynics insist is a place where nobody lives, but only serves time. On arrival in Grand Central Station there was a greeter—a handsome middle-aged black man who walked up smiling and said: "Hi, there, guy! Can I show you New York?" Not rebuffed by the congenial Lemmon turndown, the man followed him to the men's room where he kept grinning, winking, and staring.

"I remember thinking," said Jack, "that there was something a little strange about this fellow, that there might be a little 'dash' of something in there. Hell, looking back on it, he was about four and a half feet off the ground and pedaling!"

Flagging a cab, Jack headed for Broadway in search of a hotel, eventually selecting one on Forty-fourth Street where the desk clerk demanded three dollars a night for his cheapest room, a converted linen closet barely wide enough for a bed. "That three-dollar price almost killed me," said Jack, "because that kind of extravagance would soon lay waste to the three hundred bucks, and there was no telling whether that would last until I made it in show business. You know, producers are pretty stupid at times; they don't recognize us just walking around!"

Having paid the three dollars, Jack proceeded to spend the entire night walking the streets and "going in here and there—

anyplace but Sardi's. I went by there several times and looked in the window, but I didn't have the guts to actually enter. Once I saw Tom Ewell standing at the little bar, and I thought, 'Holy God! That's Tom Ewell!' Later on, I used to see David Wayne in there. Boy, did I admire him."

Already showing a near-flawless flair for dramatic timing, Jack turned up in Shubert Alley just at daybreak and paused to read the famed sign: Through This Alley Passed the Immortals of the Theater. Standing there, staring up at those inspiring words, fame and success now seemed beyond reasonable doubt. "Okay," he muttered happily, "move over! The old Boston bullet is here and everything will be fine now." That ecstatic claim preceded six months of unemployment bordering on vagrancy.

In the following weeks, Lemmon became a familiar figure in the outer (but seldom the inner) offices of agents and producers. Feckless sorties were conducted daily and by the end of the sixth miserable week the dark bird of reality had fluttered in and taken up a permanent perch outside his window. Jack soon fell into a pattern that was to continue throughout those dreary first months in New York. He would buy paperback books for a quarter, principally Ellery Queen, and hole up in his hotel or rooming house to read until dawn—then sleep away the day as an escape.

At last it became apparent that his "profligate" life at the hotel was at an end, and he would have to bundle with the proletariat—unless, of course, a friend of substance and compassion could be found; that is, one with a couch and a willingness to have an up-and-coming actor sleep on it.

Fortune has a way of slipping an understanding arm around the shoulder of Jack Lemmon in times of physical peril or payroll paucity. It cozied up this time in the person of Maury Shea, a neighbor from Wolfboro who operated a chain of theaters known as the Shea Circuit. "Maury was a marvelous guy," said Jack, "and he let me mooch a place on his sofa. He lived near the East River, a block from P. J. Clark's, which was made famous in Billy Wilder's production of *The Lost Weekend*."

During his stay at Maury's, Jack began to take long walks by the river late at night. "I would just stroll along and think and hope and dream, and then go into one of those White Tower places or some other joint and order scrambled eggs with catsup. The catsup was necessary because the food always had the consistency of soft leather."

Wednesdays were red-letter days because that was publication day for *Actors' Cues*, a small newspaper that featured casting tips.

Jack would be first in line at the newsstand on Forty-fourth Street in Times Square to lay out a precious dime and then race to various casting offices, inevitably to no avail. Seeing an agent at all was difficult and, even then, fruitless. Their legendary insensitivity was as reported by all who had fought in Broadway's trenches.

Eventually, by chance and cunning, Jack was able to wangle a meeting with one agent almost at will. This came about because Maury Shea, who traveled a great deal, owned an unusual coat which stayed home. Jack recalls that it was a splendid garment with black fur collar and cuffs "like the Russians wear." Through Maury's absence and generosity, Jack began wearing the coat.

"I didn't have a nickel," said Jack, "but I was wearing this terrific coat. One of the agents on my daily rounds was Lester Shurr, who had a big office in the Paramount Building where there were always about forty actors in the anteroom smoking and chatting and waiting. Every once in a while, Lester would come out and beckon for someone to come into his office, somebody he might have a part for."

One day the agent came out, did a double-take at Lemmon, then waved somebody else inside. Five minutes later he was back, this time crooking a finger to Jack. "Hey, kid. Come in."

Once inside, Jack launched into a nonstop spiel about how he could sing and dance and play comedy *or* drama, and was a songwriting sensation as well as a piano player.

Shurr was unimpressed. "Look, kid, you don't understand. I don't have anything for you. But what do you want for the coat?"

Taken aback, Jack stammered that he couldn't sell it. "I wasn't about to tell him that it wasn't mine, but something told me not to give him a definite No. So I said, 'I'm really very fond of this coat and I couldn't give it up. It would be an awfully hard decision. It's a very expensive coat and I had to *do a lot of shows* to get it.' "

"You sure," Shurr pressed, "that you don't want to sell it?"

"Well—I don't think so. Let me give it some consideration."

"Okay," Shurr agreed, "you think about it, and come back."

"I kept right on coming back," said Jack, "and I was always indefinite. I knew he was never going to say he had a part for me, but at least I was seeing an agent! You could live by those moments. It made me feel that at least the world wasn't one hundred percent closed to me."

Lemmon believes that some of the agents and producers knew what just meeting with them for a moment meant to young actors.

He recalls that Nate Beards of the William Morris Agency used to come out into the huge Morris anteroom three times a week, shake hands with everybody there, and say a few words. "It was wonderful that he would do that," said Jack. "He knew what it did for the kids."

In the fall of 1947 Andy McCullough, now graduated from Harvard, came to New York and sought out Lemmon. It was a meeting not soon to be forgotten by McCullough. Jack was, of course, wrapped in Maury's coat, an item Andy saw in a strikingly different light.

"Jack was wearing this abominable raccoon coat that looked like Bobby Clark's, and he was carrying a malacca cane! His appearance was very much like that of Tony Curtis in *Some Like It Hot*. He started dragging me around to agents' offices where there would be some snarling secretary who hated him, *hated* him.

"Jack would walk up to the secretary and say something like 'Gracie, darling! God, it's wonderful to see you! I want you to meet a friend of mine.' The girl would scream 'Get out, get out!' and Jack would ignore it and say: 'Hey, he's got a great little act you could use—and have you got a little thing for me?' Naturally, the girl would just keep yelling, 'No! Get *out!*' Jack would turn to me and say, 'Wonderful girl, Gracie.' "

Jack once took Andy to Sardi's, where a small group was gathered at the bar, including Bernie Hart, Moss Hart's brother, who, McCullough says, later recalled the incident.

Moving in confidently, Jack said, "Hi, there! Hi, there, everybody! I've got my old friend Andrew McCullough with me!"

"They all turned their backs on him," said Andy. "It was like 'the club bore is back.' He was kind of a mix of W. C. Fields and Cagney, and I didn't know what the hell was going on. I was kind of embarrassed to be seen with him."

According to McCullough, Jack turned to him after a while and whispered, "We don't eat here; we go to Bergen's, where they have the cheap lunch for sixty-five cents."

"Jack," said Andy, "what the fuck are you doing? What is all this bullshit?"

"Oh, it's rough," confided Jack, "it's really rough. This is the only way you can make it. I wear the coat because everyone remembers it; it attracts a lot of attention."

To Andy, the situation was puzzling because he knew Lemmon to be a sensitive person who, at Harvard, wanted to be the most popular man on campus. "Jack was kind of an off-horse, an outlander who managed to be completely accepted by the club aristocrats. If you were an Irish-Catholic at Harvard, that was much worse than being a Jew; because while there were 'white' Jews, there were no 'white' Irish-Catholics. But Jack made friends of all those who would normally be inclined to look down on him. I thought it was rather strange of Jack to do this because he had his mind made up about what he wanted to be, and I could see no connection between acting and whether the Adamses or the Lowells liked him.

"It was," said Andy, "a kind of political sense—like knowing the elevator operator's name and asking, 'How's your wife?' and so forth. Jack had that. Perhaps it's what goes to make up an actor, especially comedians, who want their audiences to love them, as opposed to a Brando who doesn't give a shit whether they like him or not.

"Anyway, here was this go-getter behaving like a character out of a Sinclair Lewis story, yet a guy who was conscious of what he was doing. He did it deliberately. Jack had a lot of ambition, a lot of drive. If there was a chance there might be a part available, he would go after it, con people, get on the phone and find out who was sleeping with the stage manager and call *her*. He played all the angles."

(*Note:* Lemmon's reaction to the above: "Fascinating, but either I've got a lousy memory or Andy's full of shit!")

During the early winter Jack relinquished his hold on Maury's couch and for a short period took a room, a walkup on the fourth-floor of an old brownstone in the upper sixties. The room, which in earlier and better days had served as a storage closet, listed as its only appointment an army cot. There were no windows, only a small skylight which Jack dubbed the "tantrum." All who dared open it were deluged with dust and soot. "It was," said Jack, "a matter of expire or go blackface." What the accommodation lacked in elegance it made up in price: two dollars a week.

The brownstone and Jack's monastic billet were under the circumspect command of Mrs. Martinelli, a motherly martinet with a Prussian corporal's passion for order. In addition to running a tight ship, Mrs. Martinelli had a small side business—an operation conducted with a stockbroker's instinct for economic leverage.

The instrument of profit was a pay telephone located on the first floor. Under Mrs. Martinelli's astute management it became the building's "answering service." Incoming calls were intercepted and callees summoned at volume in her marginal English.

With exceptions. No calls were floated up the stairwell unless the recipient had signed up for the "service" at fifty cents per week. Not listed among Mrs. Martinelli's captive customers was Lemmon, for whom the four-bit fee would have constituted deficit financing.

For those on the paid list receiving calls, Mrs. Martinelli would yell out and leave the telephone receiver hanging so that the person could come down and speak with the caller.

Recognizing that certain individuals would abstain from payment, Mrs. Martinelli devised countermeasures. Rather than refuse the calls, which would have been counterproductive, she adopted a guerilla tactic that proved highly successful in bringing holdouts around. It was a process of gradually tightening the screws.

"She would answer the phone," said Jack. "I could hear her say, 'Yes? Who? One-a moment-a pliz.' Unless it was a call for somebody taking her service she would stand there. She wouldn't yell for you, but for about twenty seconds, she wouldn't hang up, either. During that twenty seconds I would go down those four flights like a streak. Jesse Owens couldn't have made it faster. When I got there, usually in my shorts, I'd say 'For me?'—which it usually wasn't. She'd give me an enigmatic smile and walk away with: 'No, it'sa notta for you.' She was a marvelous old character and tough, but she never broke me. I never did pay."

Once in a while Jack would write to his parents, but these messages became more infrequent as weeks became months with not a single job to report. "I was terribly embarrassed," Jack recalls. "I had nothing to say and I'd make up things like: 'Guess what! I'm getting an interview tomorrow! Whoopee.' Great flashes like that.

"Every so often my father would come into town on a business trip and he'd find me—but not easily, because I never knew where I was going to be. When he did locate me I would sometimes borrow ten or fifteen bucks from him—reluctantly. He worried about me because nearly a year had passed and I still had nothing."

Nothing? Not quite. There was hope. "Somebody," said Jack, "once told me the odds against ever making it in show business were actually about a million to one against you. When you are young, you are filled with the ignorant optimism of youth. You don't know whether or not you can make it because you've never had a chance. What you don't realize is that even if you get a job, you'll still never know whether you are really talented until you're lucky enough to get a truly good part with a top company and a good director. Hell, that might never happen. There are probably thousands of fine actors who never made it simply because they never got that chance. Luck and timing—they are as important as talent."

In the search for a chance, any chance, Jack teamed with a very young girl named Mitzi Mandelbaum, who wanted to put together a revue that would tour the Catskills. Jack remembers that Mitzi was very bright and about sixteen years old. The problem with Mitzi, he said, was that she didn't have the one ingredient needed most by the small group they'd put together: money.

"For weeks a bunch of us kids worked on that thing, trying to put it together, and finally we were really down and out. Nothing to eat and no place to go. Not a one of us even had enough to get a cheap hotel room. By this time I had forfeited my place at Mrs. Martinelli's. During this period, for a long stretch, Andy McCullough's family took me under its wing. They had a home on Long Island, so at times I had a place to eat and sleep. They also had a piano and we could practice. Andy and I were trying to write songs together at the time."

One evening, the group found itself with no funds and no place at all to sleep. Pooling their money, they bought two hamburgers, carefully divided them, and then went in search of shelter for the night.

"I don't know who found the place," Jack said, "but we ended up in some godforsaken old building in Hell's Kitchen near the river on the West Side. The windows were all boarded up and had X's painted on them. We found a room on the first floor that had a couple of old mattresses and we sprawled out. I think there were three guys and two girls, and we were worried about rats and everything else.

"Things went okay until about eight o'clock in the morning, when all hell broke loose. There was this tremendous crash. I thought there'd been an explosion until I saw a big steel ball the size of a Buick come bashing through the wall and then draw back and disappear! Christ! Things started falling all around; everyone was screaming and hollering. I think the same thought hit us all at the same time, and that was that at any moment that ball was going to come back through again and then—good-by Charlie!

"Well, hell! I went right through a window that was *boarded up* and then pulled the girls out behind me. There was a wrecking crew outside and those guys were screaming at us. I don't think we stopped running until we hit Times Square and that was about ten blocks away. One of the guys lost a shoe in the getaway and ran with one bare foot. He had to go back for it later."

Jack sighed. "Those were the days. Nothing bothered you, because you didn't give a damn about physical comfort. I've forgotten where we slept the next night. We were just nomads, scrounging whatever we could—anything, anywhere."

Chapter

VII

"You're hired. There's no salary."
—*Paul Killiam, The Old Knick*

TO OPEN A SHOP is easy; the difficult thing is keeping it open. So goes an old Chinese proverb, an adage that must have seemed incredibly apt to Jack Lemmon in the final weeks of 1947. Not a single buyer had been found for his wares and he had taken to reflecting on the wisdom of those who exist in simple, honest anonymity: woodcutters in the dell and the like.

For a brief while during the summer there had been hope. He and Andy had tested some of their surefire songs on a summer stock outfit in East Hampton, but were shot down in flames. However, Andy had been acceptable and was hired as a stage manager.

"Jack came out to East Hampton with my folks to see me," said Andy, "and I lorded it over him abominably. You know—I was the working pro, while he'd had a rough summer; hadn't gotten a thing."

The glory was brief for Andy, who soon found himself in the mailroom of the Compton Advertising Agency, unable to advance an inch farther in his theatrical career for the moment.

With a stoicism uncommon outside the ranks of the Praetorian Guards, Jack kept plugging away, chipping at the wall of indifference thrown up around Broadway. A study in retrograde motion, he moved from one rooming house to another, each more wretched and correspondingly cheaper than the last.

One afternoon, McCullough's mail sorting was interrupted by a telephone call from an old army colleague who wanted to sublet his apartment while he went on the road with a touring theatrical company. Would Andy like to take over the place? Real cheap? Andy jumped at the chance. The apartment, a fourth-floor, cold-water walkup on Delancey Street, sported five rooms with a toilet down the hall. Its trappings included three venerable claw-footed bathtubs, all of which reposed in the kitchen. After surveying the new abode, Andy's first move was to reach Jack.

"It's a fantastic place to live," he assured a cautious Lemmon. "We can share it and split the rent. You'll save a fortune."

"I'm already saving as much as it is possible to save," replied Jack. "If I save any more, they'll be paying *me.* Besides, I'm in here—"

"Get out of it," persisted Andy. It can't compare. This is really a great apartment. You'll be very happy here."

Jack relented, and dazzled by the relative opulence of McCullough's dwelling, moved in despite the frighteningly high rent: $2.50 a week. The first night, Lemmon came bounding out of the bedroom wrapped in a blanket and pointing accusingly over his shoulders. "Rats!"

"Rats?" asked Andy evenly. "There are no rats. It must be your imagination."

"Rats!" insisted Jack. "The size of antelopes!"

An inspection banished all doubt. "They were all over the place," laughed Andy. "Leaping around in there like terriers. We closed off the studio and bedroom, moved into the kitchen and from then on slept in the bathtubs. By the way, there were some cockroaches of heroic size in that kitchen."

Now that a détente of sorts had been reached with the rats, it was necessary to find some means of combatting the onrushing winter. "We didn't have a pot, so to speak," said Jack, "but we went out and got a really big one and filled it with water. Then we lit the oven, stuffed the pot in, and left the oven door open. Within two hours we had steam heat."

At this point, a new method of obtaining food was perfected; the ubiquitous New York cocktail party. "Jack had a lot of well-to-do friends, people he'd known at Andover or Boston, who were always throwing these parties and we would go to their posh apartments on the East Side and Jack would play the piano," said Andy. "Well, we would live off hors d'oeuvres. The waiter would come by and we'd take the *tray.*"

Demands of the stomach having been met, other important matters could be considered: girls. McCullough recalls that there developed a "tremendous battle of the sexes." Guile, deceit, lies—all the normal weapons of romance—were trundled out and deployed. Such steps were necessary because the girls, usually naive debutantes, had to be convinced to go to the apartment—a trip requiring a bus, the subway, and one transfer.

"They always protested," said Andy. "They wanted to go out to dinner and we didn't have any money, of course. We had to get them to the apartment. Jack would do a song and dance about having to go there to await a call from a big agent or something."

Usually, these machinations were not successful. On the occasions when the girls could be lured into the trip, they often balked when they neared the apartment, taking offense at the neighborhood, the stray cats, the overturned garbage cans.

On the off chance that the girls turned out to be the hardier, pioneering types who would actually climb the four flights to the apartment, another ruse would be called into play, this one dealing with the dearth of suitable beverages.

Jack would initiate the routine by opening and shutting cabinet doors in a useless quest which ended with an exasperated, "Andy, where's the Black Label?"

Andy's line was: "Why are you asking me? You were supposed to—"

Jack (snapping his fingers), "That's right! By God, I was. It *was* my turn. It slipped my mind completely—and all we have is some cooking sherry."

"It was a dreadful line," said Andy, "and he always read it, I thought, very badly. Generally the girls left at that point because this was a little too much. But we figured that *if* they stayed—it was such a terrible neighborhood and a long walk and everything—things would be all right. But it still was a long shot.

"I remember one night I was working on this girl in the front bedroom and Jack was in the kitchen with his date and I suddenly heard her say: 'You sleep in the bathtub? What are you, sick or something? You some kind of freak?' I heard the door slam; the girl had split. I went out to the kitchen and Jack was poised there over the tub. Seducing a girl in a bathtub is not the easiest thing in the world!"

Christmas 1947 was one suffered in Dickens-like frugality, the kind the impoverished recall as one of those affairs where "you get new cardboard for your shoes." Jack sent his mother a trinket with a note: "With love, respect, and hopes that in the future I can offer more concrete things to show my gratitude and love—J. L." In the corner of the note Jack drew a small, round, smiling face.

As previously pointed out, a recurring theme in Lemmon's life is his knack of falling on a fumble in the end zone to win the game. It may be that the whole thing is more a function of pluck than luck, coupled with a scoutlike propensity for preparedness. But in Jack's case, one keeps remembering the old Arab saying that you can pitch a lucky man into the Nile and he'll come up with a fish in his mouth.

One night in January, walking back from a visit with Maury Shea, Jack rounded the corner of Second Avenue and Fifty-fourth Street and chanced to glance in the window of The Old Knickerbocker Music Hall. He saw a familiar face looking back; it was Paul Killiam, who had attended Harvard and seen Jack in one of the Hasty Pudding shows.

"I went in," said Jack, "and Paul bought me a beer and we talked. The Old Knick could hold five hundred customers and there were about twenty people in the joint. I later learned that that was a good night for them—it was considered packed."

"We're running an amateur-night show," said Paul. "Why don't you belt out a number and you'll win."

"How do you know?" asked Jack.

"Well," Paul rubbed his chin, "I don't think anybody else is going to enter. Besides, I'll just *say* you won."

Having established the ground rules, Jack sang one of his own compositions, "Lucy Isn't Goosey Anymore," accompanying himself at the piano. He was declared an unanimous winner by Killiam, beating out a thirteen-year-old juggler for the honor. "It was," said Jack, "no contest."

"That was terrific," said Paul, shaking Lemmon's hand. "You're hired. There's no salary."

The Old Knick was a modified joint venture. "There was no union in there," Jack recalls. "You would work and get a free meal—a piece of chicken and a few french fries in a basket. At the week's end you would all split the tips and profits, if there were any. You might get five dollars now and then, and one time I got seventy-five dollars; I couldn't believe it. But I was working and it was sensational."

Work was whatever needed doing. Jack served as a singing waiter and the orchestra, which consisted of a piano. Killiam would run old silent films and narrate them while Lemmon provided piano accompaniment.

"We could do anything," said Jack, "as long as we didn't repeat, because if two new customers came in, the show started over again. Christ, I made up more stuff because you might be on twenty times a night. I did a pitchman routine where I wore a straw hat and a blazer and went out into the audience with a microphone. You know, I'd put on the old nasal twang and say, 'Right this way, folks, step right in—fifty girls, fifty—some of them even younger!' Then I'd hold up a photograph and tell the audience: 'What you do, ladies and gentlemen, is strike a match and move it—in an un-du-lat-ing fashion behind the picture. Now, watch the little girlie wiggle! It's guaranteed to re-joove-enate you, or else consult your family physician.'

"Well, it was awful, but I loved it." Others began to love it, too. Columnists started plugging the shows, now and then mentioning young Lemmon's piano-playing and pitch routine. Performers who worked with Jack took notice as well.

Andy recalls how Jack Albertson, one of many name talents who worked The Old Knick, was astonished at Lemmon. "The first night he was there," said Andy, "Albertson did a skit with Jack and afterwards grabbed me by the arm and asked: 'Who is he? Who is that kid?' I told him his name was Lemmon. Then he asked, 'Where'd he get that timing?' "

When not on stage, Jack would help tend bar, where drinks were poured with elaborate care. "We didn't short anybody or water them, but there wasn't any spillage. We had the dryest bar top in New York, because Paul said if we were able to pour the absolute maximum number of drinks per bottle of booze there would be more to split up at the end of the week."

While the bar may have been honest to a fault, other operations sometimes lowered the standard a notch. Such was Jack's pièce de résistance—the singing of "By the Beautiful Sea," an audience participation act in which customers were offered a free bottle of champagne if they could sing the song faster than Lemmon. Words to the song were flashed on a screen by an assistant named Pepe, a key man in the "success" of the routine. Customers, of course, were unaware that a bottle of champagne had never been seen at The Old Knick. Lemmon was so informed by Paul, who added ominously, "Don't lose."

Jack would begin by singing the song, after which a customer was invited to do the same. Jack would offer them a stopwatch to time their performance. "The thing that got 'em," said Jack, "was the line, 'I love to be beside your side, beside the sea, beside the seaside, by the beautiful sea.' That was tricky if you were trying to do it fast, but I'd had plenty of practice.

"Now, in case somebody was pretty good and it looked like he might be a threat when he got to the last chorus, I would give just a slight look over my shoulder to Pepe, who was in the booth behind me watching like a hawk, and he would—ever so slightly—blur the words on the screen, just momentarily. It was just enough so that the guy would squint and then stumble, and I'd be there like a shot to say, 'Sorry—next!' By that time the words on the screen were clear and the poor guy would blink and look and rub his eyes. There's the outside chance that such deportment might be termed unprofessional!"

The Old Knick was host to a number of top performers, along with many like Lemmon, who would become stars in the future. In one show, Jack recalls, the cast included Albertson, Maureen Stapleton, and Darren McGavin. Others who worked there occasionally were Jack Cassidy, Gene Barry, and Cliff Robertson.

McGavin, billed as Davin McGaren at the time, worked The Old Knick to gain experience, as did most of the young actors and actresses who showed up on the bill. "I'd appeared in a couple of films in California," he said, "but I was pretty bad and figured I'd better get my tail to New York and learn something about the craft if I intended to stay in the business.

"Jack, 'Mo' Stapleton, Cliff Robertson, and the others—we were all alike: young kids on our asses in the big city scratching at the door of show business. Boy, it was a tough time. Making it was really rough.

"I do remember that even then I looked on Lemmon as supertalented. He had, and still has, that lovely light touch to his acting. It's almost a mathematical thing, and it's required to give really great comedy performances. Playing comedy is the most difficult job in acting and very few actors have what it takes to do it well. Most young actors coming up today have a dark tone to their work, not that lightness I see in Jack. Lemmon has done some fine dramatic work in recent years, but I do hope he will continue to do comedy as well."

Those who worked The Old Knick would agree with Jack, who says it was ". . . the last vestige of the kind of place George Burns remarked about years ago when he said, 'The trouble is, there's no place left for a kid to be lousy.' That was the value of The Old Knick, of vaudeville, of the circuits. You could get experience. That kind of thing existed in the early days of television, too, but no more. You could do anything at The Old Knick—and anything was likely to happen."

One of those things that happened was a robbery. Late one night, Jack was preparing to go home, and since it was Saturday he approached the club's bookkeeper, a chap with "a kind of bent nose and a funny-looking ear."

"Do we get paid this week?" asked Jack.

"Afraid not," said the bookkeeper, pulling a gun from his pocket.

"Right, sir!" replied Jack, "You are right! Absolutely!"

The man then replaced the gun and continued counting his money. "You folks just keep cool," he advised. Finally, he joined his accomplice, an aging waiter standing by the exit, and the pair walked out. "I don't know if they ever caught those two old geezers," said Jack. "I do remember that before they left, they said goodnight."

Gradually, The Old Knick began to pick up business, especially on Friday and Saturday nights, lured by such presentations as "The Old Look," starring Jack Albertson in *Vaudeville's Last Stand;* and *The Wayward Maiden*, featuring Ernest Sarracino. Jack appeared in both and wrote much of the music with McCullough.

Another reason for the growth in business, Jack believes, was the fact that The Old Knick was a theater prior to becoming a cabaret, and therefore had a slightly slanted floor. "People would have a couple of drinks and head for the john, and they'd have a hell of a time because they couldn't walk straight. They forgot about the floor; they just thought our drinks were dynamite."

An ancillary benefit of The Old Knick was that it served as a kind of watering hole for young dears and Lemmon was usually able to ensnare a pair; one for himself, one for Andy. However, McCullough did not always find this arrangement to his liking. "Jack," said McCullough, "was scurrilous in the fact that when I would come into The Old Knick, he would wait till they were showing old movies and then say, 'I've got two terrific girls for us'; and I'd say 'okay' before my eyes had adjusted to the darkness. When they did adjust, there would invariably be one very good-looking one and a dog—and the dog would always be mine."

The situation finally became intolerable to Andy when one night he was paired with "this horrible, this awful-looking gal who kept giving me surly looks while Jack was conning the other girl. My date kept saying to her friend, 'Come on, let's get out of here. I don't like this; these guys are phonies.' They finally left."

It was too much for McCullough, who turned on Jack. "Forget the whole thing," he stormed, "I'm fed up with this. You are selfish, you're a pain in the ass, and you take all the classy broads for yourself. I should be writing the great American play, anyway, and who needs all this? Just forget it. Forget it and move out; it's my apartment anyway, for crissakes!"

"Right!" said Jack, and walked out.

Two nights later at two in the morning, Andy, busy pecking out his great American play on the typewriter, heard voices and the sound of trash cans being overturned. Then there was a feminine giggle and Lemmon's unmistakable laugh, and suddenly the door opened a crack and Jack's head appeared. "I want you to know," he said emotionally, "that I'm sorry about what happened the other night, and I have made it all up to you."

With that, Lemmon threw open the door, Andy said, and there were two women—a six-foot blonde showgirl with a big smile, and beside her a hulking bull dyke in corduroys and a mustache."

Pointing to the lesbian, Jack said: "That one's yours!"

"The dyke," said Andy, "was infuriated. She turned and hit Jack a shot in the face, grabbed the blonde and left. I was in hysterics and so was Lemmon. And naturally, he moved back in."

Andy, by this time, had risen from the mailroom at the Compton agency and was directing the Lowell Thomas news program twice daily. Jack continued to work nightly at The Old Knick, spending his mornings lounging in bed, except for an occasional dash to the bathroom down the hall.

One February morning, alone in the apartment, Jack was taking his ease and enjoying the potted steam heat, when it became mandatory to make the hall trek. Wearing nothing but his shorts, as usual, he opened the door and entered the below-freezing hall for the short and hasty trip. Halfway there, he heard the bedroom door click shut, and at that moment remembered that it automatically locked from the inside—and Andy was gone.

"It's February and snowing," said Jack. "I'm in my underwear and beginning to shiver and shake, and I can't break down the door because I can't afford to fix it. But I can't just stand there and freeze to death, so I finally said, 'Screw it!' and walked down the four flights, out onto the street. It's ten o'clock in the morning and people are out shopping, and I walked through them twenty feet to my left to Isaac Gellis' delicatessen, where my landlady worked.

"I marched in and right up to the cashier's cage and asked her if she had a passkey because I was locked out. She didn't bat an eyeball, but just handed me the key. I went back out on the street and sloshed through the snow and the people to the apartment. Not a soul had said a word or even looked at me. Only in New York would that happen. Maybe people there just don't look at each other."

Within the complex makeup that is Jack Lemmon there is a meld, a curious compound of Sir Galahad and Don Quixote. At times Jack shows an almost irresistible compulsion to help people in distress. In so doing, the size of an adversary or the physical danger to himself seems not to matter. He will unhesitatingly go for the biggest windmill in sight, and charge it with a bent lance and a spavined charger if those be the only tools at hand.

A good example of this is an incident which occurred one night during his first months in New York. He had wandered into a diner, favored for its low prices and plentiful catsup, where he ordered scrambled eggs and milk with his last fifty cents. Just as his meal was set before him, a fellow diner became enraged at the quality of his spaghetti and heaved the plate, which ricocheted off the cook's head before self-destructing on the back wall. The man then burst out the door and took flight—but not alone. Hot on his heels was Lemmon.

"The guy was fast," said Jack, "but no match for 'the old Boston bullet.' After about three blocks he finally stopped and turned, and it was only then that I noticed he was about six feet, three, and must've weighed two hundred pounds. We just stood there looking at each other and I waited for him to come over and break my legs off. Finally, in desperation, I pointed my finger at him and said: 'Okay, fella. Don't move a muscle. I'm a black belt and my hands are considered lethal weapons. Make one move and they'll carry you off in a basket! Now you stand right there while I go get a cop.'

"He waited about one second and then took off like a streak—but not as fast as I was going in the opposite direction! When I got back to the diner, the mess had been cleaned up along with my eggs and milk. I went home hungry."

At The Old Knick, Jack was learning and growing as a performer. The learning came from his association with top talent which drifted through the music hall, especially Jack Albertson, who had worked in plays and musicals on Broadway and the road.

"Albertson wasn't on the same level as the rest of us," said Jack. "He got a salary. His then-wife Merle worked at The Old Knick, too, and we all became very good friends.

"I learned a lot from him. We would do old burlesque routines together or I would play the piano and he would sing and dance. He's a marvelous dancer."

While Jack was appearing at The Old Knick, John Lemmon arranged a transfer to New York and leased an apartment on Eighty-sixth Street off Lexington Avenue, explaining that the move had been prompted by the needs of business. Actually, John wanted to keep a concerned eye on his only child who, during his first year and a half in New York, had hardly turned the city on its ear.

Jack became a frequent guest on his father's couch, as John had hoped he would. More than once father searched son's pockets, found them empty, and quietly stuffed in a few dollars.

In time, John was transferred to Europe to beef up the Doughnut Corporation interests there, and Jack moved into the apartment along with Andy McCullough and Ted Allegretti, who had recently moved down to New York. Andy recalls that the apartment, oddly, contained not a bite of food except for tomato soup—three cases of it.

"So," said McCullough, "we lived on tomato soup and we threw a lot of parties, although I don't really remember how the hell we managed it. I know we bought these gallon jugs of Haitian rum for a dollar or so. It must've been condemned or something. Also, we'd get these big cans of grapefruit juice at half price because they had dents and holes in them and nobody else would buy them. It was an interesting time."

During their stay in John's apartment, Jack got his first chance at a part in a big Broadway play, Philip Barry's *Second Threshold*. "There was a lot of stealth and all sorts of strange shenanigans going on," Andy recalls. "They liked Jack but thought he was wrong for the part, that of the kid brother. Then they called him back again. I remember the night he came home from that meeting; I could tell it hadn't gone well. I asked, 'What happened?' He said, 'It's out.' Then Jack turned to me and said, 'They made a big mistake.'

"He never referred to it again," said Andy. "I think he put it out of his mind. I've known a lot of actors and I've never known one that didn't keep replaying the part they didn't get, and wondering what they did wrong. But not Jack. He never did. I think he just said, 'Okay, that's over. Next!' which was very unusual. That stiff-upper-lip thing has, I think, always been a part of Jack."

Chapter

VIII

"Right on the button."
—*James Cagney*

SOME HORSES ARE BORN to run. They don't require blinkers because nothing short of an artillery fusillade can distract them from the only thing that matters—the race. Six furlongs or six miles, they'll finish; and winning isn't as important as the running. Their reason for being lies in an open gate and a roaring crowd and if you slap them in harness they die.

Some young actors are like that. Lemmon was one. In the fall of 1947, with real success as distant and evanescent as ever, there was no thought of retreat to the doughnut company and security. In a business with a lemminglike mortality rate, it is customary for hopefuls to heed the whispering of logic after a time, and join the rest of us in rolling five eights and picking up forty. Not Jack. He was born to the stage, as much a predestinate as one conceived in the caste.

Withal, Lemmon was beginning to sense, with that instinct singular to the artist, that he was not going to become "another George Gershwin." One winter afternoon he set that half of his dream quietly adrift. Andy McCullough, who had continued to compose songs with Jack, remembers the moment.

"In trying to sell our tunes, Lemmon would get us in the door at these small agencies. He had hustled the secretary at one of these outfits and she agreed to give us five minutes with the guys who ran the place. We walked into this room and there were these three 'gangsters' with their feet on the desk. And one was on the phone saying, 'Give me twenty on the nose in the third.'

"We stood there until one of them finally said, 'What the hell you waiting for?' I told them we were waiting for them to be quiet. He said, 'Out! Get your ass out! Who the hell do you think you are?' They threw us out, but we came back a week later and the man said, 'Oh yeah. You're the guys we have to be quiet for.' He hung up the phone.

"Jack sat down at the piano and started to play. Now, there's one thing about Jack as a composer—he never plays a tune the same way twice. He wanders off a little bit, which is creative of him, but this time he forgot the lyrics! So here's our big moment, where we're playing our million-dollar song before these three gangsters and Lemmon is off on his lines. So I jumped in—but I'm completely tone-deaf, so they threw us out again.

"When we got outside I said: 'Jack, how the hell could you forget the lyrics? We wrote them!' He looked at me and said very matter-of-factly, 'I guess I'm—not going to be a songwriter.' I thought it was a joke at the time, but later I realized he was making some kind of a decision, a differentiation, because he never would have muffed it in acting. He would have known everything."

While the light was dimming in the musical corridor, Lemmon's acting career was finally shifting out of low gear. Though he was unaware of it, fortune had tossed in her hand and was beginning to lean his way. The tilt started with the word that an off-Broadway production of a Russian melodrama was being cast—Tolstoy's *The Power of Darkness*, to be directed by noted actress and drama coach Uta Hagen.

Jack read for and won the lead role, that of Nikita. He was billed as John Uhler. Darren McGavin, still known as Davin McGaren, showed up in the part of Pyotr, Nikita's father. And there were others in that cast whose names would go unrecognized today. Merle Albertson appeared on the bill as Merle O'Rorke playing Akulina.

A pretty, fresh-faced blonde named Cynthia Stone was selected to play Marina, Nikita's sweetheart. Cynthia's name didn't stick, either. In time she would change it by marrying Nikita and becoming Mrs. Jack Lemmon.

Nobody got paid for doing *The Power of Darkness.* It was a point of little importance to Jack, for whom a paycheck for acting would have been a pleasant surprise, but a surprise all the same. Anyway, there was a bonus—his introduction to Cynthia, who proved as sweet as she was lovely. Cynthia, whom everyone soon learned to call Cinnie, was as charmed with Lemmon, "this very cute boy with dark, curly hair who was awfully pleasant and nice."

Rehearsals began, and the pair saw much of each other. Jack began to take her out occasionally for coffee and a sandwich. "She was hesitant," said Lemmon, "because she was engaged to another fellow, a student at Yale Law School. But she went and we enjoyed being together. We became friends, but nothing more, during the play."

The Power of Darkness was staged at the Ethnological Dance Studio which, Jack recalls, "was not the Palace. We were on the second floor and there was a heat wave on. It must have been a hundred and ten degrees in the place, and to make matters worse we couldn't open the windows because workmen were tearing up the streets for some reason, digging, riveting, and banging.

"I had to wear high-heeled Russian boots that tilted me forward and every time I walked out on that flat stage I damn near fell on my face. I'll never forget opening night. As the curtain went up, I walked out there and said: 'I've just come up from the basement,' or some such fantastic line, and with that I looked down and saw an elderly couple in the front row keel over. Kaplow! Just like that! I still remember the thought that went through my head: 'My God, I'm killing them. I'm really killing them!' Later I realized the heat had a little something to do with it."

Among the first-nighters was Millie, who came down from Boston for the occasion. After the show she took Jack and Cynthia to a small, chic restaurant for dinner. Cynthia was nervous, a little in awe of the sophisticated Millie. "She reminded me of my mother," said Cynthia, "and I'd had some problems with my mom; but before the evening was over Millie and I were hitting it off. She had a marvelous sense of humor."

Although the play was something less than a theatrical Second Coming, Jack's performance impressed Uta Hagen, who liked "the clean simplicity of his work, something I was to see again, later, in his *Days of Wine and Roses,* the best thing I've seen him do. There was an innocent quality about Jack that I liked. He was also a fine student and his talent was obvious, even then. In the very good ones, you can see it at an early age."

For Jack, a fortunate by-product of the play was an introduction to Don Dickinson, a friend of the Albertsons and director of the summer stock company of the Hayloft Theater in Allentown, Pennsylvania. Lemmon was asked to join the troupe for the 1948 season, a pivotal break, as it turned out. He left New York a hopeful amateur. He would return at summer's end a confident professional.

The Hayloft, and everything about it, was a delight to Jack. Situated two miles from the highway down a country lane, the theater was spared problems created by the noise and interruptions of a city location. The Hayloft boasted a fiercely loyal audience that packed the theater, rain or shine, for nearly every performance. "The players," said Jack, "were really fine. It was a crackerjack company."

It was a challenge for Jack, a demanding workload that saw him do, in succession: *Three Men on a Horse; Dark of the Moon;* Oscar Wilde's sophisticated comedy of manners, *Lady Windermere's Fan; Death Takes a Holiday;* and *The Drunkard.* Some weeks there were small supporting roles, other times the lead—characterizations ranging from a ninety-year-old judge to a sixteen-year-old boy—even the odious lieutenant in *John Loves Mary*.

The allegiance of the audience was sometimes tested, but never found wanting. The Hayloft did not come by its name adventitiously. The roof was tin; the floor, dirt; and when the rains came—the result, predictable. The show would be halted in deference to the racket of rain pelting the roof. Soon a respectable brook would form and flow *through* the theater. With commendable aplomb, patrons would hoist their feet until the flood subsided, at which point the players would back up to the beginning of the interrupted scene and start over. On occasion, Lemmon bridged the unscheduled intermission with selected piano offerings.

In the 1930s, Hollywood show-biz movies always featured a mandatory "big scene," in which the fledgling actor gets his chance and bowls 'em over, flabbergasting the critics and moving hard-bitten stagehands to dab at their eyes with their handkerchiefs. This is outrageous hyperbole, of course, but like sextuplets it can happen when the right elements are there. It happened at the Hayloft, with Jack playing a naive young man having his first go at alcohol in a play called *Apron Strings.*

"This was an old war-horse of a play," said Jack, "and we decided during rehearsal that I should ad-lib a little—give the part a little goose, pad the bits. Well, this guy has his first drink and he kinda likes it. So he has a second, then another and another, just walking over and filling his glass as he talks. Eventually, he's beginning to have a little trouble with his words.

"Well, I started working on this thing and the audience began to pick up on it, started to laugh. I was throwing in bits of business, whatever occurred to me. Now, all this stuff I was doing—none of it threw *this* company. They'd just give each other those knowing looks, and once when I turned to fill my glass, one of them was trying to hide the bottle. They were just beautiful! I then started looking for the bottle, of course, in impossible places—under cushions and so forth—and the audience was roaring.

"By this time I was just flying. When I finally did collapse I fell on the sofa and it gave a little, so that I came back up and then down and bounced. I kept bouncing like it was a trampoline, and I sort of liked that. Then I started laughing and kept it up until tears were streaming down my face."

The audience by this time had been reduced to bedlam, whooping it up and giving Jack the longest sustained laugh the company could recall. The drunk scene, brief as scripted, lasted more than half an hour. The final curtain didn't drop until after midnight, and when it came down on *Apron Strings* it went up for Lemmon.

"That one shot did it," recalls Jack. "It gave me a tremendous boost. I was supercharged! From that point on I had no qualms about tackling anything. It was a great night and a great summer."

Broadway was typically blasé over the fact that lightning had struck in Pennsylvania. Jack found New York unchanged upon his return in the fall. He was still on the wrong side of the moat with nobody manning the drawbridge, and his ancient adversary, insolvency, was right there waiting.

It was Cynthia who came up with an interim hedge against poverty. Through personal contacts, she wrangled a job for the pair of them. They would be checkers for the Childs restaurant chain, undercover inspectors of food and service. The job was gratifying in all respects. They would eat and get paid for it, a situation much sought but seldom found by actors.

Jack and Cynthia would enter one of the restaurants, order a meal and then, instead of paying, leave a small card bearing the foreboding message: MR. TIPS WAS HERE. A report form was filled out, indicating whether the goods and the hired hands were Excellent, Good, Fair, Dismal, and so forth. It is not Jack's nature to knock his host for a free meal, even less so when remuneration is involved. The food, therefore, was always "Excellent" and the help "Sensational." They always left the maximum allowable tip of $1.50, even when the gratuity exceeded the bill. Three days into the job, they were fired. "I guess," Jack reflected, "our methods were not what they had in mind."

Cynthia was making her own way in the big city by occasionally modeling for Oleg Cassini and doing, now and then, small parts on radio. After a bit of coaching and nudging she convinced Jack to try for a job in radio soap opera by auditioning at sponsoring agencies.

Lemmon made the rounds, signed up at the agencies, and waited. Several weeks later he got his first audition and flunked it. He tried again and flunked that one as well; also the third. He felt totally frustrated with nothing but his voice as a tool. When a session was played back for him it sounded flat, unconvincing. Without the use of his face and body he was limited.

On the fourth attempt he passed the test and was summoned the next day to read for a role in the long-running daytime soaper "The Brighter Day." A new main character, Bruce, was being added to the cast. "I couldn't believe it," said Jack, "I was finally getting a chance at a part. I went over to NBC about four o'clock in the afternoon and by that time about twenty actors had been in and out reading for the part of Bruce. The director was Arthur Hanna, a lovely man.

"I put my hat and coat on a chair and waited. There were maybe thirty other guys in the room, reading the material and glaring at each other. It was a cage and we were the animals. When they finally called me and I got up to the microphone, I really started going at it, acting up a storm. I was sailing along in fine style when Hanna stopped me with: 'Please, Mr. Lemmon, you're knocking the needle off here in the booth. Please don't break our mike.'

"He really was very sweet about it; he asked me to read the piece over and do it a couple of different ways. I said, 'Sure thing! Right you are!' I toned it down a little and did my stuff; I played it this way, that way, every damned way I could think of, but I was so busy acting I forgot it was radio and I would keep moving away from the microphone. Hanna would very patiently stop me and explain that he couldn't hear me if I walked away."

After nearly half an hour of reading, the director stopped Jack. "Okay, thank you, Mr. Lemmon. Are you with Lexington?"

"With who?"

"Lexington, the Lexington telephone answering service."

"No," replied Jack, "I'm not."

"Well," said the director, "would you please contact them this afternoon so you can receive your messages? You will need the service unless you live with someone who can take your calls in case you're not in."

"Oh, yeah, I'll do that," said Jack. "That's a very good idea—really should have the service, you know."

"Fine. Do you have another number in the meantime?"

Jack, who had no telephone, no realistic prospects of getting one, and only vague futuristic intentions of securing a service, gave him Cynthia's number. "She's my girlfriend," he confided, "and I talk with her each day."

"That," said Hanna, "is wonderful. I guess it'll have to do. But in case you don't get a call before Lexington starts its service, check my office, because your first call will be for the day after tomorrow—ten o'clock."

"First what?" asked Jack, now thoroughly puzzled.

"The first show, for crissakes!" said Hanna. "Don't you understand what I'm talking about? You've got the part."

"Oh, yes, of course," said Jack. "Yes—well—see you Thursday!" Snatching his belongings from the chair, Lemmon walked dreamlike through the door, caught a bus, and went straight to Cynthia's apartment, where he launched into the story of his big break. Halfway through he stopped, having spotted a strange hat, coat, and briefcase on her sofa. "Whose is that?" he demanded. "Who's been here?"

"Whose is what?" asked Cynthia. "You brought it in with you."

An examination of the briefcase revealed the contents to be those of the director, as were the hat and coat. Frantically Jack called the studio. "Is Mr. Hanna there?"

"This is Mr. Hanna," said a tired voice. "I've just been waiting here for your call and I'll continue to wait. I'd love to have my hat and coat and briefcase. I'll need them for tonight."

Professionally and financially, "The Brighter Day" was a breakthrough for Jack. The pay was $25 for each broadcast appearance, and there were two or three each week. "It was sufficient," said Jack, "to keep me in the manner to which I had suddenly become accustomed."

His work on the show brought him another job, this one on the soaper "Road of Life," in the role of Butch Brent, younger brother of Dr. Brent, played by veteran radio actor Don McLaughlin. As the young Dr. Brent, Jack was a central character and often played long scenes with McLaughlin, who one day gave the irrepressible Lemmon a memorable lesson.

"The director on "Road of Life" was Walter Gorman, a marvelous man with—thank heaven—a great sense of humor. I was in the middle of a scene with McLaughlin on this particular show and Gorman was in the control booth. I read a line something like: 'Well, I still don't agree. You may be my big brother the doctor, but I say this patient has *hypocloroflitasineth* and she needs a *hyaumph!*'

"I turned the page and cruised right through the next paragraph—and only then realized I'd just read McLaughlin's part, too. I'd answered myself!

"Now my cue came up, but I'd realized my mistake too late. I was in a corner. I looked at McLaughlin, the old-timer, and got no help at all. He just stood there, serenely, gazing at me over the mike. Then he backed away and just sort of bowed and gave a little wave of his hand as if to say: 'It's all yours, my friend. Go right ahead.'

"Well, I gave out with a few of the 'ugh—ugh—ughs,' and eventually blurted: 'What was that you said? I know what you're *going* to say'—and I read McLaughlin's line, replying to *me*. Then I read my lines and then his, answering myself as best I could.

"The flop sweat was flying off me and I gave a desperate look up at old Gorman in the booth but Gorman was no longer there. Just his feet. He was on the floor in hysterics and only his feet were showing through the window, wiggling and shaking. I looked at McLaughlin and he was laughing so hard there were tears pouring down his cheeks. I did two and a half pages of that gibberish, but it worked; I got away with it. There was a lot more organ music at the end; I remember that. I guess I must have gone through that script double-time. It was a lesson I never forgot.

"It's interesting that I blew more lines on radio with the script in front of me than I've ever done on the stage or live television. I suppose it was because I never could relax, using just my voice. But it was good experience and a livelihood, mainly."

Chafing under the choke rein of radio, Lemmon continued to haunt the agencies, trying to burrow into the exciting new medium of live television. Time and again he auditioned, seeking bit parts, walk-ons—anything. In one of those happenings peculiar to show business, the first part he landed was the lead role in an hour-long "Kraft Theater" production, a takeoff on *Charley's Aunt*.

"This thing was called 'The Arrival of Kitty,' which they bought because *Charley's Aunt* would have been expensive; but they could pick this bomb up for probably fifteen dollars. Maurie Holland was the director, a guy I really admired. It took guts for him to put an unknown kid doing his first TV show in the lead spot. Kraft was a big account and it cost a bundle to sponsor an hour program.

"I was fascinated by Maurie because he was so sharp. This was the real beginning of television on a major scale, and there were no ground rules. In the rehearsal hall, Maurie had all the camera locations marked out with tape. He had a chair with four wheels and he was a genius at being able to push off and—zook! he'd glide over to one corner where a scene was being shot. When it was finished he'd say, 'Okay, fade out,' and zoom!—he'd be on the other side where the next shot would be."

The part called for Jack to wear a skirt, a requirement that would surface again years later for Billy Wilder's film classic *Some Like It Hot*. Lemmon had no concern at all about his ability to handle the role; but if he wasn't getting butterflies, somebody else was—longtime character actor Dort Clark. A man of vast experience, including many Broadway plays, Clark was concerned for the youthful Jack and spent the full week of rehearsal coaching him.

"Now don't worry," Clark would say. "You see where Maurie is sitting? The cameras will be over there; so if it's comfortable for you, try not to play the scene over here, because you're going to be too far away. Then in the final rehearsal they're going to start telling you from the booth to 'turn it here.' That might throw you."

"I really appreciated the help," said Jack. "Dort was such a fine actor and it was just one of those things—he had a supporting role and I had the bloody lead, and I'd never seen a TV camera in my life, and in those days you only got one or two run-throughs on camera.

"When we got on the air I was out there alone for five minutes and doing fine. I was playing the part of a desk clerk in a hotel. I felt even more confident when Dort came on because now I had the old pro backing me up. So help me, he walked up to the desk, leaned over and whispered, 'What's my line?' "

In television's embryonic days, young players had to live with a hard truth. The medium was live, ephemeral, one-shot. Turning in a bang-up performance one week was no guarantee of working the next—not unless a producer or director chanced to be watching. There were virtually no repeat broadcasts because of technical problems associated with production of quality visual recordings. An actor therefore needed luck—and luck it was that landed Jack his next job the week following his appearance on "Kraft Theater."

It happened that CBS was expanding at such a rate that producer Worthington (Tony) Minor was occupying an office temporarily without a door. Lemmon was not one to ignore such a providential circumstance, especially since Minor was in the process of casting *Shadow and Substance*, the superb Paul Vincent Carroll play which had been introduced at Dublin's famed Abbey Theatre in 1937.

Spotting Minor alone, Jack strolled through the convenient ingress and in a thick Irish brogue said: "How d'ye do? I'm from the Abbey Players. I'm just off the boat and I was havin' a spot 'o tea when I heard ye were castin' *Shadow and Substance*, and—"

Minor watched Jack's monologue with some fascination and when the routine was finished, leaned back in his chair and grinned. "Bull! I saw you last week on 'Kraft Theater.' But I liked what I saw so you can have the part."

Shadow and Substance became one of many shows in which Lemmon worked with Minor. "He was wonderful to me," Jack said. "Tony was influential in the business, one of the pioneers of really good television drama. He started and produced several series, including 'Studio One' which, as I recall, was TV's first big dramatic series—an hour and a half, live."

The back-to-back programs were the impetus needed to get Jack's career off center and moving. He began to work regularly—actually earning a living, a thrill in itself. "It was a wild, exciting time," he said. "I was working with a lot of great young talent that went on to the top. People like Sid Lumet, John Frankenheimer, Frank Shaffner, Ralph Nelson, and Arthur Penn. We had writers like Paddy Chayefsky, Reginald Rose, and Rod Serling doing scripts for actors like Chuck Heston, Rod Steiger, Biff Elliott, and a ton of others.

"I can remember doing a show where John Frankenheimer was an A.D. [assistant director]. His job at one point was to run around under the camera that was on me and yank my pant's leg to signal when the camera went off me, so that I could move to the next scene."

As a member of this group, Lemmon was one of several young actors who began to get the majority of assignments; perhaps six lines one week and a lead the next. "We would do anything if we didn't have a conflicting offer and have to choose. It didn't matter whether one show was better than another or a part wasn't so hot. We were just getting experience and making a living. Nobody was a star. You would rehearse a week and get fifteen dollars for the appearance. I remember one show I did when I got fifty dollars. Heston had the lead and that paid seventy-five dollars, as I recall. It made no difference; it was a terrific time."

Gradually, Lemmon began to be noticed by the public and by his peers. Almost without exception, those who watched him came away impressed. In a television comedy role he caught the attention of James Cagney. "Here," said the great actor, "was a young man who knew how to be funny without being brash, and to find a young person getting laughs and not pushing too hard—that was something to see. I was reminded of others who really push every second of the time with a brashness that is, to me, unattractive. I immediately called my brother, who was an agent, and told him about this kid I'd seen, whose name I didn't know, and I asked him to look him up. Unfortunately my brother was too busy or something and never did it.

"Later, I saw this young man again, this time playing a straight dramatic part and he was great, he was fine. Right on the button. Again I called my brother and left word at the office for him to find this boy, but nothing ever happened."

Had Cagney's brother located Jack he might well have been too late because a young agent named Charles Baker had also spotted Lemmon on the tube in a half-hour drama. "It was," Baker said, "an extraordinary performance by someone I'd never seen, heard, nor met. I did know a little something about him through my cousin, who was in the same class with him at Harvard and who used to tell me of this rather exceptional guy in terms of his activities with the Dramatic and Hasty Pudding clubs."

The Baker connection was another of those opportune incidents that seem to occur through almost Olympian guidance for Jack. A bright Harvard graduate, Baker is a man of taste and foresight who was to become one of New York's most respected theatrical agents.

Now president of Macmillan Performing Arts, Inc., Charley Baker is witty and urbane, the epitome of the Broadway entrepreneur—the sort who appears to have been constructed by Wilde to be played by Niven.

"I loved the theatrical business," said Baker. "I was in it for almost thirty years and it was such fun I could never understand why they paid me. But the atmosphere of the theater, the business itself, changed. People didn't know what they were doing. When I went into the business we had what I would consider giants—Leland Hayward, Selznick—people who knew more than I did, which made me quite happy to be the salesman and they the buyer. In the last several years it became quite the reverse."

Baker signed Lemmon to a contract on sight, although he had to survive a trauma to his sensibilities in the process. "Here was my very first client," said Baker, "and he came into my office wearing the most awful topcoat that I have ever seen in my life. It did not appear to be made of any known fabric; I rather believe it was pressed cardboard pretending to be camel's hair. I said, 'Where did you get that coat? It is the most terrible thing I have ever seen.'

"Jack confessed that he didn't have a penny and that he'd gotten it free for buying a pair of slacks in some shop, Lord knows where. I told him that he simply could not afford to be seen in it and must take it off at once, and if he caught pneumonia that would be preferable to wearing the coat. He looked like a very unsuccessful pimp and I explained that he could not sell that image of himself. One of the things Jack had going for him was a certain amount of class, and he had to appear in the proper clothes. He was a terribly attractive young man. I must say Jack understood at once and I never saw the coat again."

The first few jobs Baker secured for Lemmon paid so little that no commission was deducted. "Charley's take would have been about a dollar and a half," said Jack. "He was just starting out in the business, too, working with a girl named Gloria Saphire. They shared a tiny office at the top of the Random House building next to CBS. It had a slanting roof and one window. But that didn't figure to last, because Charley was one hell of an agent.

"At first he would get me little jobs that would pay maybe fifteen bucks. I would work shows like 'I Remember Mama,' where I'd have a small part. Eventually Charley and Gloria split up. It was all very amicable and I went with Baker because he had been doing the work for me. Rod Steiger went with Gloria in the division. Charley and Gloria only had about ten clients, but they were good ones and they turned out to be successful. They had pretty keen foresight, that pair.

"Charley was on his own for a while and then became head of the legitimate theater department for the William Morris Agency. He became just about the best theatrical agent in New York—would still be, if he wanted to work. He loves and understands theater. He became a very good doctor for sick plays. He would even help producers cast their shows with talent from other agencies if he thought their actors might be better for the play than those with Morris."

Despite the television breaks beginning to come his way, Jack's pecuniary condition and lifestyle occasionally met the legal definition of vagrancy. Thus he spasmodically continued to work at The Old Knick, unable to pass up the few dollars he might earn there.

Cynthia recalls that they had to turn down invitations to several smashing parties, including one on New Year's Eve and another later one in Washington, D.C. because Jack said he could make twenty-five dollars by playing piano at the bar. Cynthia skipped the parties and spent the evenings listening to Lemmon play requests for revelers.

"Jack wasn't starving to death," said Cynthia. "He had a place to stay, at his father's apartment, but he didn't have any money."

By 1949 Jack and Cynthia had decided they were "fairly serious" about each other, although neither was ready for marriage. "There was no deeper involvement than that," said Cynthia, "because I was a pretty good straitlaced kid and Jack was very much the gentleman with me, so we just dated more than anything else. The few times I did go out with other fellows, Jack would always be sitting on my doorstep, waiting, when they brought me home. He always outstayed them."

Chapter

IX

"... an obscure but wonderful comedian ..."
—Cincinnati Post *critic*

LEMMON'S DRIVING, Kennedy-like determination kept him hard at it in the spring of 1949 even though the show-biz breastworks had been breached and there was a steady trickle of television work. It was not enough; he'd won a lap, not the race.

When not working, Jack was preparing for work. He belonged to a small acting group that met regularly with its monitor, David Alexander, in a room above the Stage Delicatessen. Other members included Ross Martin, Nina Foch, Neva Patterson, and Biff Elliott.

"Jack was the best of the group," said Elliott. "We'd do improvisations and little scenes and Jack's genius was obvious even then. He does things so effortlessly you don't realize the work, the depth of planning that went into it. You have to sit down and rap with him about a part to recognize what a hell of a job he's done to come up with the characterization."

While Jack was always up for his acting assignments in those early days he was sometimes caught off-base by the routine events of life. A case in point: Cynthia's unnerving announcement that her parents, spires of society in Peoria, Illinois, where they owned the First National Bank, would soon arrive in Gotham and would love to meet him.

Jack was to be stretched on this rack of romance at a supremely inopportune time: he was between coats. The quasi-camel's hair had been destructed on command from Baker, and Shea's resplendent outerwear was now unavailable. On the wintry eve of the scheduled confrontation, which was to take place at the elegant Plaza Hotel, Lemmon was still coatless.

"I didn't own a hat," said Jack, "and that was bad enough. But to enter looking like a walking snowman would have made me look like a bit of a jerk. I didn't know what to do, but knew there were some cut-rate clothing stores way downtown and some on Eighth Avenue in the forties and fifties, so I started walking and looking."

Presently a sign caught his eye, a garish but heartening pronouncement: SPECIAL SALE—$13.00. Adjacent to the sign in the window was a polo coat! With a rush of hope, Jack audited his wallet. Twenty dollars! He crossed the street to the store, which bore the cryptic name Sa-Ray. The window and interior were bathed in a strange amber light.

"There was this old lady at the cash register," said Jack, "and when I came in, she turned and hollered out back: 'Say—Ray! Ya gotta customer!' It sort of cleared up the mystery of the name. When Ray appeared I told him I was interested in a coat like the one in the window, if he could fit me."

"Tan?" asked Ray.

"Tan," repeated Jack, "like in the window."

"Beautiful!" said Ray. "I have got such a beauty for you, a tan polo coat."

Ray produced the coat and a mirror. In the gloaming aura of the room, the coat seemed adequate. "Feel the material," Ray encouraged, gathering a sizable portion of the back, "and just look at that fit!"

"Are you certain that's the same color as the coat in the window?"

"Positively," Ray assured him. "That's tan; that's the regular tan camel's hair."

Jack forked over the sales price. "The coat felt a little loose when Ray let go to take the money. It felt a lot looser when I got out on the street, but I figured if I kept my hands in my pockets and my arms kind of tucked in, it would be okay; I could have it

Little Jackie Lemmon, age eighteen months, already exhibiting the charm that would one day captivate millions of moviegoers.

Jack aboard his pony, Pepper. "A meaner little cuss I never rode. All I did was fall off and cry."

Jackie, shortly after taking up track to overcome being a ninety-pound weakling. He later set two New England high school records.

At eighteen Jack was preparing to enter Harvard and had already decided on his career. He would be "the new George Gershwin and the world's greatest actor."

Jack with his mother Millie at their summer home in Wolfboro, New Hampshire. At this time he was fifteen years old and a student at Andover Academy.

There was no salary but Jack got free chicken-in-a-basket at The Old Knick Music Hall in New York, where he landed his first show-biz job—entertaining and waiting on tables. (TOMMY WEBER)

A turning point in Jack's career came when he joined the Hayloft Theater Summer Stock Company in Pennsylvania in the summer of 1948. Here he hams it up with a member of the troupe.

Jack with his first wife, Cynthia, on the New York set of their television series, "The Couple Next Door." Stealing the scene is their dog, Duffy.

Jack was an overnight success after his first film, *It Should Happen to You*, starring Judy Holliday, shown here with Lemmon in a scene from the movie. (CULVER PICTURES)

An unforgettable scene from a classic motion picture, *Mister Roberts:* William Powell adds a secret ingredient to their homemade Scotch as Henry Fonda (Roberts) and Jack (Ensign Pulver) supervise.
(CULVER PICTURES)

The filming of *Fire Down Below* in Trinidad provided some memorable adventures for Lemmon. He is seen here with others from the cast: (*left to right*) Lemmon, Rita Hayworth, unidentified actor, Anthony Newley, and Robert Mitchum.
(CULVER PICTURES)

Jack and Glenn Ford on location in New Mexico for *Cowboy*, a picture Ford had to trick Lemmon into doing by getting him drunk and calling him "chicken."

Tony Curtis and Lemmon in drag for their roles as Josephine and Daphne in Billy Wilder's classic film, *Some Like It Hot*. To test their outfits the boys entered the ladies' rest room. They went undetected.
(CULVER PICTURES)

Some Like It Hot: Joe E. Brown dances with his new "fiancée," Daphne (Lemmon).
(CULVER PICTURES)

Lemmon with Hope Halliday in a scene from Billy Wilder's picture, *The Apartment.*

The Apartment: Jack and Shirley MacLaine.

In *Days of Wine and Roses* Jack gave a performance which many believe to be the best of his career.

Director Richard Quine watches closely as Jack and Kim Novak rehearse a scene for *The Notorious Landlady*.
(BOB WILLOUGHBY)

Jack poses with his father between takes during the filming of *The Notorious Landlady*, in which Lemmon, Sr. had a small nonspeaking part.

Jack and his new bride,
Felicia, following their 1962
marriage in Paris, after a
five-year courtship.

Beautiful Virna Lisi studies the work of cartoonist-husband (Lemmon) in *How to Murder Your Wife*. (CULVER PICTURES)

taken in later. All this was before I walked under a white streetlight; then I saw it. The coat was *orange*—the most god-awful, brightest orange in the world.

"Ray missed his calling, because he would have been a sensational lighting man. He'd fleeced me out of my thirteen smacks for this thing, three sizes too large and made of I don't know what, but not camel's hair. By this time I was already ten minutes late and I had to get all the way to the Plaza. I started running and by the time I got to the lobby I was pouring sweat. Nobody had paid much attention to the coat in the street, but in the Plaza it seemed to me that everybody in the place was looking at me and whispering to each other. Now you'd think a twenty-four-year-old guy would have had more sense, but I wandered around not knowing what to do about that coat. I finally took it off, went idly by a newsstand in the corner, and when I didn't think anyone was looking, threw it behind a potted plant. It worked out, because we had dinner in the hotel anyway."

Lemmon says that he never saw the coat again, but this may be a mental block, a psychological curtain that can drop, obscuring from the mind moments of horror too painful for recall. Others remember seeing the coat with Jack *in it* on various occasions after the Plaza incident.

Coat or not, Jack did not on this occasion make a memorable impression on the Stones. He was a struggling actor and, therefore, in a class bounded roughly by mid-range restaurant help on one side and, on the other, by military personnel not having attained field grade. On the other hand, Cynthia was, in the words of Andy McCullough, "a marvelous girl, the WASP princess. She was a cross between Anita Louise and Grace Kelly—that kind of look—and was the debutante type, having gone to Finch and Foxcroft. Cynthia was the kind of girl a lot of my friends at Harvard married, and, I thought, *the* girl for Jack."

The Stones harbored other thoughts and, as the year wore on, took evasive action common to parents of well-bred daughters burdened with the vapors or, as in this instance, an inappropriate swain. Cynthia in hand, they embarked on an ocean voyage calculated to erase Lemmon from her thoughts. When the vessel docked after a two-week cruise it was met by a young man bearing whistles, balloons, party hats—and wearing a luminous orange polo coat. "I give up," said Mr. Stone. "She's going to marry him."

"After they got to know him," said Cynthia, "my folks were crazy about Jack. They still are. But in the early days they saw him as just another hungry young actor."

It was becoming clear as 1949 neared a close that the struggling was about to become a thing of the past for Lemmon. Charlie Irving, an actor and radio producer who was branching out into the new field of television, approached Jack to appear in a series in the planning stage, "The Kid from Kalamazoo," a title later dropped in favor of "That Wonderful Guy."

"Charlie was a very bright guy," said Jack, "and I remember that long before anyone else would even entertain the notion, he was saying that somebody ought to be filming television shows because kinescopes wouldn't hold up. I stopped him in the middle of the street once when he started talking about that and said: 'You must be insane. You've lost all your marbles! Film? On television? Film stinks. You gotta do things *live*, with sustained performances. Film is for curly-haired pretty little boys and who cares about it anyway?'

"I used to sit in Walgreen's drugstore, out of work, with a nickel cup of coffee, and shoot the breeze with other actors about how ridiculous it was for anybody to ever go to Hollywood or even want to do a film. Oh, there were certain films I loved and actors I respected; but in general I had no thought of ever doing a film. To me the only thing was the thea-tah or TV, which was live and great."

Cynthia and Eva Marie Saint read for the part of Jack's girlfriend in "That Wonderful Guy." Cynthia won out and was signed to work with Lemmon on the series, the first for either of them.

"It was the story of a naive, crazy kid like the songwriter in 'June Moon,' " said Jack, "a boy who comes to New York wanting to become an actor. He's broke and doesn't know who to see—just like I was. He answers an advertisement by the foremost drama critic, who is looking for a houseboy, and bulldozes his way into the job. Of course, he screws up everything.

"Neil Hamilton was the star of the show but I played the lead, actually. Neil is a delightful man who'd been a star in Hollywood years earlier. The show was a big deal for its day. We had a thirteen-piece orchestra and the program was live, using three cameras, including the first boom camera used in a big studio. Imagine! The music was live and integrated with scenes and bits of business. The entire show, as I recall, cost thirteen thousand five hundred a week. That's for everything—the whole nut. God knows what it would cost now."

"That Wonderful Guy" ran for seventeen weeks before ABC canceled the series because sponsors could not be found to support it. There was, Jack remembers, a general belief that broad comedy could not be done successfully on television. "I think," he said, "that it was about two minutes later that someone named Lucy did a show for CBS! Still, I can understand how intelligent people could think that. Nobody knew where television was going, what it would become, or how fast it would move. And then came Uncle Miltie. All of a sudden TV was an enormous thing."

During rehearsals for the series, a slim brunette girl slipped across from an adjoining studio to see what was going on. "What I saw," she said, "was this skinny young man dressed like a soda jerk, pushing a broom and repeating his lines to himself. We struck up a conversation and hit it off beautifully, because we were both young and trying to make a go of it in television." It would be twenty-five years before the pair, Jack and Anne Bancroft, would have an opportunity to work together, under the direction of Mel Frank, in the film version of Neil Simon's hit play, *The Prisoner of Second Avenue*.

Reviewers were generally kind to "That Wonderful Guy." They were kinder yet to Jack. *Cincinnati Post* critic Mary Wood called the show "a program which grows on you by the week—nothing spectacular, mind you, just very, very funny." She added that it "stars an obscure, but wonderful comedian named Jack Lemmon."

The fun of the series, and working with Cynthia, was dimmed for Jack by reports from Boston. Millie, lonely and unhappy—and too proud to admit it—was beginning to seriously diminish the bar stock at the Ritz-Carlton. Even in torment, however, her unflagging sense of humor surfaced. She decided that, upon her demise, it would be a perfectly marvelous idea to be cremated and have her ashes placed on one corner of the Ritz bar. In furtherance of that plan, she sent her check for $400 to the Ritz, with instructions that it be used to purchase posthumous drinks for her friends. They, in turn, would toast Millie.

Predictably, the Ritz management was less than enchanted with Millie's proposition. They returned her check, along with a terse rejection of her plan. Undaunted, she fired off a second letter, this one a caustic missive calling attention to her regular and unstinting presence in the Ritz bar, and the salutary effect this had on the hotel's credit ledger. The Ritz answered with a firm and final No. Millie then responded with a volley, setting forth her intention "never to step foot in the Ritz again." The decision did not reduce Millie's alcoholic intake, only her companionship. Most of her drinking now was done in her apartment—and alone.

In mid-April, following a luncheon at CBS with scriptwriter Russell Beggs and Andy McCullough, now a director, Jack suggested that he and Cynthia return to her apartment in a taxi. "When we got in the cab," said Cynthia, "Jack handed me a small, crumpled paper napkin. On it was printed 'I guess we ought to get married.' I looked at it for a moment and then said, 'Yes, I guess maybe we should.' That was the proposal."

A May 7 date was set in Peoria, to be attended by family and close friends. Among those *not* attending would be Millie. An emergency telephone call from Bud Noel brought Jack the sad news that his mother was in the hospital.

"It was a narrow escape for her," said Jack. "She obviously was disturbed, was drinking way too much, and had begun taking pills to get to sleep. Whether her frame of mind was a menopausal reaction, I don't know—but I do know her health was bad and she'd forget to eat.

"On this particular night she got up and tried to cook something. She was drowsy and had probably had a belt of something along with the sleeping pill. She turned on the stove but never did light it. Neighbors smelled gas and came in. She was on the floor with food spilled around. They got her to the hospital just in time, where she awoke to find herself being fed intravenously. It scared the hell out of her. The doctor told her she would either take care of herself or she'd die. It was probably a good thing, because after that she began to straighten up."

Clearly, Millie had not tried suicide. "That wasn't her style," said Bud. "Millie loved life too much. Sure, she was getting older, she was separated from the man she would always love, and her son was off in New York. But this was an accident from too much booze on top of pills in a weakened condition. After she was out of the hospital I really laid it on the line to her, raised hell. After that she was better, began to be her old self, crusty as ever."

Jack and Cynthia traveled to Peoria with John Lemmon. "It was a proper wedding," said Cynthia, "because my folks were very proper people; but it was bright and very gay. About seventy people attended. I'll never forget—when Jack and I left the reception,

Jack's father left with us, because the train was the only way to leave Peoria at that time, and everyone looked stunned. They thought he was going on our honeymoon with us!

"When we got to Chicago we went to the lovely old staid Drake Hotel, where my parents had made arrangements for us to have the bridal suite. Here we were, two naive kids, and when we got to the room it was decorated in a leopard-skin motif—spots everywhere. The bed looked like it should have Kim Novak lying on it. We spent our honeymoon on the beach in Miami and then back to New York and work."

The marriage was as pleasant and free of conflict as when both had been single. "We always had fun," said Cynthia. "There was never, ever, a cross word before or after the wedding." To friends and family it was a match "made in heaven"—perfection. No one saw in this the seeds of discontent or pondered Chamfort's unassailable observation that "bachelor's wives and old maid's children are always perfect."

The happy couple moved into a tiny but very nice apartment on the third floor of a brownstone. "It was adorable," said Cynthia. "There was a small bedroom and living room with a fireplace in each, and a kitchen that had been converted from a closet. It was charming, really delightful—just exactly what you would imagine Jack and I would have lived in."

With "That Wonderful Guy," the wolves of want ceased to snuffle at Jack's door. He wasn't rich yet, but there was enough, and more on the way. Even as "Wonderful Guy" was folding, another opportunity was in the wings, awaiting its cue. He was finally rolling sevens.

A new show being prepped for the CBS network was in need of a master of ceremonies and Jack auditioned for the job and got it. The program, "Toni Twin Time," was designed to promote the Toni home-permanent product by highlighting twin girls and the slogan, Which One Has the Toni? The format of the show was latter-day Major Bowes, a showcase for young up-and-coming talent. Only infrequently would guests be either up *or* coming, although as Jack recalls, there were some "interesting people." Among them were Gary Morton, Lucille Ball's husband, and Bob Fosse and his wife, before Fosse became a famed choreographer and director.

Critics were, at best, split over the show. *Today's Advertising*'s reviewer thought the first program was the "smoothest premiere" he'd ever caught. He was dazzled by Lemmon, seeing that he was "only a few short years out of Harvard." He then added: "There's a great difference between being an MC and being a sock comedian. There's a place for both on the visual air. Lemmon is an MC."

The critic at *Advertising Age* saw it differently: "Toni has a lemon in its new Wednesday night TV show over CBS at 9—and it isn't Jack, although as a master of ceremonies that gentleman comes mighty close to living up to his name."

Jack sided with the latter review. "I've seen some rotten emcees, but I was really it. I'll say this, though, they stuck with me at least. I was perilously close to being fired after every show for the first four or five. I was one of about eighteen summer replacements for Arthur Godfrey, who was an enormous star and all over radio and TV."

Andy McCullough, who was on hand for one of the shows, remembers that Jack had to do "this awful kind of Milton Berle stuff. He introduced 'the marvelous twins' and out came these girls tap dancing on roller skates!"

The experience was not lost on Jack, who has since carefully avoided the role of master of ceremonies. "It's not my bag. I'm always being asked to guest-host the "Tonight" show but I wouldn't think of it. Maybe I could get away with it, but I don't think I'd be any good. It's the same as going to Vegas, where I have a standing offer. My God, you can make a fortune there; but I just don't want to do it. I'm an actor, good, bad, or indifferent."

From the first program, the Toni president had proclaimed that Jack would be a "star," indicating an artistic prescience hardly indigenous to the business world, and a hope that both the program and the company product would be embraced by the hirsute. All the same, Lemmon hedged his bet by performing in other TV productions at every opportunity. He was becoming one of the most sought-after, highly regarded young actors working in the medium, and by the time "Toni Twin Time" was the subject of cancellation rumors, another series was beckoning—a program that would again include Cynthia.

To plug a five-week hole in the schedule resulting from a regular TV network series going on hiatus, CBS and the Benton & Bowles Agency came up with "The Ad Libbers," a show based on the idea that actors would be given a bare-bones situation for which they would improvise lines and action. It is the theatrical equivalent of bullfighting without a cape: exhilarating in execution, exciting to behold, but given to occasional disasters. One needs phenomenal agility.

Improvisation is a widely used exercise for high school and college drama students. It is not commonly practiced at the professional and commercial level for the obvious reason that most actors, even the very good ones, are not creatively nimble enough to make it work well or often. Jack and Cynthia were selected as members of "The Ad Libbers" cast, along with Earl Hammond, Charles Mendick, Joe Silver, and Patricia Housely. The master of ceremonies was actor and raconteur Peter Donald.

Donald would accept ideas from the studio audience and assign actors to flesh them out with ad-libs and pantomime. The show was produced live, and the skits were performed on a bare stage with only an occasional prop. Show-business publications *Variety* and *The Billboard* praised the attempt but predicted a short life for the series, which imposed "impossible demands" on the performers.

When "The Ad Libbers" left the air Jack and Cynthia became victims of that hazard shared by creative folk and dirt farmers—the dry spell. The telephone became grimly silent and they drifted for several weeks in the occupational horse latitudes, during which their savings evaporated and the $210 rent on their apartment began to appear an impossible obstacle.

The drought broke spectacularly with a telephone call from ABC producer Ward Byron. "Would you and Cynthia," he asked, "be interested in doing another series?"

"Well," said Jack, with elaborate calm, "that's a—possibility. What did you have in mind?"

What Byron had in mind was a fifteen-minute segment sandwiched within a new, hour-long daytime show, which would run five days a week and star Don Ameche and Frances Langford. Said Byron: "Does a thousand a week sound okay to you?"

Covering the receiver, Jack relayed the news to Cynthia, who had been watching his face wide-eyed, sensing that something big, like a way to meet the rent, was afoot. "Oh my God!" she exclaimed, and flopped back on the bed.

The show ran for seven months. "In all my life I'd never thought of making that much money," said Jack. "We saved a lot and it was just terrific. I couldn't believe it! I had three new suits and I would just stand in front of the mirror and look at myself. I had it all: shirts, ties, underwear, sportscoats, and argyle socks—a whole drawer full, to go along with the beautiful new shoes. We even bought a car, a Nash Rambler. We were really living at last and it was sensational."

The Ameche-Langford show was big-budget for its day—

$37,000 a week, prompting a two-column headline in *Weekly Variety*. The producer, working under Byron was Roger Kay, a man, said Jack, with the "guts of a burglar. He was a highly imaginative guy who would try daring stuff and turn some people off. They tried to fire him about eighty times, but Byron stood behind him. We did some crazy things."

In "The Couple Next Door" segment Jack and Cynthia portrayed newlyweds encountering and, of course overcoming, the trivial problems abounding in the post-honeymoon period. For the series they were happily united with writer Howard Rodman, who had a knack of turning marital minutia into a quarter-hour of quality comedy material. The Lemmons, for their part, were able to make the most gossamer of situations stand up for the full fifteen minutes. The first show, for example, consisted entirely of Jack and Cynthia trying to untangle the mystery of how one ice cube could have been removed from a solidly frozen tray.

Critics acclaimed "The Couple Next Door," although the rest of the program came in for some lumps. Lemmon gave great credit to Rodman. "He wrote some really beautiful scripts," said Jack, "but there was one problem—Howard would occasionally get mad as hell at the bureaucracy of large corporations such as ABC. He would come to work in an old hunting jacket and boots, and he'd be wearing a beard. He would pinch paper, pencil, paperclips—whatever he could—to needle them. He told me once he was thinking of snitching a typewriter, but couldn't get up the nerve.

"One day Rodman disappeared when we were three scripts ahead. He was gone for four days and we had not only run out of scripts, I had ad-libbed one whole segment because Cynthia was sick. I'll never forget *that* show. It was reminiscent of *Apron Strings.* We used a situation where I had forgotten it was our anniversary, my wife calls to say she's bringing her parents home for dinner, and the house is a mess. For the balance of the show the cameras followed me cleaning the place up.

"The bit worked fine, but it did seem to me the audience thought it was a good deal funnier than I did. After the show I found out the reason for all the hysterical laughter. I had done the whole segment with my fly open. The cameraman had noticed it, luckily, and the poor guy had exhausted himself trying to hold the shots tight, from the waist up.

"Anyway, here we were, sitting around the studio wondering what we could possibly do for the next day's program when we heard footsteps on the stairs and in came Rodman with three scripts. I asked him where in the world he'd been. 'I got teed off at the bureaucratic bastards,' he said, 'so I went out and walked around for a couple of days. I decided that I had integrity, by God, and I would get an honest job where I don't have people trying to bastardize my work!'

"I asked him what happened," said Jack, "and he said he had applied for a job as an apprentice at Singer Sewing Machine Company, starting at $42.50 a month—and had been turned down because he lacked experience. I'll always remember that moment. Howard was furious at being passed over by Singer. Now he was being forced to return to work as a writer for our show at ABC and for other programs such as 'Studio One'—a job that was earning him about $1,300 a *week!*"

For Jack and Cynthia 1952 was an idyllic interlude. The reviews were good; there were no financial worries, they were liked and respected by their associates and their public. They were "the couple next door," and the newlyweds at home very closely resembled their counterparts on television. Fans wrote, telling how they wished their own marriage could be so perfect. "They thought we had the marriage, the kind of life every young couple wanted," said Cynthia. "The pink cloud."

At the point when ABC decided to drop the Ameche-Langford show, Jack and Cynthia had already reached a decision either to take a hiatus or resign. "Doing a daily show with just two people and an occasional guest like Wally Cox finally wore us down," said Jack. "The closing of the show didn't matter to us, financially. We'd saved some money and I was working other programs. By this time I could command four or five hundred dollars for one appearance, so we were doing okay."

By late summer a new series was being assembled for CBS, another vehicle that would star the Lemmons as young marrieds. It was being fashioned entirely by advertising agency executives and carried the inspired title, "Jack Loves Cinnie," this in an attempt to somehow tap and bleed off the success being enjoyed by "I Love Lucy." It was perhaps predictable that the show would deposit an enormous egg, hatched as it was by that segment of American industry best remembered for its seeming inability to spell catsup, and its unimpeachable if somewhat redundant claim that "pain mounts up."

"Heaven for Betsy," as Madison Avenue elected to christen it, was as dreary as "The Couple Next Door" had been bright. The opening episode involved Jack mistaking a bowl of vichyssoise for a pot of wallpaper paste with all the anticipated results. Critics, wheeling and turning over the television industry, descended at once on the new CBS entry and set about pecking at the bad spots.

"The Lemmons fulfill their obligations toward the show," reported *Variety*, "but there isn't much show to speak of." Said Harriet Van Horne: "It's a glossy, skillful production, this 'Betsy' charade. But its frilly, silly notion of humor may cause some tummies to turn." Jack O'Brian wrote it off as a "sticky-sweet soap opera caught masquerading in nighttime TV . . . as adult entertainment." Mary Wood complained of feeling like "I'd gulped down a quart of whipped cream in a hurry." When the final show concluded, the cast and even some of the technicians had tears in their eyes, perhaps of relief. As it turned out, "Betsy" was the last series for Jack and Cynthia, and from that point the pink cloud began a subtle shift into the cobalt spectrum.

Chapter X

"I was taken with this fellow, Lemmon . . ."
—*Max Arnow, Columbia Pictures, 1953*

DURING WORLD WAR I a ship loaded with ammonium nitrate, a "harmless" fertilizer, suddenly exploded with "unparalleled violence." In 1923, G. N. Lewis, head of the College of Chemistry at Berkeley, explained *why* in his book *Thermodynamics.* Calculating the entropy, free energy, and heat of reaction he proved ammonium nitrate unstable, and concluded that it therefore had done precisely what it was supposed to do—explode.

The fact that the substance seldom does blow up remains a scientific curiosity. People continue to buy it by the bag and spread it among their flora. Apparently certain conditions are required to bring about a blast, and nobody knows just what those might be.

And so it was with Jack and Cynthia; two perfectly explodable entities for whom there was amiable coexistence without ignition. The circumstances necessary to enflame the heart are no less mysterious than those which kindle fertilizer, and the great philosophers are as much at sea for an answer as the scientists.

There were signposts along the way, of course, early indicators that the couple's "perfect" relationship might be a hollow one, as Cynthia was later able to discern. Such warning signals are often invisible to the principals involved, but are sometimes picked up by friends from their position of detachment.

Andy McCullough remembers that Jack had an oddly romantic attitude in his relationship with Cynthia. "It was unusual," said Andy, "because Lemmon had been quite a guy with the women. Now, all of a sudden, it was like this was the 'nice' girl. Another friend and I tried to talk about it with him one night but in a Dink Stover-kind of way he let us know that 'a gentleman doesn't discuss that sort of thing,' and he walked out."

To some, their eventual marriage was hauntingly reminiscent of a time long past when matchings were a matter not of the heart but of practicality, and couplings were calculated to preserve the breed or the kingdom's solvency. Observed one friend: "I thought they made the greatest brother and sister act going." The families on both sides were thoroughly satisfied.

In the winter of 1953 Jack and Cynthia moved to fashionable Sutton Place, an exclusive residential area of New York City, similar to, but north of, Beekman Place. "It was a super duplex," said Cynthia, "rent-controlled and all decorated in yellow. We were situated above Richard Avedon, the photographer. He had the first three floors; and we, the top two. It was a walkup, but just fabulous. We loved it and so did Duffy—Lady MacDuff, an adorable wirehaired terrier the Albertsons had given us."

Cynthia soon found herself alone much of the time in their new apartment as Jack plunged into a heavy schedule of television work. "It was a very sad and lonely time for me," she said. "Jack was out so much and I wasn't working, so there was little for me to do except wander around my big, yellow rooms. And that led to some serious thinking about just what our situation really was.

"It was during this period that I came to understand that what we appeared to be on the outside, we were not as a married couple. We were great friends, we did love each other, but it was all a performance. We had great fun together, and I'm sure to onlookers we were 'the couple next door'; but we did not have a successful marriage."

For Cynthia one thing was clear: the best times were when they were together. There was fun then, and loneliness kept its distance. The chance for togetherness came unexpectedly with the announcement that the old frenzied farce of the 1930s, *Room Service*, was being resuscitated for another stand on Broadway. Jack was offered the lead role, that of Leo Davis, the naive young playwright just in from Oswego.

Instinctively, Jack sensed and calculated the risk. George Abbott had engineered a smash with the play in 1937, but could it be revved up enough to make in the 1950s? The odds were it could not, he told Cynthia, "but it's a Broadway play and I've never done one, so I ought to do it."

Charles Baker, perhaps in recognition of Cynthia's need, insisted that a part be found in the play for her. She was hired to handle the role of the prostitute, which was not unlike casting Gloria Jean as Lucrezia Borgia. "I lasted three days," Cynthia said, laughing, "and they told me they were sorry but I just wouldn't work out. I heartily agreed, because there simply was no way I could play the part; I didn't know how. Tony Randall, who had been cast as the director, got fired at the same time, so we went across the street to Sardi's and had a couple of martinis while Jack went on to work."

As rehearsals got underway, Lemmon began doubling up to meet television commitments and hence spent even less time with Cynthia than before. It was a situation she found increasingly desperate. "I knew somehow," she said, "that being together, working together, was all we had—that if our marriage was to survive, we had to solve that problem of being apart so much."

At three o'clock one morning Andy McCullough received a telephone call from Jack. "I was staying alone at the Harvard Club," said Andy. "I guess I was 'between girls' or something. Jack asked to see me right away, said he had something he wanted to talk about. He came on over and we sat up the rest of the night with a bottle. He told me he didn't know what to do because Cinnie was going to leave him unless some way could be found for them to work as a team.

"He asked what I thought about it, and I said I felt that Cinnie was a marvelous girl, pretty and sweet, but not a great talent. I said I felt something of what Hemingway did when he told Fitzgerald not to let Zelda or anything else interfere with his writing: 'You're a writer—so write.' I told him that I believed he was an artist and the idea of trying to work as a team was insane. It probably wasn't what Jack needed at the time, because he was quite shaken by the whole thing; but I was appalled by this development."

Andy convinced Jack to take the lead part in a "Danger" TV episode he was directing a couple of weeks later. "It was the last time I saw Cynthia and Jack for perhaps a year," said McCullough, "and I remember it well because, believe it or not,

Jack missed the opening scene. 'Danger' always had a 'teaser' up front before going to the first commercial break. In this one Jack was supposed to be seen sliding across a window outside a diner; he was playing a young killer.

"Well, I opened the show and panned across to the window. There was a big 'sting' of music—but no Jack! At the break I went tearing out of the booth yelling and looking for him and I finally located him in the dressing room—being interviewed by a reporter from the New Brunswick high school newspaper! He was sitting there like Olivier, expounding on the importance of dedication in an actor. I screamed at him and he jumped and said, 'What's wrong? What's wrong?' I said 'For Christ's sake, you've blown the opening!' He shot out of there and did the show and was just excellent.

"Toward the end, Cinnie slid into the booth, and when the program was over I turned and asked, 'How'd you like it?' She said, 'I thought it was fine—but Andy, you're wrong about Jack and me.' She walked out then, and I knew they'd been talking it over again. Jack hadn't mentioned it to me, but when he's rehearsing he never thinks of anything but the job at hand."

In March, Lemmon co-starred with Diana Lynn in a "Robert Montgomery Presents" television play that was to change his career and his life. At the same time it presented him with a graphic demonstration of the fervor with which advertising executives support a client's product, whether it annihilates frizzies, balms hemorrhoids, plops rather than merely pours, or has nothing more to recommend it than being grown at high altitude.

One scene called for Lemmon to pull out a cigarette while chatting with Miss Lynn at a bar. During rehearsal Jack extracted the cigarette and casually tapped it, at which point an assistant account executive for the sponsor, Lucky Strike, vaulted from the booth and ran bellowing across the set, halting the rehearsal. "Don't do that!" he rasped, grasping Jack by the shoulder.

"Do what?" asked Lemmon, astonished.

"Tap the cigarette," he hissed. "We *never* tap a Lucky. They are round and *firm* and fully packed!"

"Okay," said Jack, "sorry about that." The rehearsal continued with the agency man hovering at the edge of the stage. When the show went on the air live, Lemmon forgot and did what he had been doing all week in rehearsal. He tapped the cigarette.

"I heard this gargling scream," said Jack, "just as the camera was going off me for the next shot, and this guy came running at me. He had that wild, feverish look in his eyes and I thought he was going to try to kill me. He literally yanked me from the barstool, saying, 'I told you not to tap a Lucky!' Well, the mikes were open and everything was going out over the air, so I did the only thing I could do—I clapped my hand over his mouth to shut him up. I thought he was out of his mind."

Late that month Max Arnow, head of talent for Columbia Pictures in Hollywood, happened to catch a kinescope of the show and immediately jotted down the name of the unknown young man playing opposite Diana Lynn. "I was taken with this fellow, Lemmon; with the strong personality coming off the screen," said Arnow. "In those days most of the stars were the typical leading-man types—the handsome young man rather than the sort who could get by on character and personality. Jack was handsome but not the typical romantic image."

Columbia was looking for someone to play the male lead in a picture starring Judy Holliday, and Arnow decided it might be a good idea to test Lemmon for the part. He ordered a kinescope of the show sent to the studio, where he screened it for studio chief Harry Cohn and George Cukor, who had been signed to direct the Holliday film. Both men agreed with Arnow; Lemmon would be offered the test immediately. Columbia scouts in New York were assigned to catch Jack's performance in *Room Service*, which was in the final rehearsal stage.

The play opened the first week in April 1953 at the 48th Street Playhouse—and closed after eighteen performances despite a generally civil reception from critics. They applauded the cast, which included Everett Sloan, John Randolph, and Alexander Asro. Asro got special praise for his "gem of a performance" as Sasha Smirnoff, a role he had played in the original *Room Service* production at the Cort Theater.

Reviewer William Hawkins singled out Lemmon as being "particularly amusing as the naive writer" and called the evening a "good, loud funny one." The *New York Herald Tribune*'s Walter F. Kerr said, "Much too much of the evening is spent pushing a willing old warhorse beyond its actual energy," adding that "the best of the evening is kept from all-out exhilaration by the stubborn heaviness of playing and staging."

Time magazine felt the cast was "conscientious and willing," but went on to lament the lack of the "ingratiating touch" of the original players, Sam Levene, Philip Loeb, and Teddy Hart. "Not up to being a good joke at Broadway's own expense," said *Time*,

"*Room Service* can only fire away as resolutely dizzy farce. But it is not really up to that, either; things are never sufficiently under control to seem to get uproariously out of hand."

Reflecting on the play, Lemmon believes the audience failed to respond "for one simple reason. A bunch of guys stranded in a hotel room trying to raise five thousand dollars for a play [*God-speed*] and seriously considering getting bread crumbs to entice pigeons within reach so they can cook and eat them, was no longer funny. It was undoubtedly funny in the Depression, but not in the fifties when acquiring a few thousand dollars just wasn't that difficult. It was a good production, but not believable."

For Jack and Cynthia there was no ready solution which might right their listing marriage. After weeks of discussion they consulted a doctor but received little help and less encouragement. "Probably we were a little late," said Cynthia. "We had been together for about five years, including the period when we were dating, and we were somewhat set in our ways, I suppose. It was my hope that the problem might go away; but such problems just don't go away."

It was Cynthia who made the suggestion that they separate. "Jack never would have," she said. "He never was able to admit defeat; I was more the one to do that, so I told him I thought we should be by ourselves and really think about what we intended to do with our futures. He agreed, and I remember he made a little joke about it, but it was pretty serious; he knew that and so did I."

Cynthia called her family in Peoria to tell them of the separation and that she would be coming home for a while. "It was," she said, "the hardest thing I have ever done in my life."

During the brief run of *Room Service*, calls began coming in from Columbia Pictures. Jack agreed to be tested but asked that terms of the anticipated contract be negotiated in advance. Arnow tendered a forty-week agreement, which Jack rejected. "Lemmon wanted a picture deal instead," said Arnow, "a contract calling for him to appear in a certain number of pictures each year, and we consented to that. The final contract that he eventually signed required him to do two pictures a year, and we had an option for a third. As I recollect, I worked out the deal with the William Morris Agency before the test was made."

The seven-year contract was nonexclusive, affording Jack the right to appear in four plays during that period regardless of how long the plays might run. The time consumed by the plays would then be "tacked on" to the seven years of the contract—a procedure that later proved illegal in litigation not involving Jack.

With Cynthia in Peoria, Jack spent most of his evenings at Cheerio's, "a marvelous joint that was located on Fifty-second Street below CBS. It was run by a couple of terrific guys named Mario and Dick Ratazzi, and everybody in radio and TV went there. You could hardly get in unless they knew you; it was a favorite hangout, especially for writers, producers, and directors.

"Old Mario would be behind the bar and he'd mix these enormous deep-dish martinis. On every table, in case you weren't working too regularly, there were crackers and huge jars of cheddar cheese. I can remember a few nights when that was all I ate! I went over there after I got word that I was going out to the West Coast for the screen test and I called Cinnie. She was happy for me, but we were separated and that was that. When I went to California, I went alone."

Chapter

XI

"Yes, dear boy, yes! Don't act!"
—*George Cukor*

WITH A SCREEN TEST SCHEDULED and his signing of a contract nearly certain, Lemmon's arrival in Hollywood lacked the storied color of some less fortunate hopefuls, who feel compelled to enter in the manner of Louis IV visiting the provinces—with the maximum pizzazz possible.

Jack disembarked without pomp at the Los Angeles airport and took a cab to the unpretentious Hollywood Roosevelt Hotel. After dinner and a martini he spent the evening in the lobby, sipping a ginger ale, listening to Bill Pannell's music floating in from the Cinegrill, and watching touring Kiwanians check in. He retired early to study the script he already knew.

The next morning he called Columbia Pictures and reached Max Arnow, who said, "Come on over."

"How do I get there?"

"Well," said Arnow, after a considerable pause, "you take a taxi or walk down Hollywood Boulevard to Gower and take a right." Still wary of the vagaries of the business, Jack hiked to Columbia and saved the two bucks.

"I was a little worried about the scene," said Jack. "I knew what I wanted to do and I felt good about that. But I was anxious because I didn't know Cukor, although I'd seen his work and I had great respect for the man. I had anticipated doing the test that same afternoon, but Max told me we would not get around to it for a couple of days. He said, 'Come on, I want you to meet someone.'

"He took me down the hall to a small office and introduced me to a couple of young guys named Richard Quine and Blake Edwards, who were writers hoping to become directors. I recognized Dick because he'd been an actor and I had seen him on film, usually playing the gawky young schnook. Quine had made one picture that was a ripper. It was called *We've Never Been Licked* and he went down in an airplane. To this day, when I see that this beauty is going to be on the tube—usually about three in the morning—I call up Quine, get him out of bed, and say, 'Dick, baby, your biggie is coming up!'

"We started shooting the breeze, and I found that, like me, Quine also played the piano and wrote songs, so we hit it off beautifully. Later on, when he got going as a director, he always ended up writing the title song because they were his pictures."

Jeff Donnell, who was under contract to Columbia, was selected to make the test with Jack, which pleased him because "she was not only a sweet girl, but a fine actress." Jeff remembers the test well. "Jack was nervous. He wanted the part, so he was a little on edge—but kind and appreciative and thoroughly professional. It was a comedy part, but Jack played it straight. He got laughs—even from the stagehands."

Quine, who directed the test because Cukor was out of town for a few days, said: "I adored Lemmon from the first moment; he had that quality about him. I was a young, high-waisted director. In spite of the fact that I was not a veteran, someone in whose hands he could place his career, commit hara-kiri for, he just said, 'Here I am—take me.' In that situation there could very easily have been mistrust or doubt on his part, which would have been understandable."

After the first test Arnow decided to give Jack another, this one for *The Long Gray Line*, a story about the West Point Military Academy to be directed by John Ford. The part required an actor that could portray a man through the years from age twenty-five to seventy-five. Jack would be tested both ways.

Again Quine directed the test. "As the young man, Lemmon absolutely put me away! I was boggled at what I was seeing; he was bloody brilliant. I think, up to that time, the only actor I'd ever worked with who could knock me over like that was Mickey Rooney, who was a genius. Jack and Mickey had something else in common that I don't recall running into with anyone else. We had a kind of shorthand communication from the beginning. We never spoke a paragraph. Both guys had a tendency to go a little over on a scene, and I would say, to either of them, 'When you make that move over to the—' and that's as far as I'd get. They'd say, 'Yeah, I know what you mean, and you're right.' I hadn't said it yet, but they would know what I was going to say.

"That sort of thing spoils you as a director. I almost wish I had never worked with Jack, because once you direct him there's no way you'll ever be happy with anyone else. It really isn't direction as much as collaboration. I mean that from the bottom of my shoes; it's incredible, the man is so facile."

To prepare for the second part of the test in which he would appear as an old man, Jack spent five days with Clay Campbell, head of makeup for Columbia. Straws were inserted in his nostrils and a plaster cast of his face was made, after which the cast was used to form rubber facial elements. After these were applied he was outfitted with a uniform.

"I was going cuckoo by this time," said Jack. "They were getting this angle and that angle and I didn't know what was happening because I didn't understand film, only live TV. I was getting tired because I couldn't sit down during lighting changes, which took an hour. I'd walk up and down and repeat my lines to myself and every once in a while I'd glance over at Quine, whom I liked because he smiled a lot and seemed to know what the hell he was doing."

At length Jack began to worry because Quine was giving him little or no direction. Finally, Lemmon had to find out why. Walking over to the director, he said: "Listen, you're not giving me much direction. Do you *know* what to tell me—or is it that you don't *want* to tell me, or what? Why aren't you saying something?"

"Because," said Quine, his smile broadening, "I like what you're doing."

Quine, as mentioned, did like what Jack was doing but the grin was there because "he was so ludicrous with that makeup on that baby face that he cracked me up; I couldn't look at him. He was marvelous in the performance, but just hysterically funny. I knew then and there that there was no way he was going to play this part and I think he knew it too, but he was in there pitching."

While Jack was in California Cynthia returned to their apartment in New York. "I had decided," she said, "that I would do something about myself, make myself far more appealing. I went out and bought a new black dress and a black sweater with rhinestones on it. I was going to be really smashing when he came home. Everything was going to be fine; usually it *was* fine, but not perfect, and we were perfectionists.

"I thought I looked pretty neat when he returned and I guess he did, too. Of course, we'd been through this period of separation and I guess we looked awfully good to each other. Things were better between us."

Out in California, an assistant film editor named Maurice Max was resorting to modest subterfuge to guarantee that Lemmon's test for the Holliday picture got the full attention of Harry Cohn. Max was joined in the plot by producer Freddie Kohlmar and Columbia vice-president Jerry Wald, who had seen the test and wanted Jack for the role.

A ploy was necessary to circumnavigate the legendary brevity of Cohn's attention span in the screening room—a matter of seconds unless something electrifying was happening on film. Cohn was likely to get fidgety because he'd seen the same scene several times. A number of actors had been tested for the part over a period of months; none had worked out. Since Jack's test ran four minutes, starting slow and building to a high point, Cohn had to somehow be kept in his seat for the entire 240 seconds.

It was Cohn's custom to get his office work out of the way during the day and then have tests and dailies (rush prints of scenes from various of the studio's productions shot that day) brought to his home in the evening, where they were shown in his private projection room. It was Max's job to take the films to Cohn's home.

Recognizing that there was little chance of inducing the studio chief to view the entire test under such conditions, Max substituted a segment from an old Three Stooges comedy for Jack's test on the evening it was scheduled to be shown. When it came up on the screen, Cohn reacted: "Where the hell did that come from?"

"It's a mistake," lied Max. "Somebody put the wrong reel in, Mr. Cohn. Would it be okay if I showed the test in the morning at the studio, since it's so late now?"

Cohn agreed. Max had already advised Kohlmar and Wald to be on hand at 10:00 A.M. the following day. It was their job to keep their boss watching. They took seats directly behind him in the screening room. As expected, Cohn became restive after thirty seconds. "Let's go to the next reel," he said. Wald and Kohlmar balked, urging him to hold off a moment and watch a little more. They coaxed him through the entire four minutes, after which Cohn, perfectly aware by this time that he'd been set up, said: "Okay, okay, goddammit, so he's good!" Lemmon got the part.

A few days later, on May 15, Jack received a letter from Wald:

> Just these few lines to tell you how delighted I was with your tests and to tell you that in my small way, I'll be sitting in the back of the car while you drive swiftly, pleasantly, and calmly to stardom.
>
> You can't miss!

One of the young actors Jack beat out for the part was his friend from The Old Knick, Darren McGavin. "I asked Jack after he made his test if he thought he would get the job. He said he didn't think he had much of a chance. Well, I went in there and tested and they threw my ass right out. The next thing I heard was that Lemmon had the part."

The fact that Judy Holliday's leading man in her new film, *A Name for Herself* (later changed to *It Should Happen to You*, with no loss of vacuity), was a first-timer in movies stirred up a rash of mentions in the show business columns. Louella Parsons took note, as did Thomas Pryor. Among the clippings was one that proved Lemmon a better actor than he had suspected. The hot-air Irish balloon that he'd inflated at CBS five years earlier in trying to con Tony Minor out of a part in *Shadow and Substance* had apparently come to earth on the desk of columnist Edith Gwynn. She filed the exclusive word that "Lemmon is well known in the N.Y. theater—and was with the famed Abbey Theatre in Ireland, too."

At Columbia an ill-at-ease Lemmon was introduced to Judy and immediately dispatched to wardrobe for an overhaul. "I weighed about a hundred and fifty pounds," said Jack, "and *she* weighed about a hundred and fifty pounds. She was a tall girl, too, about five feet eight or so, and when they put her in heels we were nearly even. They put me in lifts that made me feel like I was constantly going down a hill and they gave me a coat with shoulders padded out four inches.

"Judy was very gracious and sweet. She knew I was embarrassed and this was my first time around for this kind of thing. They put us through these awful wardrobe tests, where we would just stand in front of the camera side by side or put our heads together and grin. You felt like an idiot, turning and smiling.

"I felt it was imperative to get to know her so that I'd be more comfortable, so I screwed up my courage and asked, 'Want to go to dinner?' She said 'Sure!' She told me how to get to the house she had rented, where she was staying with her mother and baby. Her husband had not arrived from New York at that time."

That evening, they got underway in a car Jack had rented. Judy gave him directions which would lead to an Italian restaurant. The route, as Lemmon recalls, led over some mountains, which indicates that the cafe must have been located in the nearby San Fernando Valley. "I didn't have the faintest idea where we were," he said, "but somewhere in those mountains that damned old rental car got a flat tire. Well, I was immobilized; didn't know what the hell to do. Judy suggested we just wait, that someone would be along to help. 'No!' I said. 'I see some lights ahead. Must be a service station. You stay here and lock the doors and I'll go get somebody to fix it.'

"Well, I figured the lights were half a mile away—no big deal for the old Boston bullet, the cross-country ace, ya know. I started running and those damned lights turned out to be a mile and a half away, and when I got there it was a little diner, a drive-in. The people there said there was a station on down the mountain, two blocks to the right, and one to the left, and so on.

"I decided not to keep going; I might never find my way back to the car. By this time I was panicky, hysterical, not knowing what to do. I kept thinking, 'Oh, my God; oh, my God! *Judy Holliday*, and I've left her all alone!' "

Racing back to the car, Jack found Judy calmly waiting, very much alive. She unlocked the door and said, "Do you have a handkerchief?"

Lemmon was stricken with remorse. The poor girl must have been hysterical, crying and all that. He pulled out the handkerchief and gave it to Judy, who began wiping her hands. "What—what happened?" gasped Jack.

"Nothing," she said. "We're all set—let's go."

Finally it dawned on him. The "helpless" Judy had jacked up the car and changed the tire! "After that" said Jack, "she was *my girl.* A sweet, wonderful, terrific lady."

For several days prior to the start of production director George Cukor spent every available moment with Jack, walking, at lunch, or just driving around. "I knew what he was doing," said Jack. "He wanted to get to know me. Rather than just showing up for the first day's shooting he took the time to figure me out. I loved him for that. Finally one day we were driving along and he said, 'I know how you work now.'

"To this day I don't know what he was talking about but somehow he'd figured out how I approached things and how to get to me. I loved working with Cukor; he's one of the better 'actor's directors,' a sensitive, bright man. He got the reputation of being a 'woman's director' but in reality he's simply a great director, period. I was fortunate to break in with him, rather than with someone who might have been cut and dried, didactic."

Lemmon's role in *It Should Happen to You* was that of a young documentary producer/cameraman shooting on location in Central Park. Cukor assigned a photographer who understood 16mm cameras to work with Jack for two days, walking through parks, photographing people, and learning to handle the equipment so that in the picture he would look natural.

Jack's acting techniques, calibrated to the live theater and television, were a bit broad and sweeping for the big cinema screen, as Cukor soon discovered. "Cukor kept ordering retakes," said Jack. "He had this way of ending his sentences with, 'Don't you see?' I'd finish a scene and he'd say, 'Less, less, my boy. Less, don't you see?' "

Finally, Jack stopped in exasperation and said: "What is it? What's wrong? Are you trying to tell me not to act at all?"

Cukor, with the look of a man whose migraine had just let up, raised his hands heavenward in gratitude. "Yes, dear boy, yes! Don't act!"

Jack learned much from George Cukor. "He taught me not to worry about technique, explaining, 'If you have technique, it will take care of itself; never think of it or how you are gesturing—just do it.' He was quite right, because when you are concentrating on your lines or technique you're not in the scene; you're doing it technically and it will never be as good."

Lemmon's superb sense of comedy and timing, which had won him the respect of critics and actors in New York, produced an idea that made one scene from *It Should Happen to You* a highlight of the picture.

"The movie concerned a girl named Gladys Glover," said Jack, "a girl who is buying billboard space and plastering her name and picture all over New York. I played her boyfriend, who just can't believe what this ding-dong girl is doing, because there's no reason other than to see her name in print. In this particular scene in her apartment he gets so frustrated he finally can't talk to her anymore, and he leaves. I realized as soon as I read the script that he should make a false exit, then come back in the door for the final line. I suggested it to Cukor and he bought the idea immediately.

"In the scene the guy finally says, 'Do you remember my name? Well, forget it!' and leaves, slamming the door. She kicks a stool and the door opens again. He says, 'So is it still on for Saturday night?' She says, 'Of course,' and he snaps, 'Thank you very much,' and repeats the exit.

"Well, there's no way you can keep from bringing the house down with that—but only if you make the exit before the end of the scene and then reenter. It worked so well that people who saw the picture still remember that bit and comment on it."

When the day came to shoot that particular scene, it was still early on in the filming schedule, and Lemmon started worrying about it the moment he came on the set. The camera was pointing over his shoulder at Judy. New to the film world, he had forgotten that most scenes are usually shot in several takes from different angles. As the filming progressed, Jack became convinced that he would never be seen, that Cukor had forgotten their plan and was blowing the whole splendid concept of his exit.

"I was really worried," said Jack. "I kept thinking that I'd come all this way to make a movie and nobody would see me! I was just dying and I found myself sneaking upstage. George kept saying, 'Please stay on your marks.' It got to the point that I couldn't stand it anymore, so I walked over and explained that nobody would be able to see me do the big exit. He said 'Are you out of your mind? They'll see you—but at the moment we're shooting *her*. Later, we'll move over here and shoot *you*—don't you see?' "

Jack saw. "It was terribly embarrassing, but I had it in my head that we were doing it like we would on the stage—one time and that was it. I had a lot to learn."

Working with Cukor and Holliday had been a revelation for Lemmon, who was fast becoming enchanted with the movie business. At the same time the California climate and the relaxed West Coast lifestyle had captivated him, and he and Cynthia, now reconciled, decided to make their home in the Southland and began shopping for a house.

They located their cottage in Brentwood on Kenter Avenue off

Sunset Boulevard. "It was a cute little place," said Jack, "but there was the problem of the down payment which I didn't have. The contract at Columbia, as I recall, was for about ten thousand dollars per picture—but I couldn't buy a house. They wanted twenty-eight thousand for the place, which seemed like a lot at the time.

"Cinnie had some money in a trust, so we called her dad and asked if he thought using that for the down payment and putting the house in her name would be a good idea. He agreed it would be, and it was. Later on she sold it for a lot more than we paid."

At this point, principal photography had been completed on *It Should Happen to You*, so Jack and Cynthia returned to the East, visiting friends in New England and getting in some fishing. Shortly afterward, Jack was summoned back to California for two days of retakes.

In the middle of a scene on the second day, Max Arnow walked up. "Come on," he said, "Harry Cohn wants to see you."

"Okay," said Jack, "soon as we finish this take."

"Are you kidding? This is *Harry Cohn*. You come *now!*"

Although Jack had been on the Columbia lot for months, he had not met Cohn. "After we got through the row of secretaries out front, Max and I entered that big office of his. The first thing that struck me was the lighting. He had four or five windows fitted with venetian blinds. The first was nearly closed, the second a little more open and so forth. The one directly behind him was wide open and had the effect of spotlights hitting right on his bald head.

"I also firmly believe there was a slight *tilt* to the floor so that you had to walk up toward the 'throne' and were affected by this, unconsciously. Harry was hunched over his desk, a short bull of a man who reminded me of The Angel, a wrestler that used to be popular years back. Max had already taken a chair, so I walked up to the desk, acutely aware of this 'presence' in front of me."

Jack proffered his hand. "How do you do, Mr. Cohn? I'm Jack Lemmon." Cohn brought up *his* right hand and in it was a riding crop which he brought crashing down on the desk. "Nobody," he growled, "can be in films with that name!"

"What?"

"The critics will use it like a baseball bat," snapped Cohn. "They'll kill you, they'll crucify you." Jack watched, more in fascination than fear as Cohn harangued him about the name Lemmon, occasionally smiling and then bellowing, bringing the crop cracking down on the desk for emphasis.

At length Cohn subsided and Jack said. "No, there is no way I am going to change my name. Nobody mentioned this when I signed the contract. I don't want to change it. I like it."

"You know," said Cohn menacingly, "that we can drop you?"

"You certainly can," agreed Jack. "I have a ticket on a seven o'clock plane for New York and I may never be back—but I'm not going to change my name any more than I intend to cut off my right arm."

"They'll say that Lemmon is a lemon," insisted Cohn, "and that the picture is a lemon and they'll go, ha, ha, ha!"

"I've done a lot of TV," Jack countered, "and I've been on Broadway and on only a couple of occasions have critics played with that name. It's a one-shot joke and no critic worth his salt will use those puns. Besides, it's L–E–M–M–O–N not L–E–M–O–N. What about Walter Pidgeon? There's a name for you! What about Humphrey Bogart? He's supposed to be a big tough guy—with a name like Humphrey?"

"That's beside the point," argued Cohn. "I took a young girl in here years ago and she became a star because I changed her name to Ann Sothern."

"What was her name before that?"

"Harriet Lake."

"That," said Jack in disbelief, "is the greatest name I ever heard. I can see it in lights on Broadway: Harriet Lake!"

"It was terrible," said Cohn.

"If the picture's great, then it doesn't matter what the actor's name is."

"You're wrong," said Cohn, "and anyway, all I want to do is change the two m's to n's in your name. That's all."

"That's all? You want to change my name to Lennon?"

"That's it."

"No," said Lemmon jokingly, "they'll think I'm a Russian revolutionary."

"That's Le-NEEN," shouted Cohn, cropping the desk top. "I looked it up!"

Lemmon was dismissed with Harry's instruction to "think it over, take your time—but let me know by tomorrow morning."

Jack returned to New York, where he and Cynthia prepared for their move to California. He ignored a barrage of telegraphic demands for an answer on the name change and without realizing it had made precisely the right move in standing up to Cohn.

"If you didn't talk back to Cohn," said Arnow, "he would grind you into the earth. He had no respect for you. That's the kind of person Harry Cohn was; you had to talk back to him to exist there, and I think he liked Jack because Jack was very direct. The fact that Jack turned down the name suggestion impressed Harry. If Lemmon had gone along with Harry, then he might have not cared too much for Jack. Strange approach, huh?

"I know that in all the time I was with Columbia I never heard Cohn utter one derogatory word about Lemmon. He liked him; called him 'my Harvard man.' "

Chapter

XII

"I'm Ford and you're Pulver!"
—*John Ford*

THERE ARE CERTAIN nettling constants in life, small democratic sufferings that bond pipefitters, movie stars, and kings alike into a kind of brotherhood of the harassed. Moving day is one.

In the summer of 1953, Jack and Cynthia stuffed their luggage in the Rambler, called a van and storage company and prepared to leave their much-loved yellow apartment for a new life in California.

The apartment had been outfitted with expensive antiques; furniture, china, silver, and some fine and rare eighteenth-century German procelain, notably Dresden and Meissen. Most of the items were gifts from Cynthia's parents.

Jack, therefore, greeted the arrival of the movers with deep misgivings, envisioning disastrous incidents in the transferral of their goods down four flights of stairs.

"The foreman took one look at our stuff and said, 'I better call the office.' He got on the phone and said, 'Hello, Mac? Listen Mac, we gotta lotta Drezzaden and Mizzaden here, ya know? Mac, I been around dis here business for fifty years and I know dem art objects when I see 'em. Whatta we gonna do wit dis crap?'

"When I heard that line," said Jack, "I gave up. I figured everything would be busted. I could just hear the furniture bashing against the walls as they carried it away. I tried to ignore the whole thing and when they'd finished loading it, we closed the apartment, climbed in the Rambler with Duffy in the back seat, and took off across the country. It was fun, that first part of the trip, because I'd never done that before and neither had Cinnie."

Duffy the wirehair had an uncompromising nature, the kind dog lovers describe, inadequately, as "feisty." He had faint regard for his own kind and when he encountered a dog in Peoria, where the Lemmons stopped to visit the Stones, he took instant umbrage. An armistice seemed unlikely, so Jack left Duffy in the Rambler back seat overnight. As a deterrent to any such future affronts, Duffy ate the seat.

"When we came out the next morning," said Jack, "we found a winter wonderland. After he'd finished off the seatcovers and padding, the springs let go and pashew-w-w!—foam rubber went everywhere. I longed to strangle him but didn't dare. He snarled when I came near. Duffy would bite a mastadon, anything."

Jack believes the early Nash Rambler to have been a sensational machine, with but two faults: the motor and the convertible top. In warm climates the engine overheated at ten-minute intervals. The top was rigged with an ingenious system of wires and pulleys, which would have been a triumph of automotive engineering had they functioned. For Jack and Cinnie, their trip through the desert lands of the West was memorable.

"We'd go a little ways and then we'd have to stop and get a motel room for an hour to cool off, take a shower, or hop in the swimming pool if there was one. The engine kept boiling over and we couldn't get the top up. It was an awful journey, but we made it—pulled up at our little house late one afternoon. Everything was going to be okay now, because our furniture would be there and we could start living. I jumped out of the car and ran next door where a lady had our key."

The lady advised him that, unfortunately, the furniture had not arrived nor had the mover called. "We had gas, lights, and a telephone," said Jack, "but not one stick of furniture. Nothing."

A call to the local office of the van and storage company produced the distressing word that they had never heard of Jack Lemmon *or* his furniture. There must be some mistake, they said.

This was true; the furniture had been transferred to another truck in the Midwest and sent on its way back East! It would be a full month before it was shipped back to Brentwood.

It was now 6:00 P.M. and Jack suggested they go to dinner and think about what to do next. Entering a small restaurant on Sepulveda Boulevard just off Sunset Boulevard, they spotted Peter Lawford, dining alone. "Pete had worked with me on the Judy Holliday picture," said Jack. "We joined him and later he took us up to his place and loaned us a mattress, some cups, plates, forks, linens—things like that. The next day I went out and bought a lot of stuff.

"We put Pete's mattress on the floor and slept on it for two or three weeks until I couldn't stand it anymore and went out and bought a bed. Sleeping on the floor in a bare house can drive you a little crazy."

It Should Happen to You was a hit and Jack got praise from the critics, who sensed a star in the making. So did Columbia, which decided to hold its bright newcomer off the screen until the right script could be found for his second film. For the next seven months Jack waited in vain for something to do. "I was like an athlete who was being told to stand by, but not to work out; just wait for the game."

After several weeks he accepted an offer to star in a half-hour television drama in New York. The role brought a fee of $700 which dwindled to a net of $200 after taxes, expenses, and the agent's commission. The pay didn't matter; *doing* something did. For fun, and as an actor's exercise, Jack played the part while using only his left hand. Nobody noticed, not even the director.

Upon his return to California Jack found the situation unchanged. Columbia still had not scheduled him for a film. "I was going stir crazy," he said. "It was one thing to be out of work when you're trying to find a job and can't, but here I was with a contract and nothing to do. In desperation I finally went out in the back yard and went berserk over gardening! I had the most gorgeous little plot in town; got to know all the Latin names for plants. I was spending three or four hours a day out there—a man of the soil."

At last Columbia came up with another picture for Lemmon, *Three for the Show*, a musical directed by Henry Potter. In the film with Jack were Betty Grable and Marge and Gower Champion. "It was fun to do," recalls Jack, "but not as exciting as the film with Judy. I just wasn't that wild about the movie or the part.

Betty Grable was divine and the Champions are, of course, two of the nicest people around. Jack Cole, the choreographer, was a strange and fascinating guy and Potter was a very knowledgeable director, a nice man, but the picture just wasn't exciting to me. Perhaps no picture would have been, because it wasn't that first time. There's not much to say about it; it was a Hollywood musical."

As the year began drawing to a close, Cynthia advised Jack that there would soon be three for the show in the Lemmon household because she was pregnant. "It was," said Cynthia, "to be one of the happiest times for us. Jack was successful, I was pregnant, we had the pretty little house with pink geraniums in the front yard. It was back to the 'Couple Next Door'—perfect."

Delighted with the situation at home and at the studio, Lemmon plunged into his second picture with Judy Holliday, *Phffffft*, which was written by George Axelrod and directed by Mark Robson. "It was a good film—almost a *very* good film," said Jack. "The thing I remember best about it was an 'emergency' break that was called while we were filming a big ballroom scene. Mark Robson had to shut everything down while he went to a front-office meeting.

"There must have been a hundred extras, plus all the technicians, just sitting around waiting for two and a half hours with money just pouring down the tubes. When Mark finally came back, he was in hysterics. I asked him what the meeting had been about, what was so urgent? 'It was a meeting about a title change,' he said. 'They changed it from *Phffffft* to *Phfffft*. They took out an *f*.' "

It was not Lemmon's first encounter with the antediluvian types who seem to occupy most of the positions of power in television and the motion picture industry. Possessing not one whit of creativity, they control the creative industries for the most part. Their utterances are legend:

"We can't use this script. It's relevant, but we did relevance last year."

"The leading man won't do. He doesn't have any statue."

As *Phffft* was in the final stages of production, Maurice Max was busily cranking up another ruse that would get Lemmon noticed—this time by the great director, John Ford, who was to direct *Mister Roberts*. Ford had refused to even look at Jack's test for *The Long Gray Line*, selecting instead Tyrone Power, in the belief that he needed an established star for the role.

One afternoon when Ford was screening dailies Max spliced Lemmon's 'old man' test onto the end of the reel. Ford watched it and when the lights came on, stood up. "That kid," he said, "makes the worst old man I ever saw. But he'd be a hell of a Pulver."

Pulver, the frenetic, blowhard ensign in *Mister Roberts*, was a part Jack had wanted to play above all others. "I stood outside the theater in New York for four days," said Jack, "trying to get in to see Josh Logan when they were going to do *Mister Roberts* as a play. Never did get in; I wanted to read for one of the sailors' parts—one line, anything. The play starred Henry Fonda, of course, and David Wayne played Pulver and he was great."

Sauntering around the Columbia lot one afternoon Jack decided to visit the set of *The Long Gray Line* to watch a little of the filming and perhaps catch a peek of John Ford, whom he'd never met. He found technicians busily yanking cables and preparing to light for the next scene. He stood next to an ancient "grip" who wore a patch over one eye and had his brow shaded by a nondescript baseball cap. His tattered coat, missing most of its buttons, made no pretense of matching his baggy khaki trousers. He was chewing on the corner of a handkerchief.

"You Lemmon?" the old-timer asked.

"Yeah," Jack answered, trying to recall whether the old duffer had worked on the crew of *It Should Happen to You*.

"I've been watching you," he said, removing the handkerchief from between his teeth. "You know something—they're going to make *Mister Roberts* soon and you'd make a good Pulver."

Jack laughed skeptically. "Spread the word."

"You want to play that part?"

"In the world, there is no part I want to play more."

"Okay," he said, "spit in your hand."

"Huh?"

"Spit in your hand!"

"What are you talking about?" asked Jack, perplexed.

"It's an old Irish custom," the old fellow insisted, and spat. The expectorant landed neatly in the center of his palm. He extended his gnarled hand.

To humor him, Jack followed suit, as delicately as possible, and shook hands.

"There," said the old man, with finality. "I'm Ford and you're Pulver!"

It would be months before the stunned Lemmon would hear

anything more about *Mister Roberts* or Pulver. In the meantime he played a secondary role in *My Sister Eileen*, directed by his new friend Richard Quine. "It was the smallest part Jack has ever played in films, I'm sure," said Quine. "I think he only did it out of friendship for me and to get one of his picture commitments out of the way. The girls, Janet Leigh and Betty Garrett, were the real stars.

"I had acted in the Broadway play," said Quine, "so when Blake Edwards and I wrote the screen version I began to enlarge, unconsciously, on the part I'd played before—Frank Lippincott. It got bigger and bigger and Jack's part got smaller. It was the actor in me; I forgot I was going to direct it, not play it. As it ended up, Bob Fosse played Lippincott and had a bigger role than Lemmon. Jack sang in the film for the first time and he was very good at it."

On June 22, 1954 a son, Christopher, was born to Jack and Cynthia. He weighed nine and a half pounds, the largest child born that week at Cedars of Lebanon hospital. The birth was Caesarean.

"When Jack first saw Chris," said Cynthia, "he said 'My God, my child has a pointed head!' That was true, he did; but the doctor massaged it and the next day he was perfectly normal—and so was Jack."

Lemmon was as normal as it was possible for him to be while waiting for the part he'd always wanted and seeing the months pass with not a word. Finally one Sunday morning the telephone rang and Cynthia answered. "Jack," she said, "it's Leland Hayward on the line."

Leland Hayward! One of the great producers of all time, both on Broadway and in motion pictures. Jack took the phone with due deference. "Jack," said Hayward, "I'm in town for just a day or so at the Beverly Hills Hotel, and John Ford tells me that you are supposed to be Pulver, which is just fine—but I don't even know who you are! I think it would be rather nice if we met each other, since I'm supposed to be the producer. Do you suppose you could drop over here for a little while?"

Upon meeting Hayward it became obvious to Jack that the producer was completely "thrown" by the fact that Ford had elected to go with a relative unknown in a key role. "He was so nervous about it," said Jack, "that he read the entire play to me, now and then asking that I read a few lines for him.

"The man was wringing wet, scared to death and I could tell that he thought Ford had lost his marbles. But Ford was a giant and nobody, not even Leland Hayward, was about to second-guess him. Otherwise, I don't think I'd have gotten the part."

Chapter

XIII

"I had never been more impressed."
—*Henry Fonda*

Mister Roberts was that near-perfect gallimaufry of rare ingredients laced with just enough discordant spice to make a classic motion picture. The timing was almost supernaturally right, coming at a point when Jack was professionally capable of handling the role, yet in the spring of his career. Those who knew both Lemmon and the play suspected from the outset that he might be the ultimate Pulver—and an Oscar nominee in the bargain.

These lofty possibilities didn't occur to Jack, whose big dream had already come true. He was in an advanced state of rapture over just being part of a cast that included the likes of James Cagney, Henry Fonda, Ward Bond, and William Powell—all under the direction of the famed John Ford.

Mister Roberts was a major motion picture in every sense of the word: big budget, with a cast and crew to match. The film was to be shot on location in Hawaii and at Midway Island, scene of a decisive 1942 U.S. naval victory over the Japanese. Cinematographer was Winton C. Hoch, who had won the Oscar for his work on two other Ford pictures, *She Wore a Yellow Ribbon* and *The Quiet Man*.

The company assembled in Los Angeles and flew to Hawaii,

redezvousing with others of the production complement before pushing off for Midway. Among those who had gone to Hawaii in advance of the main party was James Cagney. "I had read in the newspaper that this young fellow I'd admired on TV had been signed to play Pulver," said Cagney, "so I went down to meet the plane when it landed; and there was the lad."

As he shook hands with Jack, Cagney asked, "Do you still use only your left hand?"

"Huh?"

"Your left hand. I saw you on a TV show and in my life I never saw a man more left-handed."

Suddenly Jack understood. Cagney had detected his "acting exercise" two years earlier and had remembered. "From that moment I was in awe of that man," said Jack. "What an incredible eye for detail, what retention! As far as I know, Cagney was the only person who saw that show and caught my little experiment."

On Midway, Jack found himself with plenty of free time, as did the other leading players. Ford was shooting scenes involving members of the U.S.S. *Reluctant*'s crew. Noting that Cagney spent his spare time practicing dance routines to keep in shape, Jack asked to join him.

A former hoofer, Cagney delighted in taking Lemmon on as a student. "We found a big empty room at the officer's quarters," Cagney said, "and I taught Jack a time step, which turned out to be one of the funniest time steps I've ever seen. He's very loose-jointed, you know, and I would say that his control is rather lacking. He did learn a time step, but it was a truly eccentric one.

"There are time steps and there are *time* steps, but there was only one set pattern for Jack; that was to fling his right leg out uncontrollably. He had no command at all over the left, which limited the action of that one! Later, when he was doing a picture up in Chester, Connecticut, with Doris Day, I sent her a wire: DEAR DORIS. TRUST EVERYTHING IS GOING WELL, BUT DO KEEP AN EYE ON LEMMON'S LEFT FOOT. IT DOES STRANGE THINGS MOST OF THE TIME."

After spending some time with Jack, Cagney began to worry about a key scene in *Mister Roberts* in which the captain of the *Reluctant* (Cagney) chances to meet Ensign Pulver, the "laundry and morale officer," for the first time. "With the coloring Lemmon brought to that part," said Cagney, "I knew I was going to have trouble keeping from breaking up with laughter. I told Jack about it and he said 'I've been thinking about the same thing.' I said I thought we'd better get together and work it out."

The pair located an empty cabin aboard the AKL * serving as the *Reluctant* and "went at it." The critical part, as Cagney recalls it, went something like this:

CAGNEY: Young man, are you one of my officers?

LEMMON: Yes, sir.

CAGNEY: How long have you been aboard, Pulver?

LEMMON: Fourteen months—sir.

"Now," said Cagney, "when he delivered that last line, he'd get that silly look on his pan and I'd break up—we both would. I hadn't seen one of my own officers in *fourteen months*, which meant he was a very able dodger."

Lemmon lays the blame on Cagney for not being able to get through the scene. "When he'd ask me how long I'd been on that boat, there'd be a long pause, because Pulver was in no hurry to answer that one, and I'd finally look up and Jimmy's eyes would be twinkling and going around and around like cherries on a pinball machine. He convulsed me. Eventually we reached an agreement; we wouldn't look each other in the eye. I would stare at his Adam's apple and he'd fix on the brim of my cap. That's the way we finally did it."

The means of divertissement on Midway were few and usually homegrown. "There was Sand Mountain, which was about thirty-five feet high and you could climb that," said Jack. "Or you could watch the goony birds, which was great fun because after they landed they'd fall ass over teakettle. Then they'd stand up and pretend it never happened, preen and hold their heads high, and go stumbling off down the beach.

"The other big attraction was watching for colored glass balls that would float in. The Japanese used them for fishing-net floats and when one broke loose it would travel all the way across the Pacific. Guys would sit on the beach with binoculars all day, and when they spotted one, they'd scream and go swimming off like madmen to fetch it. The guy with the most balls on his mantle was a big man on Midway."

Fonda, Cagney, Powell, Lemmon, and Bond formed a group that was highly resourceful at creating Machiavellian amusements and was not at all diffident about turning on one of its own if it served the moment. Such a moment arrived once, and Ward Bond was served up to it.

"We were sitting around in Bill Powell's quarters one Sunday

* Auxiliary Kargo Light—a light cargo vessel used by the U.S. Navy as a supply ship in World War II.

just before sunset," recalls Jack. "Bill was fixing some coffee and hors d'oeuvres. We called him our den mother because he was always tidying up, making little snacks and whatnot. If there was a flower to be had on that island he'd find it and stick it in a Coke bottle. He was just marvelous—the only man I ever saw who could walk around in fluffy house slippers and shorts and maintain a regal dignity like he was on his way to the coronation.

"Anyway, we'd been swapping tales. The guys would tell wonderful stories about the business and I'd relate some of my adventures—which must have been thrilling for them! Fonda was complaining that his yarns were drowned out by the snoring of Bond, who'd gotten a little sloshed on beer and had gone across the hall for a nap. Finally Hank said: 'I believe I have come up with a brilliant suggestion; we should wake Ward up and tell him Ford is doing a dawn shot and where the hell is Bond because he's supposed to be in the scene with the crew.' "

The others agreed instantly that they'd never heard of a better idea and voted to act upon it at once, inasmuch as the sun would be setting momentarily. Lemmon was selected to be the "actor" who would deliver the urgent and awful news to Bond, who could be heard snoring, blissfully unaware, in the next room. Cagney and Powell quickly began scrambling eggs, pouring coffee, and setting the table for "breakfast."

"I played the young Pulver bit," said Jack. "I grabbed Bond by the arm and began shaking him, all excited. He came up saying, 'What—what—wha—' I said, 'Wake up! Wake up, for God's sake! Pappy's furious; he's furious! He's all lined up for the dawn shot—don't you remember the dawn shot?' Ward looked at me with no comprehension at all and said, 'Dawn shot? What dawn shot?'

"I said, 'Come on, for God's sake, he's waiting! They've got three jeeps cooking outside and everything, and Ford's up there on the bridge of the ship waiting to shoot the dawn shot where you're supposed to have the whole crew behind you while you're talking about Roberts.

"Well, poor old Bond was floundering. Now he was getting petrified because he realized he'd been drinking and Ford was waiting for him and all hell was going to break loose. He just *knew*, because Ward and Pappy Ford had been close for years.

"Ward had left his clothes in Bill's room; so, dressed in shorts and socks, he came bulling in, his big belly bouncing, his enormous red eyes popping out and watering. He took a look out the window at the sun, which was just about to dip below the horizon and he said: 'Holy Jesus, it's already up!'

"He sat down with his back to the window. Hank Fonda didn't crack a smile. He just sat with his back against the wall and watched as Bond started pulling his pants on. Ward was giving a running monologue and trying to see to put his shoes on. He was mumbling, 'That goddamned Ford never leaves you alone—always tryin' to pull something—Chrissake, been the same way for thirty years.' Then he looked back outside and said, 'Jesus—gettin' darker, isn't it?'

"Fonda was marvelous. He looked right at Bond and didn't crack, and once in a while he'd say something to Ward like: 'You better hurry it, baby, 'cause we've both been there for a long, long time and we know what that man is going to be like when you show up. And every minute that you're late is just another year of hell.'

"When Bond was finally looking for his jacket and it was too dark in the room to find it, he said, 'What the hell? Is it going to rain?' He looked out the window and by now, of course, it was dark. He stood there for about a full minute trying to figure it out, and then it hit him. He turned around and said, 'Oh, my God, that one's a beauty—you dirty sonsabitches!' and then broke up with the rest of us."

For the most part the actors spent their evenings at their quarters. It was safer. Midway was a military base, an isolated outpost populated partly by "nervous in the service" GI's. The few women on the island were wives of officers and enlisted men who could prove a specific need or who were qualified by reason of rank or longevity to have their dependents with them.

The presence of the women among so many "rock happy" men generated a situation of constant tension. It was not unusual, when a man with a wife drew night duty, to have an armed friend walk guard duty in front of his quarters to protect the little lady from amorous outsiders; or perhaps vice versa.

Lemmon found out just how touchy the situation was one evening at an officer's club party. He was, as usual, playing the piano, singing, and having fun. During the group singing of "Down by the Old Mill Stream" an officer's wife seated herself on the bench next to Lemmon and, draping an arm around his shoulders, joined in. A moment later Jack heard a commotion and found himself lifted bodily from the piano. He was hustled out the screen door, into a jeep, and driven back to his quarters.

"What the hell happened?" asked the confused Lemmon.

"Get in your room and stay there!" said his escort. "That broad's husband was heading for you with a butcher knife."

After that episode the group sought out less risky pursuits. Fonda spent many of his afternoons fishing, and eventually hooked a strange and large marine creature that he'd never seen before. Cagney examined the catch and pronounced it "the best 'eating fish' in the world."

"We picked up some vegetables at the post exchange," said Fonda, "procured an enormous pot, and Cagney proceeded to make the most delicious fish soup you ever tasted. We kept that pot on continuously and when the contents got low we'd just add more milk and vegetables."

Life in the *Mister Roberts* company was not without occasional abrasive moments. Jack recalls hearing a ruckus one night: "It woke me up, and I could hear a lot of hollering going on up the hall. I got out of bed and padded over to see what was going on. Through an open door I saw Hank Fonda and Pappy Ford in the middle of the room, yelling at each other. It was a funny sight because old Pappy was in his shorts, seven inches shorter than Hank and looking about a hundred and ten years old.

"As I stood there gaping, Ford yelled, 'You're not gonna tell me what I can do, goddammit!' He pushed Hank back with one hand and swung from the floor with a right! He damn near connected but Fonda just shoved him back on the bed and told him to shut up and calm down. Old Ford came right back up, slapping away. Hank wasn't fighting back and Pappy was just flailing air; Hank was so much taller and younger, he could just hold him away.

"Now these guys had been close friends and co-workers for years—and continued to be—but Ford had been making changes in *Mister Roberts* and it was killing Hank, who had starred in the play for years on Broadway. He had his soul in it; the original script was his Bible and he really did know it, but Ford was Ford and he was going to do it *his* way. I turned around and went back to bed to mind my own business."

After nearly two weeks on location Jack still had not worked in a scene. Each evening following dinner he would check the call board only to find that the schedule had been changed and Ford was planning to shoot some other segment in which Jack did not appear. Lemmon began to suspect that the director was dangling him. Ford had a reputation for trying to keep actors off balance, throwing them into a scene they had not expected to do until another time. It was a stunt that occasionally brought the director an outstanding performance.

"Pappy Ford did not like actors to think or make suggestions," said Jack. "A couple of times I went up to him and said, 'Mr. Ford, I've been thinking—' He said, 'No, you haven't.' The only way to get an idea across to Ford was on film. You had to *do* it; then he'd either accept it or have you do it over his way. He had a giant ego but he had enormous talent to go with it. He was a tough man, like the captain of a ship, and every decision was going to be his alone."

One evening Jack checked the board and found that, as usual, he had been removed from the following day's work schedule. The next morning he slept late and was aroused at nine-thirty by the roar of a jeep. He was confronted a moment later by the driver. "Get up. Hurry!" he said. "Ford wants you right away; they're going to shoot." Jack jumped into his uniform and climbed into the jeep.

"Ford is steaming," confided the driver. "It's not your fault, but somebody cancelled this scene last night and they weren't supposed to. They've been ready and waiting for half an hour, and Ford's in a rotten mood; so look out.' "

"Okay," said Jack, remembering all the Ford-the-tyrant stories he'd heard and getting a little nervous.

Arriving on the deck of the AKL Lemmon found the camera in place, Cagney standing by, and Ford looking ominous. Jack recognized at once that the director had switched from the scheduled scene to one that was not supposed to be shot until much later—the confrontation between Pulver and the captain.

"You make your entrance up there," said Ford, pointing to the bridge, "and you slide down the stairs to here."

"Is this the scene," asked Jack, "where I first meet the captain?"

Fixing Lemmon with his one eye for a long moment Ford said, "Of course. You know it, don't you?"

"I think so."

"I came down that ladder so fast," said Jack, "that I think my pockets were smoking. I spotted the captain, whom I'd been hiding from, and started right back up the stairs. Naturally, the captain says, 'You there—come down here. What's your name?' I'm trapped. I tell him I'm Ensign Pulver, laundry and morale officer. Well, all this time I was looking at his Adam's apple because I knew if I got a look at his eyes I'd blow the whole thing."

As it was, Cagney barely scraped by. "I just made it," he said, "and *only* made it! Just managed to sit on the laughter and not let go. I was like a bloody amateur, but this was one of those scenes; never happened before with me, but I knew this was going to be one."

When it was over, Ford said, "Cut," gave Lemmon a suspicious look and then said, "Once more." They went through the scene a second time. "Ford didn't say anything more," said Jack. "He just went on to the next scene but I know he'd been expecting to catch me off-guard, maybe unprepared and nervous or something. I remember thinking it was a damn good thing Cagney and I had been working on that particular bit for days. I could have given it to Pappy eighteen different ways."

Fonda, who worked with four different Pulvers during the years the play ran on Broadway, was impressed with Jack's portrayal of the goldbricking ensign. "I confess," said Fonda, "that I had some preconceived notions about Pulver and how the character should be played, and I didn't know what Lemmon would do with the part until the first day he worked.

"Leland Hayward had called me after seeing Jack in *It Should Happen to You* to say he thought Jack would be a tremendous Pulver. After they screened the film for me I agreed that he would be great in the role.

"The first time I heard him 'talking Pulver' it was new to my ear, yet I had been listening to this dialogue for years. Now, they weren't the same lines anymore . . . they were great! I had never been more impressed. Lemmon gave Pulver another dimension, something more. He didn't take away from the character, he added to it.

"I don't know how Jack does it, or even what it is that he does, but it is the thing that makes him the actor that he is. Part of it is in his delivery. If, for example, you have a line of dialogue that has eighteen words in it, I—and most other actors—will learn that line, those words. I will say that line to the best of my ability to make it sound real, as though I hadn't memorized it—like it was just coming off the top of my head.

"Jack Lemmon will take those eighteen words and add syllables, even repetition of syllables; not stuttering, mind you, but something else—and it's unique in Lemmon. He *was* Pulver; you couldn't beat him."

Jack says that his was not a carefully pre-planned Pulver, that much of the characterization "just fell in place." Lemmon had seen Pulver as played by David Wayne and Murray Hamilton, both of whom he felt were excellent in the role. "As soon as I knew I was going to play Pulver," he said, "I dropped a curtain to the point where I actually could not remember what they had done. I psyched myself out so that I wouldn't consciously do what they had done or do the reverse—try so hard *not* to imitate them that I'd go way out in right field the other way.

"I always felt one thing about Pulver; there was a naiveté about him. He was younger than the other guys, a babe in the woods in many ways, and always trying to prove himself. He wanted to be accepted by his idol and by everybody else. He wanted to be a hero and yet he'd never done a thing in his life; didn't make the football team, didn't do this, didn't do that—probably ran around the campus and got in as head of the cheerleaders. *That*, Pulver would do. He'd be out there jumpin' around like a jackrabbit trying to be accepted. I was the top cheerleader at Andover—did I ever tell you that? I wonder why. (But I never had a malacca cane—McCullough's full of crap!)

"Anyway, Pulver's frenetic behavior, as I saw it, came out of this tremendous drive to prove himself to Roberts and, secondarily, to everyone else—to be accepted. It's that simple. A lot of acting is sheer instinct. I could say I worked out every little thing, but an awful lot of it—like Pulver's strutty little walk—just came out, that's all."

One scene in *Mister Roberts*, the blowing-up of the laundry, put Lemmon in bed for two days; and the stunt man, Dick Crockett, was out for nearly two weeks. The scene called for Pulver to make his way through a long tunnel of soapsuds. Since real soapsuds didn't provide the mass, consistency, or durability required, a chemical substitute was used, a substance that proved highly irritating to humans.

A risky segment called for Pulver to descend stairs obscured by billowing mounds of foam. Crockett doubled for Lemmon. "It was a wise move," said Jack. "I like to do my own stuff when it's feasible, but an injury to a main character can shut a production down for a while and that can be inordinately expensive. When you insist on taking those chances, it's just an ego trip.

"Crockett was in that foam ten times longer than I was and he got a lot sicker. Just from the amount they threw on me for my entrance my eyes swelled and my throat closed, so I couldn't speak and my skin was burned."

After four weeks at Midway the company returned to Hawaii where the famed segment of the *Reluctant*'s crew on liberty was filmed. Production proceeded smoothly enough until a stunt man balked at riding a motorcycle off the pier for a key scene.

"They were shooting the night sequence where all the sailors were coming back so drunk that they were loading them on the ship with a cargo net," said Jack. "The script called for this one guy to show up on a motorcycle, gloriously swacked, wearing his hat down over his eyes—and he's supposed to sail right off the dock and into the drink.

"They had brought a stunt man all the way from Hollywood to do this thing, but he wasn't about to take a shot at it. It was blowing like mad and pouring rain. The wind was whipping up the water and you could see the whitecaps. That stunt man took one look and said, 'I ain't gonna do it. You think I'm nuts? Weaving on a motorcycle on this slick pier, and then going forty feet out and fifteen down into *that* ocean? You wouldn't even see me out there if I'm dazed or something.'

"Now most other directors would have wrapped up the whole thing and rescheduled it for the next night. Not Ford. He thought it was great, with the storm and all. As it happened, there was a drunk car dealer standing there watching and he said, 'I'll ride it! I'll ride that thing.' This guy had never been on a motorcycle in his life, but Ford took him up on it and had the guy sign a waiver—an agreement not to hold the production company liable if anything went wrong. I think he got paid seven hundred dollars for it.

"I do recall they had to teach this character to ride the cycle before they could even try for the take. Ford had a camera set up on a raft out in the water and when he yelled, 'Roll!' that guy came down the pier. Now, never having ridden a cycle before, he forgot how to work the throttle. In trying to slow down he turned the handle to wide open. He sailed way out and rolled off the motorcycle just as it hit the water; otherwise he probably would have been injured. He disappeared for close to a minute and the six Hawaiian divers they had standing by dove in to search for him. Suddenly we saw him bob to the surface; he hadn't even lost his sailor hat! They fished him out, a little stunned but otherwise okay.

"The shot was spectacular. I felt kind of sorry for the camera operator because he's out there on a bobbing raft and there's just one chance—but he got it, center screen all the way. Who but Ford would take a chance like that, betting he could pull it off at night in a storm, using a drunk who'd never been in a film or on a bike? He just assumed that God was on his side—and maybe He was.

"The people who worked with Ford had a love-hate relationship with him. I suppose he could be a tyrant at times, but he was a great director, a giant. I'd get to thinking of what a persnickety old cuss he was and then I'd remember the control tower on Midway that I walked out to see one day. That thing had more holes than a ping-pong net. It got the hell shot out of it in World War II. Ford was in that tower during the Battle of Midway. When his camera operator was killed he picked up a sixteen-millimeter hand-held camera with a long lens and kept rolling until his film ran out, bullets be damned. He was a hell of a man, Ford was."

Back in Hollywood, bad luck hit *Mister Roberts.* Jack walked onto the set one morning and the place was in turmoil. During the night, John Ford had been rushed to the hospital for gall bladder surgery. Another producer/director, Mervyn LeRoy, had been contacted and had agreed to finish the film for the ailing Ford.

"The studio screened everything for him that had been shot," said Jack, "and we got underway again. Mervyn made no attempt at all to insert his own ideas; he tried his best to set up the shots the way he thought Ford would have done. I give him ten points for that. I doubt that very many people were able to tell which director staged a particular scene. LeRoy later told Ford he didn't want any credit, but Pappy insisted that they share screen billing for direction—and they did."

Many of the long shots of the exuberant Pulver walk carried the sound of the ensign singing the old ditty "If I Could Be with You." The hot-cha Lemmon vocal was an afterthought by someone at the studio, who was alert enough to recognize that those scenes needed a little "business" to help carry them. Jack came in to the studio and dubbed the song, which was later added to the soundtrack. The touch worked so well that the old tune enjoyed a brief revival following the picture's release.

Certain scenes filmed in the island were reshot in Hollywood on the studio lot. Among them was the one where Frank Pulver reads to the crew a letter he has received from Mister Roberts. The original shot had been marred by wind noise.

When John Ford was released from the hospital to recuperate at home, Jack made an appointment to visit him. When he entered the bedroom, Ford's first words were: "I understand they reshot the letter-reading scene—that you weren't happy with it."

"Who told you that?" asked the surprised Lemmon.

"An editor. He said you were upset with it."

Jack explained that he'd been asked whether he would *mind* a retake of that scene and he'd replied that he'd be glad to do whatever was needed. "Oh—okay," said Ford.

"The idea," Jack said, grinning, "that any punk actor would dare to second-guess John Ford was sacrilege. Geez, he was a tiger."

When production concluded on *Mister Roberts* at Warner Brothers, Jack returned to the Columbia lot where he learned he was scheduled to co-star with June Allyson in a remake of the old Frank Capra comedy, *It Happened One Night.* The new version would be called *You Can't Run Away From It*, a title that had the hard ring of truth for Jack and Cinnie who, in the months after *Mister Roberts*, decided to stop running.

Chapter

XIV

"He has a lot of joy."
—*Robert Mitchum*

Mister Roberts was generating Oscar table talk in 1955 while it was still being preened for release. The smart-money was on Jack Lemmon for best supporting actor. It looked that way to publicist Arthur Jacobs, too, who snapped up Lemmon as a client and placed the new account in the hands of an associate, Richard Carter.

In meeting Carter, Jack got another of those fortuitous breaks. The two were much alike in several important ways. Carter was bright, talented, compassionate, and, like his celebrity charge, impeccably honest. It is one of those historical misfortunes that Diogenes didn't run across the pair. He could have pawned his lamp and stopped sleeping in a tub. The Carter-Lemmon relationship was to be one of Hollywood's longest and most fruitful.

With the exception of his marriage, which was failing in the second act, life was improving for Jack. Millie, now in improved condition, had moved to Brentwood, where she had her own apartment on San Vicente Boulevard. Autonomous as ever, she stubbornly fended off the encroaching years, insisted on living alone, and flatly refused to give Jack a key to her apartment.

When he came to visit he could, by God, knock at the door the same as anyone else.

"She was a ripper," said Jack. "Couldn't do a thing with her. Her arteries were beginning to go but she paid no attention to the doctor's orders not to eat salt. 'Screw him! What does he know?' That's what she said and she poured a ton of salt on everything she ate."

In the 1950s Hollywood was beginning to siphon growing numbers of creative and technical talent from New York as more and more television shows began to be produced on the West Coast. Andy McCullough pulled up stakes and headed West. Freddie Jordan, who had been working with the J. Walter Thompson Agency in New York, took a part-time assignment in Southern California. He stayed. Both Andy and Freddie picked up their friendship with Jack where it had left off a couple of years earlier.

Mister Roberts was released in July 1955 and was nominated for three Academy Awards: for best picture, best sound and, as expected, best supporting actor—Jack Lemmon. Some within the film industry were disappointed, feeling the film version fell considerably short of the stage production. The public loved it.

Richard Quine, who attended a preview of *Roberts* at a Los Angeles theater, was "distressed" by the picture but added: "Those were my embryonic days and I was critical of everything. I wasn't as exuberant about Jack's performance as I should have been. He was phenomenal, but then I just naturally assumed he would be great."

The brilliant Fonda, a *Mister Roberts* purist, called the play the finest he had ever read. The picture, he contends, "was not the picture it should have been; it wasn't fifty percent as good as it should have been. But still it was so good that you can't tell people who saw it *twelve times* that you wish they could have seen it the way it should have been done."

James Cagney confessed that he has never seen the film, has in fact viewed no more than twenty percent of the pictures he has made. "I lose all curiosity about them once I've finished the job. While I'm at it I'm doing it to the fullest, but after that's over I forget it."

It was a keyed-up Lemmon who watched the approach of the day when the Motion Picture Academy would make its awards presentation. "I knew I had a good chance," said Jack. "I thought it would be between me and Arthur O'Connell, who was a nominee for his fine work in *Picnic*, but there was some other stiff competition. Arthur Kennedy was up there for his role in *Trial*, Sal Mineo for *Rebel Without a Cause*, and Joe Mantel for *Marty*."

Oscar day dawned bright and sunny. Nick Adams, who'd appeared as one of the *Reluctant*'s crewmen in *Roberts*, made it even brighter when he dropped by the Lemmons' house to wish Jack good luck and to drop off Ensign Pulver's hat, which he'd lifted from the wardrobe department at Warner Brothers.

Cynthia had spent the day finding "the prettiest princesslike dress you ever saw" for the ceremony. She was attired and waiting when Jack came home late in the afternoon, "a nervous wreck."

Lemmon was nearly dressed in his tuxedo when he was stalled out by a shortage of apparel. "Cinnie!" he yelled, "Where's my shirt?"

"What do you mean, where's your shirt?"

"What I mean," said Jack, in a tone of rising panic, "is I don't have a shirt!"

"Oh, my God!" she gasped, "I must have sent it to the laundry!" A frantic telephone survey of dry cleaners failed to turn it up. By this time, the clothing shops were closed and it was beginning to look like Jack might accept the Oscar in tails and T-shirt. At the last moment Cynthia remembered. "Our cleaning lady has it! She took it home to launder it." Jack bolted for the door and raced across town to arrive just as the shirt was finished being ironed.

They made their appearance at the glittering affair exactly on schedule. "By this time," Cynthia said, laughing, "Jack was a mess—drenched in perspiration." As they navigated through the surging mass of fans and cameras to a small raised platform from which they would be introduced, Jack realized with a sinking feeling that even with a shirt he might not get to attend the affair. "I'd forgotten the tickets! Left the damn things at home in all that panic over the shirt. Luckily, when we did get to the door they had a list of the nominees and who was sitting where, so we got in.

"Now as we got to this platform outside where we were supposed to say a few words and have our picture taken, I made another mistake. I leaned on the rail, trying to appear casual, and then discovered they had painted it at the last minute so it would look good for the cameras. I got red paint all over the right side of my monkey suit and on my right hand. Cinnie was wearing white gloves and she got messed up, too. Of course there were signs all the way up to the ramp warning that the rails were freshly painted, but I didn't see 'em. I was so charged up I didn't see anything."

During the presentations, Jack seemed in shock. "He was a bundle of nerves," said Cynthia. "We were sitting right across from Arthur O'Connell and he and Jack kept staring at each other. It was the first time I had ever seen Jack speechless. He couldn't even lean over and say a 'funny,' which he usually could, to me. He didn't utter one word during the entire program.

"Finally, they were ready to give the supporting-actor award. Eva Marie Saint came on stage, opened the envelope, and said, 'The winner is—Jack Lemmon—for *Mister Roberts!*' "

After the ceremony, Jack and Cynthia attended a party at Romanoff's. "It was the wrong party," said Jack, "because most of the winners showed up at a swinging affair over at the Beverly Hills Hotel. I think I was the only one at Romanoff's who'd come away with an Oscar, so there were a lot of long faces. But I was having a ball, and we spent the evening at a table with Lee J. Cobb, a lovely man whom I'd admired for a long time.

"Afterward, about three in the morning, we went home, and the telephone started ringing. Relatives and friends were calling from Boston, and the papers were looking for interviews to make the early editions. I don't think I ever did get to bed that night. I had diarrhea of the mouth and I was loving every minute of it."

One afternoon, a few weeks after the awards, Cynthia quietly visited a friend of Jack's who was an attorney, and filed for divorce. "Jack and I had discussed it many times but hadn't done anything about it," she said. "We were both reluctant to make the move.

"The attorney drew up a little paper. There was never any unpleasantness over the division of property or anything; neither of us cared about that. If you can have such a thing, I guess you could say we had a very successful divorce. I packed up little Chris and went off to Las Vegas where I could get the divorce on grounds of incompatibility, because that's what it really was and I didn't want to call it anything else."

Lemmon met with Harry Cohn and explained that he and Cynthia were splitting. "Okay," said Cohn, "don't let it worry you. We'll take care of it; you won't end up the heavy." At that point several studio executives entered for a meeting and Jack left. On the way to his car he stopped. What had Cohn meant? Was he going to pull something like the stunt that used to be common in the old Hollywood, where the studio handled such situations by leaking stories that threw blame on the star's spouse? He turned around and went back, interrupting Cohn's meeting. The others stepped out for a moment and Jack said, "I don't know what you have in mind about my divorce, but I don't want anything said or written that might imply that Cynthia was at fault. She wasn't; nobody was, it was just one of those things." Cohn agreed.

A few days later Louella Parsons got wind of the breakup and printed a tongue-clucking story about young actors who, at the first blush of fame and success, waste no time in jettisoning their wives. Lemmon was angered and dismayed. He'd just gotten his first look at the price tag on eminence.

Fire Down Below, an action adventure yarn for Columbia, was Jack's next picture. He looked forward to it. He would be working with two great stars, Robert Mitchum and Rita Hayworth, and he would be out of the country for several months on location in Trinidad and England. Maybe he could forget, shake the first reactions to a failed marriage.

From the moment the airliner door was flung open in Trinidad, *Fire Down Below* was lively fun. A huge crowd of fans, dignitaries, and reporters greeted the plane. Someone promptly asked the devil-may-care Mitchum what he was carrying in his flight bag. Figuring the inane query deserved a like response, Mitchum announced that he had "two kilos of marijuana" in the bag. He then added that in his veins he was carrying "a quart of Jewish blood" that he'd taken by transfusion, "so I can stay even with those guys."

On the ride into town Mitchum was in a car with an official's wife who, he said, advised him, "You will enjoy very much Trinidad. On Trinidad there is not one virgin past the age of thirteen, and after carnival there are no virgins at all on the island." Mitchum says he "perked up at that!"

By the time the cast and crew had settled in their hotel rooms Mitchum's airport comments had bounced all the way to Washington and back. "He damned near caused a riot," said Jack. "We were practically barricaded in our rooms for three days. The State Department got into the act and there was talk of throwing us off the island. Old Mitch couldn't understand what all the fuss was about. He said, 'Don't these people have a sense of humor?' "

To occupy his time Jack employed the diversions men have favored throughout history—booze and broads. His first ladyfriend came by way of Mitchum, who had run across a comely girl in a red silk dress perched upon a pile of lumber on the dock. She agreed to meet him in her convertible at the hotel back door that very evening. At the appointed hour, Mitchum was in the hotel bar with Jack, who was himself in search of companionship.

"Go right out that door there," said Mitchum. "There's a girl in a red dress in a convertible. Tell her I can't make it." From that moment, according to Mitchum, Jack took the girl everywhere with him. An islander, who noticed this, approached Mitchum one afternoon. Pointing to the girl he said: "You know how she's called? They call her *dogola.*"

"Oh, really? What's it mean?"

"Like it sound. Dogola—dog! How you think she come by the car and all the silk dresses?"

That evening Mitchum put on a solemn face and cornered Jack. "You can't be squiring this girl around town, for crissakes, and be taking her to the governor's mansion!"

"Why not?" retorted Jack. "That's the most ridiculous thing I ever heard! Why not?"

"Because," said Mitchum, "everyone *knows* her—she screwed the entire U. S. Navy!"

"That's only thirty-two guys," Jack shot back.

Mitchum shook his head knowingly. "No, Jack, I mean when the facility was in full operation here. They had ten thousand of them then!"

Lemmon pondered the new equation for a moment, then said: "The hell with it. That's their problem. She's my girl, now."

Having survived the arrival flap, *Fire Down Below* director Robert Parrish was now plagued by incessant rains, which stretched on for weeks. For the actors and crew there was little to do. The company had now moved to the island of Tobago, northeast of Trinidad. "There were days," said Jack, "when we spent our time betting with each other over who could spot the biggest lizard."

It was during this period that Mitchum vanished for three days. Nobody had seen him, so Lemmon was elected to find out where he was holed up. "I figured he'd be in his room," said Jack, "although nobody had been seen entering or leaving. I pounded on the door and after a half hour I heard his voice. 'Who is it?' he asked. I told him it was 'little Jackie Lemmon, movie star.' He was suspicious. He said, 'Say some more words.' I did and he opened the door a crack and motioned me inside.

"It was all dark, and in the center of the room was the damndest contraption you ever saw. It had copper tubes and a pot with a little flame under it with fluid dripping into it. It was a still of some kind. With him in the room was his stand-in and two young native kids, a boy and a girl who looked about fifteen years old. They were sitting in chairs, solemn as judges. What was happening, I found out, was that Mitchum and a buddy had heard about this stuff that could be found in the jungle—something that had the properties of an aphrodisiac. They were distilling it and giving it to these natives as an experiment! Which figures, because Mitchum always was inquisitive."

According to Mitchum, it was his friend who'd run across the story of a special bark which could be synthesized into a splendid sex stimulant. "They called this bark *bois bundy*," said Mitchum. "I don't know the exact translation, but whatever it is I think it means *hard*—hardwood. So my friend went out and bought a whole bunch of this crap. I told him I'd heard all sorts of stories about *bois bundy* and we ought to be careful. We were boiling it down; we didn't really know what the hell to do with it. Nothing ever happened. It was just a sackful of bark—and he'd paid about thirty dollars for it."

According to Mitchum, there were thirty thousand people on Tobago, including one Chinese family and eighty-seven white. Out of the eighty-seven, he recalls, there were two girls. "I was invited out on a picnic by a family my wife had met when she was down there. The picnic was held at Golden Grove Lagoon, where Princess Margaret later spent her honeymoon, and I met this pretty girl. She had a sister, just divorced, who'd been in a nursing home in Trinidad. She said her sister's problem was mostly emotional, and the 'most manifest symptom is nymphomania.' I thought to myself, 'That would be for Jack.'

"She was really a pretty girl," said Mitchum, "and she and Jack hit it off. He'd come to work all red-eyed and he couldn't see! Meanwhile, we had a cameraman who would put every possible light and reflector he could find on us. He had a hat with a big brim and he'd put the light meter under there and say in that clipped British accent: 'Pitch black. Cawn't see a thing!' Then he'd add more lights. Jack was suffering, but he was toughin' it out. Nothing fazed him. He was happy as a clam."

Back in California, Cynthia had begun to date actor Cliff Robertson, an old friend from the days in New York. Robertson had been a part-time singing waiter with Jack at The Old Knick and had taken acting classes with Jack and Cynthia. "There *was* a spark between Cliff and me," said Cynthia. It was a spark that would later lead to their marriage.

In Tobago the rains persisted, throwing the production of *Fire Down Below* weeks off schedule. Jack's new girlfriend had left the island and he would often fill his time walking on the beach, continuing the lizard census, and chatting with members of the cast and crew. It was here, one rainy day, that Mitchum confided: "Did I ever tell you about my friend who humps sharks?"

Jack shook his head, speechless. With appropriate gravity, Mitchum then related the story of how this friend had been walking with him on a beach once when they spotted a shark lying on the sand. On a dare from Robert, he performed the act.

"I told that story to Faith Domergue once," sighed Mitchum, "and she was appalled. Said she didn't see how he could do it with that old dead thing. I told her my friend is a sport, not a necrophile; that shark was throbbingly alive! There were other stories going around that it was a male shark," he added gravely, "but I don't think it really makes that much difference in a shark. Anyway, it wasn't a serious affair. I mean, he didn't kiss it or anything."

Months later in Hollywood, while making another film, the payoff came on the shark yarn. A man approached Jack on the set and introduced himself as Mitchum's "friend." He asked, "Could I see you alone for a moment?"

"Sure," said Jack, "come on down to the dressing room." There the man looked at Lemmon questioningly for a moment, then asked: "Did Mitchum tell you I hump sharks?"

Flustered, Jack mumbled, "Yeah, but I didn't pay any attention or take him seriously. It was just a gag."

"It *is* serious," he said. "He tells that story to everyone he meets and I have to go around behind him, explaining it."

"Don't worry about it," said the embarrassed Jack. "Forget it."

Having set his man up, Mitchum's accomplice delivered the kicker: "I can't forget it!" he shouted. "How would you like it if someone was going around telling that story about you? I tell you, it's not fair. You hump *one* little shark and from then on—!" Jack insists that he has not fully recovered to this day.

According to Mitchum, not long before the *Fire Down Below* crew finished shooting in Tobago, Jack turned up with a new girl. "The hotel would sponsor a barbecue down on the beach once a week and they'd have music and dancing. Most of the others would go to it, because there wasn't much else to do. I didn't hang around much with those people because they always want to talk about the script or the picture, you know, and the minute I clock out—screw that. I don't want any more of it.

"Anyway, Jack saw this girl dancing by herself in the moonlight, and that really got him. She was a tiny thing—Christ, she was so small she could burrow up through the drains. I didn't think the poor guy was going to make it, but he did."

Returning to the subject of *Fire Down Below*, Mitchum said:

"It really was an enjoyable picture, and Jack was so good, he touched you. When he is given the freedom to develop a character his own way, as he did in *The Apartment* with Shirley MacLaine, he's at his best. When he does anything that demonstrates his own sensitivity he is very convincing, very moving. He has a lot of joy."

The weather on Tobago brightened eventually and the final scenes were shot, after which the company packed up and headed for England. Since Jack was not keen on air travel, the long over-water flight was not something he was looking forward to.

"At the start of the picture, when we left New York," said Mitchum, "Lemmon and I were sitting together, along with my wife Dottie and our infant daughter Trina. Jack was nervous on takeoff, kind of clutching things. We had barely gotten out of New York when there was a big fart of black smoke out of one of the engines. Jack looked at me and asked, 'What was that? What does that mean?' I said, 'That means Boston. We'll probably make it to Boston.' "

The plane actually made it to Gander, Newfoundland, where it was grounded for twenty-seven hours while a new engine was shipped out from the Boeing factory in Seattle. Billeting was on a first-come, first-served basis, with women and children having priority. When everyone had been settled for the long night ahead, only one had been left without quarters—out in the cold, as it were—John Uhler Lemmon.

The operations officer explained that since there were no more beds, Lemmon would have to sit up all night in the terminal. "How about out in our plane?" asked Jack. "There are berths in the plane and I can sleep there."

"Absolutely not," said the officer. "They're working on the plane and nobody can go near it." Convinced that they were serious, Jack walked to the center of the terminal and began to undress. The shirt, shoes, and socks were off and he was unzipping his pants, when the officer rushed over.

"Good Lord, man! What are you doing?"

"I'm going to bed."

"You can't sleep here!" the officer gasped.

"It's this or the plane," said Jack, continuing to remove his pants. The officer relented and Jack was taken to the plane. "I went out like a light," he grinned. "Didn't hear a thing."

The next morning Mitchum entered the terminal to find Lemmon "bright-eyed, fully dressed, and in his right mind. He'd had that whole plane to himself, including the liquor cabinet. I spent the night being kept awake by a fleet of Canberra jets being ferried out to Australia. Resourceful guy, Lemmon."

Arriving in London, Jack checked in at 22 Grosvenor Square along with Mitchum, who had a flat across the hall. Lemmon promptly went out and bought a sunlamp. "He'd been in the islands for weeks," commented Mitchum, "but I don't think he ever went out in the sun. Every time the director said, 'Cut,' Jack would roll up in a ball and disappear. He was very pale; looked like a worm."

After glancing at the instructions, Jack hooked up the lamp and tried it out. Afterward, he showered, shaved, and went out to a birthday party being thrown for columnist Louella Parsons, also in England at that time. Halfway through the affair Jack's eyes began to burn and his face felt raw and swollen. Soon the tears began to pour and he could barely see. Excusing himself, he rose to leave. As he stumbled out he heard Louella say: "Isn't that the sweetest thing? It's my birthday and that dear boy is crying."

By the time he reached his flat, Jack's eyes were nearly swollen shut. A doctor was summoned and Lemmon was put to bed at once, a victim of severe burns. "I'd set that damn lamp wrong—at three inches for thirty minutes instead of three minutes at thirty inches or some dumb thing. I was out of commission for days."

A sympathetic Mitchum was quick to pay a visit to his fallen colleague. "He was a mess," said Mitchum. "His eyes looked like a tennis ball cut in half." Thinking to cheer him up, Mitchum returned to his suite and fashioned a bouquet, a wondrous work featuring varicolored condoms artfully interspersed with stink weeds. It was delivered later the same day.

A week later Lemmon arose, skin still peeling in spots, and set out to attend a cocktail party at the residence of a friend, Sharman Douglas, daughter of the former American ambassador to England. Jack went forth in his convalescent state because Princess

Margaret was scheduled to attend and he looked forward to meeting her.

He had just entered the Douglas brownstone when someone said to him, "Have you met Margaret?"

"Margaret who?" said Jack, as he turned. Directly behind him was Princess Margaret, who seemed to find his words amusing. They did not appear as amusing the next day when they appeared in the London papers.

"We'd been chatting away for about ten minutes and I was having a fine time," said Jack. "I noticed that people were leaving, drifting into the next room. I didn't notice, but Sharman had been trying to catch my eye to let me know that, according to protocol, I was supposed to leave. Finally, Princess Margaret said, very politely, 'Are you staying for dinner?' I said, 'I don't know—am I?'

"I turned and there was Sharman across the room, just shaking her head, so I said, 'No, I'm not!' When the princess went on in for dinner Sharman explained that it was a sit-down affair with a precise number of chairs. She suggested I go out for a bite and then return later."

Jack hiked over to the Les Ambassadeurs, a nearby club, and instead of eating, downed a few drinks and chatted with friends about how he had just met Princess Margaret. An hour and a half later, he returned to find the dinner finished and a handful of guests sitting around chatting.

"It was very informal," he said. "We were lounging around on the floor and some couches. I remember one incident that was interesting.

"Now Princess Margaret had shown herself to have a sense of humor; she was very bright, but she adhered to protocol under most circumstances. There are certain things that you just don't do in front of royalty, and that's that.

"There was one fellow there who got a little too relaxed. He was lying back on his elbow, and he started a sentence with, 'I remember when your sister—' Without missing a beat, Princess Margaret said quietly, 'I presume you mean the Queen?' Well, this guy left about sixty seconds later! You do not refer to the Queen as 'your sister.' As an English subject he should have known better."

Gradually the other guests departed, leaving only Princess Margaret, Jack, Sharman, and a young minister. Sharman suggested that instead of using the royal limousine, they grab a taxi to Les Ambassadeurs, where they could continue the party.

"We slipped out, piled into a cab, and went over there," said Jack, "arriving unannounced. Well, they went into a total flap! The place was packed upstairs but they got a table ready in a hurry. The joint went crazy, with men bowing and women curtsying. The orchestra immediately dug out the sedate music. We sat down and I ordered a couple of bottles of Scotch, which everybody else was drinking. I had a bottle of wine.

"We started talking and I was telling the princess all about everything—acting, music, everything—and waving my hands. Well, I hit one bottle of Scotch and over it went in her lap. The whole bottle, all over her dress! It was nothing new for me, and I always do it to the biggies. Only the biggies. Ask Mary Benny about her white rug. I did that with red wine, of course, otherwise it wouldn't have been any good. Anybody could do it with white wine.

"The princess was very gracious, of course, and told me not to be concerned. But an army of waiters was there instantly with enough napkins for an eighth-floor jail break. So what do I do? I said, 'Do you want to dance?' She said, 'Certainly!' We got up to dance and everybody moved ten feet away from us.

"So there we were and I danced fairly close, like I normally dance. I didn't think anything of it but it must have stunned the rest of the people because the next day the papers made a big thing of the princess dancing cheek-to-cheek with the American actor. Meantime, through all of this, Lemmon has not eaten—and Lemmon is having a ball, flyin' away!

"When we finally got ready to leave, the doorman was thunderstruck that the princess was going to ride in a cab, but he finally whistled up one for us. The cab driver simply could not believe it. The princess! In his cab! I took the jump seat with my back to the driver and Sharman and the princess were in the seat with the minister, and off we went for the palace.

"Now I was obviously a little tiddly with the grape and I began to lecture her, you know, about who she was and how she had to be extra careful about how she behaved because she was in a different position than the rest of us. Can you believe that? Schmuck Lemmon is telling *her*. Well, the whole thing struck her funny. She got hysterical and so did Sharman, and the tears were running down their cheeks. Old Lemmon just kept right on going. I thought 'Boy, am I making a hit!'

"Every once in a while I would hear the cabbie talking to himself, saying, 'Me old lydy ain't never goin' to believe this. The bloomin' princess in *my* cab.' That cabbie was driving slow because he was savoring this thing, but we finally got to the palace.

"All of a sudden the cab stopped and here came the guys with the big fuzzy hats and the guns. Before the princess could do anything, I rolled the window down, leaned out, and said, 'Would you open up, please, I've got the princess here.' Now you know what those guys are thinking! The princess? At two-thirty in the morning? In a *cab?* Not a chance! They lowered the guns and advanced. One of them said, 'Look 'ere—watcha think yer doin'?' They meant business; thought we were going to crash the gate or something.

"At that moment, pushing out *above* me was Princess Margaret saying, 'It's me! It's me!' Well the guards cannot believe it. They are outside holding a caucus and the princess is yelling at them to please let us in and laughing at the same time.

"They finally opened the gates and we pulled through. When we tumbled out of the cab, suddenly, for a brief moment, all the levity stopped. The princess stood very erect, offered her hand, and said, 'Thank you very much. I do hope we see each other again.' I bowed and said, 'Thank you for a lovely evening'—and we left, Sharman, the minister, and I. It was the last time I ever saw the princess."

Chapter XV

"I think you're just chicken . . ."
—Glenn Ford

TIME, DISTANCE, ALCOHOL, WOMEN—all the established male recourses for snuffing out the past—had proven enjoyable and successful for Lemmon. Nevertheless, returning from London after completing *Fire Down Below*, he had tentative thoughts about his marriage. Possibly, he and Cynthia should "give it one more try," not only to make sure their decision was right, but because of Chris, whom Jack had missed terribly. They were thoughts that ignored the fact that those left behind do not remain in fixed suspension, like bugs in brine.

A telephone call found Cynthia friendly but realistic. She had begun pulling together the strands of a new life, one that included Cliff Robertson. Jack was left to contemplate Byron's tart caveat to the voyager: "Wives in their husbands' absences grow subtler, and daughters sometimes run off with the butler."

A couple of days later Lemmon got another lesson in relativity when he was joined by Freddie Jordan to take little Chris for his first haircut. The months Jack had been away translated to a major part of the boy's lifetime.

"There was the ususal fuss," said Jordan. "It was the first time Chris had seen a barber's chair and he was hollering and screaming and running—but *not to Jack.* He was coming to *me,* because I'd been around and Jack hadn't. Well, Jesus. I felt so sorry for Jack; I knew the sadness in him. It was like everything had gone out of his life; even his child was deflected somewhere else. Yet it was typically sensitive of Jack that he picked up on the situation instantly. Before I could offer a word he said, 'I understand.' Some might have seen something more in what had happened, but not Jack. He's like those little monkeys: see no evil, hear no evil, speak no evil. Yet he is not naive, and I'll be damned if I can figure that one out!"

The failure of the marriage had a demoralizing effect on those around the couple. Millie, who adored Cynthia, was heartbroken, as were Cynthia's parents, who had grown very fond of Jack.

As for Lemmon, he put up another "wall," took a deep breath, and plunged into a new picture for Columbia, this one a zany war story about soldiers attempting to throw a party. *Operation Mad Ball,* directed by Richard Quine, remains one of Jack's favorite films—perhaps because he had great fun making it, fun that he desperately needed at the time. Critics didn't find it so hilarious. In Leonard Maltin's movie guide it received a modest two-star rating as a "weak service comedy" with dull stretches and not many gags.

Mickey Rooney and Ernie Kovacs worked with Lemmon in *Operation Mad Ball* and that made the production something special for Jack, who ranks both men among the great talents. Quine tells of one scene with Rooney that required thirty takes because Lemmon kept breaking up in helpless laughter. "Mickey never did the scene twice the same way," said Quine, "and every time he'd add a new touch, Jack would just fall over backwards. It was the only time I ever saw Lemmon unable to handle an acting chore. He only had one line and I don't think he ever got it out."

Quine believes that on the screen Lemmon relates to men better than women. "If you look back over his most successful roles you can see it: *The Fortune Cookie, Mister Roberts, Some Like It Hot, The Odd Couple.* It's tough to make him believable in a love scene. You put him with a femme fatale and for some reason she will seem to overpower him; maybe because of the boyish quality he has.*

"On the other hand, put him with guys, and brother! it's home and mother! Kovacs is a good example. If Ernie had lived, the Lemmon–Matthau team might well have been Lemmon–Kovacs. They reminded me of a sophisticated Laurel and Hardy."

* Says Lemmon: "Quine is full of crap. As screen lovers go, I'm a biggie."

In the months following his return to California, Jack began dating a succession of girls, none of whom he took any more seriously than his paramours in Tobago. Most evenings, with or without a date, he could be found at Dominic's restaurant, in company with Quine or musician-composer Freddie Karger.

It was Karger who kept touting Jack on a friend of his at the studio. She was, he insisted, an actress of surpassing beauty, a girl certain to lift his drooping spirits; her name was Felicia Farr and she was as smart as she was pretty. The sales pitch worked and Jack joined Karger one afternoon on the set where Felicia was working.

It was a fateful meeting, not unlike the encounters favored in musicals of the 1930s where the rising young star bumps into the ingenue. As Jack was soon to discover, mystical conditions were at work, and this time around, the "ammonium" was going to raise all kinds of hell with the "nitrate."

"They were shooting a test, a Western scene. Felicia was sitting on a prop trunk off to the side, waiting for a lighting change. I remember she was wearing an old-fashioned dress, an ankle-length gingham gown. She was just sitting there kind of wiggling her legs around. Well, I don't know what happened, but I took one look at her and—bow! That was it! Boy, oh, boy, I have never been hit like that.

"Now I was very reticent with her. Despite all those stories Mitchum tells, there's always been a reluctance about old Uhler where the ladies are concerned. I've always wanted to make very sure I was welcome in a territory before I made the big move."

Karger suggested that Felicia join them for dinner and, to the immense relief of the bewitched Lemmon, she accepted, agreeing to meet them after returning home for a change of clothes.

"Freddie and I went along to have a drink and wait," said Jack, "but Felicia never came. Finally Freddie called and found that she wasn't coming, after all. A girlfriend had a problem and she wanted to see her. I was really disappointed, and when Freddie called her the following week and got a date, I was absolutely crushed."

Providence, always riding shotgun for Lemmon, took a hand a couple of weeks later when Jack attended a party at the home of Quine. There, on the arm of Karger, was the fetching Felicia. When a group, which included Karger and Felicia, broke away from the party to catch a new show at the Coconut Grove, Jack tagged along—stag.

At the Grove Jack lost no time in steering Felicia to the dance floor. "She was so beautiful it was incredible, really incredible! When we danced, that did it. It was the end of me forever; a total wipeout."

According to Felicia, Jack's reticence was nowhere to be found that evening. "He was naughty! On the dance floor he got very feisty. Very! However, instead of being insulted or upset with him, I liked it. It shook me up that I enjoyed it and when I walked back to the table I remember my knees felt funny. I'd never had a reaction like that to anyone and it really felt strange. I thought 'My God—hmmmm!'

"Apparently, Jack was able to sniff out that reaction, because later in the car he was playing kneesies with me and then I really got a little upset with him because it wasn't too terrific a thing to do with a friend's date."

Jack was now hopelessly smitten. "From that moment," he recalls, "there was no way out for me. She was mine! Even today, if any other guy started coming around I'd get 'im. I'd have him done in, as Mitchum would say, by indifferent marksmen!"

Bringing the clever Felicia to heel, however, was not to be that easy. Jack had been seeing another girl and made the tactical error of confiding to Felicia that he thought he should "break it off slowly because people might become suspicious." Responded Felicia: "Suspicious of what?"

Jack's statement had rallied Felicia's formidable feminine instincts. "When he said that, I thought to myself, 'Oh, no, you don't. No, no, no!' He had given me a clear way and I started seeing just everybody—and drove him crazy. I had dates going at all hours. In the middle of the evening I would suddenly say, 'Sorry, I have to leave you now. I have a late date.' And even though he'd been forewarned, it drove him absolutely nuts!

"I was having such fun. For a long time nobody was getting hurt, then one of the fellows started getting serious and it became very sticky. But for a while there it was—the most fun I'd had in any social relationship. For the first time I knew what men felt while playing that game."

As though corraling the frisky Felicia were not perturbation enough for Jack, Harry Cohn was bent on putting his Harvard man astride a horse. With memories of the cussed Pepper yet fresh and painful, Lemmon was balking. There was no way, Jack contended, that the movie-going public would buy him in a cowboy suit. Furthermore, he argued, a horse was a spectacularly ob-

The source of Jack's mobile features is apparent in this shot which caught him and his mother Millie during the filming of *The Great Race.*

The nefarious Professor Fate (Lemmon) plots more dirty deeds with sidekick Peter Falk in *The Great Race.*

The Lemmon children: son Chris proudly holds his new half sister Courtney, 1966.

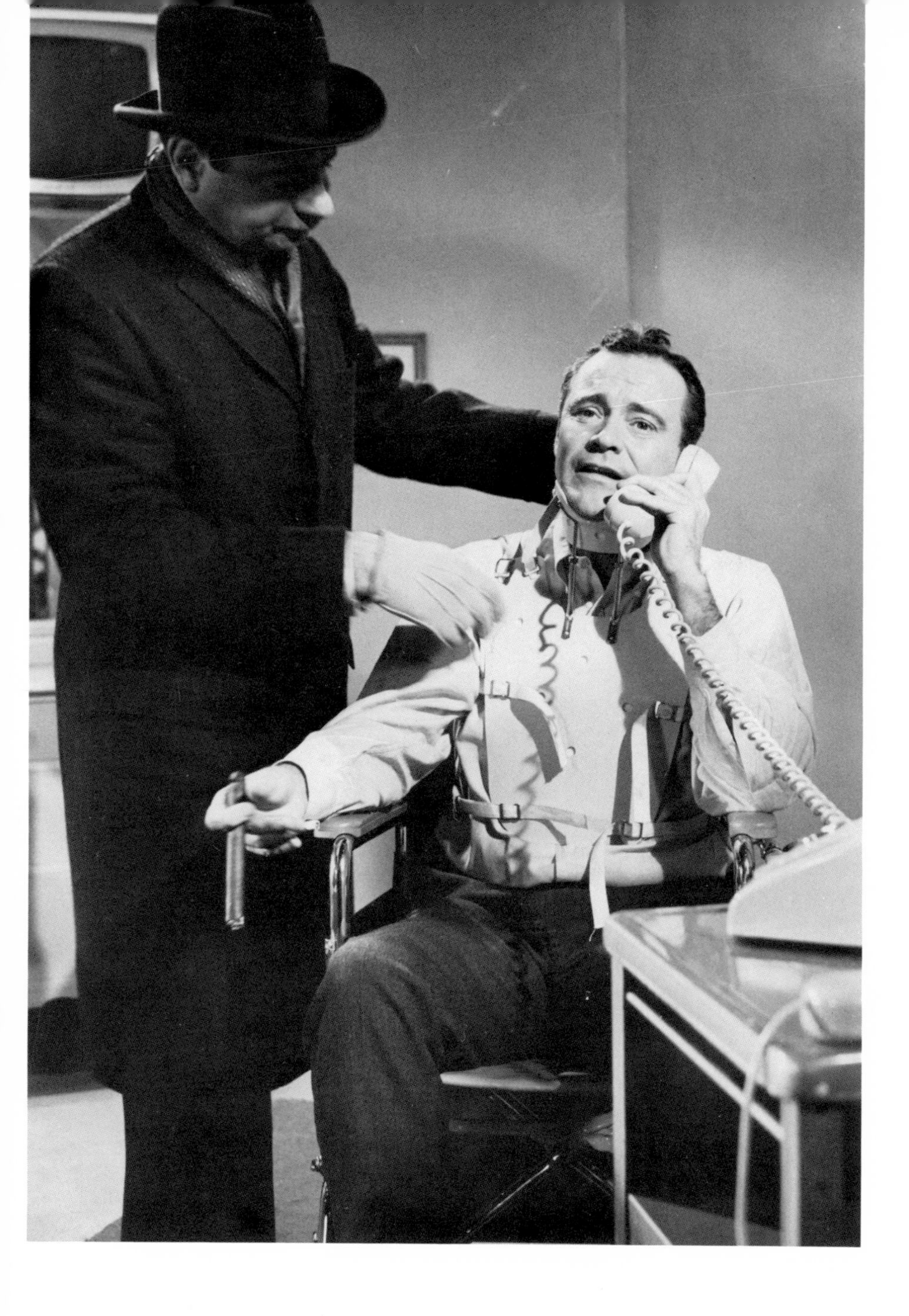

In *The Fortune Cookie*, shyster lawyer (Walter Matthau) instructs client Lemmon in the fine art of fleecing an insurance company by faking injury.

Elaine May and Lemmon in *Luv*. (CULVER PICTURES)

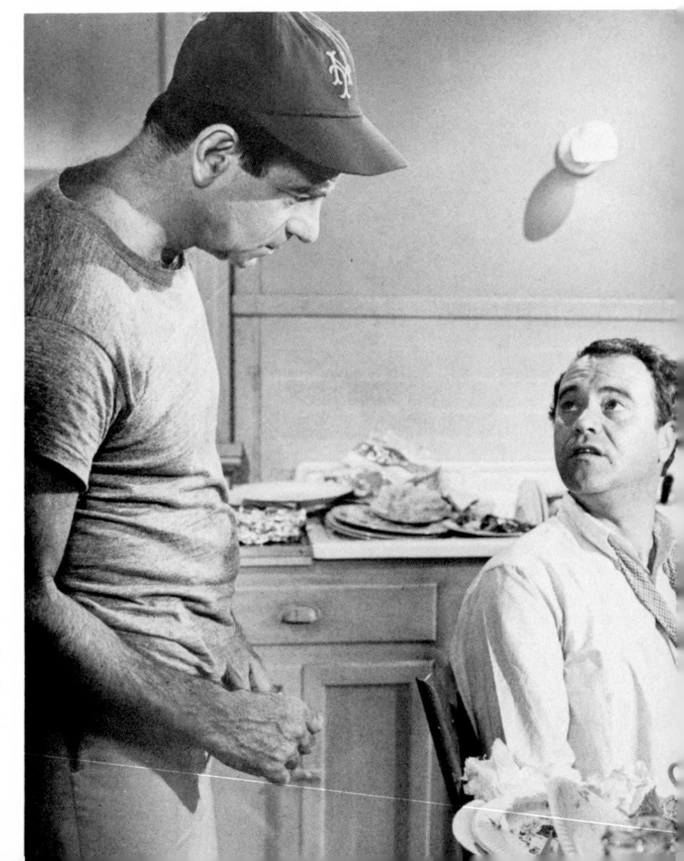

Walter Matthau as Oscar and Lemmon as Felix in Neil Simon's hit, *The Odd Couple*.

All the evils that can befall a visitor to New York were jammed into *The Out-of-Towners*, which paired Jack with Sandy Dennis.
(CULVER PICTURES)

On location during the filming of the Emmy-winning documentary on ecology with producer-writer Don Widener.
(LEIGH WIENER)

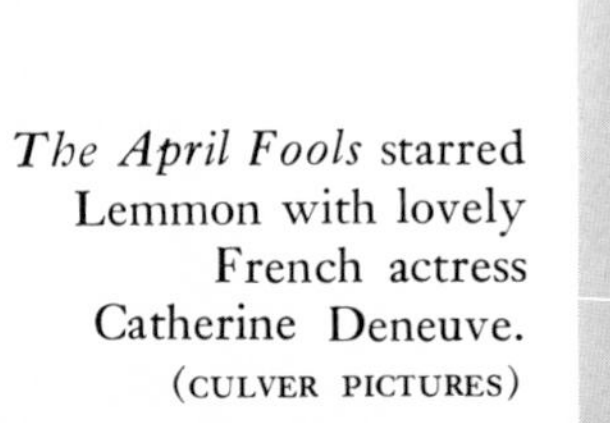

The April Fools starred Lemmon with lovely French actress Catherine Deneuve.
(CULVER PICTURES)

Lemmon in a tense scene from *Save the Tiger*, the picture that won him an Oscar as Best Actor. On the phone in the background is Jack Gilford; lying in the foreground is Norman Burton.

Jack in another scene from
Save the Tiger.

On stage at the Ahmanson Theater in Los Angeles in Robert E. Sherwood's 1936 play, *Idiot's Delight.* Jack's performance as Harry Van got rave notices.
(PAT DARRIN)

Portrait of a star—Jack Lemmon, 1972.

Producer Richard Carter with Walter Matthau, star of *Kotch*.

Lemmon and Fred Astaire teamed up for a 1972 Gershwin television special that won an Emmy.

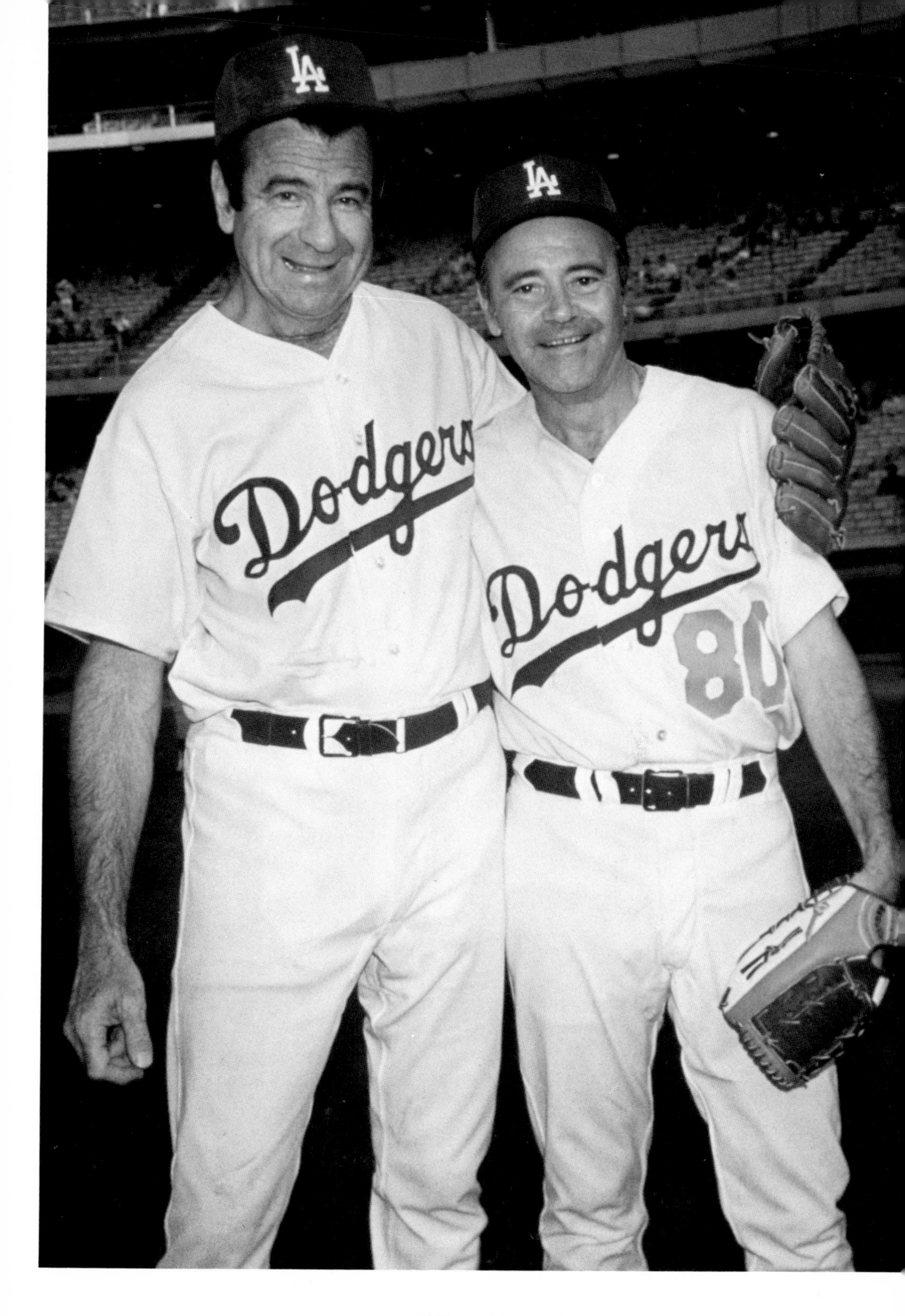

"The odd couple" suited up for an annual charity ball game in 1974.

Jack and Felicia at home.
(RODDY MCDOWALL/LEE GROSS INC.)

Jack Lemmon and his favorite actress, Anne Bancroft, in an artistic shot taken of them during the filming of *Prisoner of Second Avenue*, in which they co-starred.

"Captain" Jack Boyle (Walter Matthau) and Joxer Daly (Lemmon) in Sean O'Casey's *Juno and the Paycock*. The pair co-starred with Maureen Stapleton in the 1974 revival of the play at the Mark Taper Forum in Los Angeles.

At fifty and at the top, Jack celebrates his birthday at a party in New York with former co-stars (*left to right*) Shirley MacLaine, Susan Sarandon, and Sandy Dennis.

tuse animal and the dangerous necessity of climbing on one had ended promptly with the invention of the internal combustion engine.

The crafty Cohn shrugged. A secondary plot was already operational—a scheme which would get Lemmon aboard a cayuse, and of his own volition. Cohn had already entered into collusion with actor Glenn Ford, who also believed Jack would be perfect as Frank Harris in *Cowboy*, the film version of Harris' memoirs—the reminiscences of a tenderfoot on a big cattle drive. Ford was already set for the role of Harris' boss, the tough Tom Reese.

"I believed," said Ford, "that Jack was the one guy who should play Harris. I had great respect for him, as did everybody else in this town, so I made a deal with Harry; he would assign the role to Lemmon if I could convince Jack to do it. I thought about it for quite a while. It wouldn't be easy, because Jack had already told me he didn't want to do it, and I knew he was a little leery of horses."

Early one afternoon, Ford hit on an idea, consulted with Cohn, and then invited Jack across the street to The Naples, a restaurant, for "a few drinks and to have a talk." The first round of drinks led to others. "We were having vodka," said Glenn, "and after the first couple I began to pour mine in a potted plant when Jack wasn't looking. He just kept putting them away, but I needed a clear head for what I had to do."

After an hour of steady drinking Ford could see that the vodka was beginning to do its work on Lemmon. "I got him on the subject of *Cowboy* and then said: 'What is it Jack? Is it that you don't have the guts to do the picture?' I could see that the question rankled him. Hell, you don't say something like that to Lemmon."

"Glenn," said Jack, "I don't even know how to get on a horse. I can't do it. Forget it."

After another couple of drinks, Ford was at it again. "I guess maybe you can't do it," he needled. "Fact is, I think you're afraid to do it. I think there's reasons you won't tell me about."

Well on his way to getting bombed, Jack was in no mood for Ford's thrust. "Whatta ya mean, I can't do it?" he asked, fixing Glenn with a boozy stare. "Dammit, I can! I can do anything that you can do!"

"Of course you can. That's the whole point!"

"What's the part about?"

"You've read it."

"I didn't read most of it. It's got horses in it—and cowboys—

and you're gonna shoot in Santa Fe. I don't wanna go to Santa Fe."

"Well," said Ford, "I think you're just chicken and that's the reason you don't want to do it."

Jack leaned across the table, squinting. "Whozat yer callin' chicken?"

Noticing that Lemmon was now getting madder and madder, Ford sank the harpoon. "Okay, you say you can do the part of Frank Harris. Will you go over right now and tell Harry you can do it?"

"Damn right! Where's Harry? Bring on Harry. You just get me there," said Jack, struggling to his feet, "and you'll see. . . . They ought to get another plant—that one's dying."

Holding the irate Lemmon's arm, Ford led him across Sunset Boulevard to the Columbia lot. "I don't know how we made it, but we did. I was afraid Jack might decide to leave because his car was in the lot. Cohn was located on the second floor of the administration building and I'll never forget the door to his offices. There was a big circle of paint missing, eaten away by the sweat of frightened palms belonging to the people who had to go in there. I once told Harry *that* ought to be Columbia's escutcheon.

"When we got inside, Harry was ready. He played his part perfectly. He looked at Jack, who was standing there kind of weaving, with that steely look in his eyes, and said, 'I understand the reason you don't want to do *Cowboy* is that you're scared.'

"Jack drew himself up and said, 'What the hell you talkin' about? I'll do that part! What is this? Why's Glenn here sayin' I can't do that part? I can do this Frank Harris. I can do—' and that's as far as he got. Harry said. 'You've got it!'

"I didn't stick around; I maneuvered Jack out of there, but as I left I glanced back and Harry was giving me the old 'okay' sign. I got Lemmon to his car. I don't know how the hell he ever made it home, but I know I was delighted. I'd done it. Jack Lemmon was Frank Harris and I knew he would be just great."

The initial eight weeks of production on *Cowboy* involved all the scenes with horses and cattle, and Jack arrived on location in New Mexico without so much as a canter through the park to prepare for the saddle. "The first thing they did," he remembers ruefully, "was fix me up with the fastest damn quarterhorse you ever saw. Sunday his name was, but he could run all week. The second you got on him he took off like a gazelle, and he had a way of stopping like he'd hit a tree. Every time he did that I went ass over teakettle."

Ford remembers the horse. "Jack got the worst of the lot. Once when Lemmon wasn't around I got on and tried to ride that animal—and the horse won. I don't see how Jack stayed on him.

"One day we were waiting to ride into a scene when that nag reared and threw Jack, who landed in the dirt. He really hit hard and I know it hurt him; I've been through that before. I sympathized with him, but I didn't get down or offer to help him. He looked up at me and I guess he saw a twinkle in my eyes, because he was muttering under his breath while he brushed himself off. He gave me a look that could kill, climbed back on that horse, and did the scene. He did it, brother, without a word of complaint. He was a real pro."

The veteran Ford saw in Jack's anger and frustration an opportunity to enhance *Cowboy*. "I knew Jack had to feel some antagonism toward me; after all, I'd gotten him into this thing. I wanted to go over to him and say, 'Aw, come on, Jack, we're friends,' because I really liked him. On the other hand, that antagonism was showing up on the screen and that's what the picture was all about—Harris' hate for this cruel Tom Reese. I decided to keep this thing going."

In various scenes Ford deliberately pushed beyond the requirements. "Once I threw a branding iron and hit him in the legs. Man, he threw it right back. Another time I held him down into a campfire, choking him, until his clothes were literally smoking! I don't want to use the word 'hatred' because I don't think Jack knows how to hate, but he was coming close. I wanted to let up but I didn't because I saw this guy giving one of his finest performances. I was fascinated watching him work; he was a real professional. The thing that struck me was that with all he was going through he never once—and I mean never once!—complained."

From the first day on location, Jack was leaving blood on the saddle. During most of the eight weeks in Santa Fe he was wearing a Kotex napkin, a fact soon uncovered by the rowdy cowhands hired to work in the picture. "Those wranglers," said Lemmon, "were the real thing; they were rough and tough. They rode hard, drank hard, and played hard. They didn't give a damn about Hollywood actors. They had a good-paying job and they were playing cards and getting stoned every night. It surprised me that they were really as ornery as the movies portrayed them. If they'd been carrying loaded six-guns, they'd have been shooting up the saloons.

"When those guys found out about the Kotex I was wearing because I had to be on that horse eight hours a day, they grabbed me and did just what they used to do in the old days. They slapped me down on my belly, pulled my pants down, spread my cheeks apart, and emptied a quart of rotgut whiskey on me. One of them said: 'Toughens it up, pardner!' "

A few nights later Jack nearly got into a brawl with one of the cowboys who got drunk and surly during a poker game and decided to beat up on him. A professional stunt man who was in charge of the riders intervened and Lemmon took the opportunity to vanish from the premises. "There was one hell of a fight, with bottles being thrown and chairs crashing. I don't know who won, but both guys were a mess the next day.

"It's a good thing I got out of there, because I wouldn't have had a chance. I have no confidence that I could beat up a butterfly! I think maybe I'm a coward at heart and that may be why I took up cross-country running at such an early age. I have an aversion to fighting, except in my fantasies. Then I move with the lithe grace of a jungle cat and I can knock the bejesus out of anybody, including Superman and Brooks Slocum, who used to live next door."

Lemmon's self-effacing talk of cowardice brings a laugh from those who know and work with him. Says Quine: "You have to literally hold him down. The silly bastard will try anything. He has the guts of a bandit." Ford remembers a scene during the making of *Cowboy* in which Jack had to enter a railroad boxcar full of steers. "That was truly dangerous."

The incident is branded in Jack's memory, as sharp as if it happened last week. That it should remain so ingrained after nearly twenty years is not surprising; the scene almost cost him his life.

The cattle car had been loaded with twenty longhorn steers, descendants of the rangy, mean-tempered cattle that roamed the brush-covered arroyos of Texas and Mexico in the nineteenth century—progeny of Coronado's Andalusian stock brought from Spain. The script called for Jack to enter the car, locate a downed steer, and wrestle him to his feet.

Representatives from the Society for the Prevention of Cruelty to Animals had administered shots to the animals, a sedative to keep them calm. One, the fallen steer, had been given a heavier dose; he was lying down, but conscious.

Director Delmer Daves had set his camera to shoot through the slatted siding of the enclosed car. Jack said, "I was supposed to go in, try to raise the animal, and then get pinned. Glenn would then arrive to rescue me. That's what was *supposed* to happen, but an error was made somewhere.

"Apparently, someone misjudged the sedation dosage and how the steers would react when they came out of it. It wore off sooner than expected and when they recovered, they reacted violently. Once I got in there under the downed steer, I couldn't get out, what with walls on four sides about ten feet high.

"Anyway, there I was, tugging away at that steer, when all of a sudden the other cattle started coming out of that sedative at the same time. They began really thrashing around and their horns—I don't need to tell you how long and sharp those are—were flashing by me like sabers. We hadn't done a thing to blunt them because it would have shown on the big screen.

"At that moment the steer I was holding started recovering from his shot. Instinctively, I jammed myself against him, with my head directly between the horns, as he brought his neck up. If I hadn't done that, he'd have ripped me to pieces. I hung on for dear life and as I looked around, wildly, I could see nothing but horns and hooves. Those steers went beserk; they were tossing their heads, and kicking like mad.

"Glenn was in there by this time, as much to try to save me as to appear in the scene. I could hear guys yelling and trying to figure out some way to get us out before it was too late, because at this point things were totally out of control; one slip and we're hamburger.

"I don't remember the end of it, how we got out of there, but it's funny what you *do* remember. I can recall the horror of the moment and one thing that was just hysterically funny. Del Daves, the director, not knowing what to do and helplessly watching everything about to go down the tubes, stood flat against the slats and screamed again and again at the *steers:* 'Cut! Cut! Cut!' "

Ford calls *Cowboy* one of his all-time favorite films, not an insignificant statement for a man who has made 167 of them, along with 38 television specials. Movie buffs and most critics agreed; the film is now considered among the handful of classic Westerns. Ford gives much of the credit to Lemmon. "He was so easy to work with, so completely professional. I can't tell you how much respect I have for that dear man. I hope that Jack has forgiven me for getting him into that picture and for needling him. I'll always treasure the memory of him looking up at me out of the dust and saying, 'For crissakes, stop looking at me that way, you big stoneface!' He always called me that—Stoneface."

Lemmon admits that he was absolutely miserable during the making of *Cowboy*, but insists that he never was mad at Glenn.

"Once in a while I'd say, 'You dirty so-and-so, why did you get me into this mess?' but I wasn't really mad. Drunk or sober, I never would have made that film unless I thought I could do it. I was worried because I felt I was not the right guy for the part. I'm glad that I did do it; *Cowboy* was a hell of an experience.

"As for Glenn, I have great respect for him as an actor and as a man. Over the years he developed an extraordinary film technique; a method of approaching his parts that is unique to Ford. He has a marvelous, distinctive way of delivering lines and he brings that to each role, yet he doesn't make them the same, as some actors do. Glenn manages to nail down the character. He's a fine, intelligent actor."

Glenn will be happy to hear those words. "I've always wondered," said Ford, grinning, "if maybe one of these days I might not ask Jack to have another drink, get him bombed, and put him on another horse alongside old Stoneface." *

* Says Lemmon: "When with Ford, don't sit near a plant."

Chapter

XVI

"He is a person first and an actor second."
—*Charles Baker*

THERE WAS an aristocratic streak in Millie Lemmon. She was a product of American gentry and, as such, inherited a trait that runs through the landed and titled. She could be common without *being* common. A stockyard expletive from Millie gained by association, taking on an unfamiliar elegance—like home brew poured from a Ravenscroft pitcher.

Within months after her arrival in Southern California she had taken the measure of Beverly Hills and found it an acceptable, if less civilized, extension of her Boston environs. Effortlessly she captivated her new circle of friends.

Richard Carter and his vivacious wife Ruth quickly became part of a Millie cult, delighting in her sometimes outrageous behavior and ever-ready one-liners. Ruth tells of an instance when Millie was shown a nightgown during a shopping spree. "What on earth would I do with that?" asked Millie. "I sleep in the nude!"

The saleslady was aghast. "But Mrs. Lemmon, what if there was a fire?"

Said Millie, carefully timing the punchline, "I wouldn't go!"

One afternoon when Millie was visiting Jack she stopped sipping her martini long enough to announce that she'd decided she might "marry again, and I'll tell you one thing—he's going to be damned young!"

"He's going to be young?" asked an awed Jack.

"You bet your ass, he is!" she snapped.

"Do you think you can handle a young man?"

Millie grinned wickedly. "Of course! It comes back to you, just like swimming."

Jack returned from his perilous adventures on *Cowboy* just in time to be on hand for another of his mother's traumatic moments. Jack was watching a show at the Mocambo while Millie was dining with an old family friend, Walter Kronke. A call came through to Jack, alerting him that his mother had just suffered a serious accident at the Bel Air Hotel.

Within ten minutes Lemmon arrived on the scene, where he found Millie. "There she was, just sitting on the curb," said Jack, "waiting for an ambulance. I could see that she had fallen. Her shoulder was dislocated, hanging down about three inches. It looked horrible—like there was no shoulder at all, as if it started around her breast or something. She looked up and grinned, and I saw that one tooth was missing. She still had a drink in her hand and I'll never forget her first words. She said: 'Look out for that first step; it's a bitch!' Even under those circumstances she couldn't resist it; she had to come up with a one-line nifty."

As an afterthought Millie decided to sue the Bel Air Hotel on the grounds that she had slipped and fallen because somebody had been watering the lawn. Jack's reasoned argument that it was unlikely the gardener was doing such a thing at eleven o'clock at night provided not the slightest deterrent to Millie, who had made up her mind. "Some son-of-a-bitch," she snapped, "must have been out there with a hose."

With a sigh, Jack contacted Bob Eaton, an old friend who was a lawyer. "The medical bills came to about eleven hundred dollars," recalls Lemmon, "and she was convinced she could make the hotel pay. Now I had to pick her up and drive her to the lawyer's office because she didn't drive—and thank God for that, because none of us would be around today. She was very nervous and also hard of hearing."

Attorneys for the Bel Air Hotel arranged a meeting to take Millie's deposition and Jack picked her up for the drive to Beverly Hills. "All the way there," he said, "I kept getting this stream-of-consciousness diatribe about how 'sure as hell they're going to say

I had something to drink. I know goddamn well those bastards are going to say I was drinking. Ridiculous!' Now, I knew she'd had a few—like about half a quart! I told her to just answer their questions and tell what happened."

In the attorneys' office, Millie was even more nervous and was having trouble hearing the questions. "What is your name?" asked one of the lawyers, politely.

"Well, for God's sake," said Millie, "you know my name. You have my card."

"Please just tell them your name," prompted Jack.

"It's Mildred," she snapped. "Mildred Larue Noel Lemmon—Junior, for God's sake!"

"When," asked the attorney, "did this accident occur?"

"Don't you know *anything?*" she asked.

"Of course, but we have to get it down for the record."

"It was the other night," said Millie, "at the Bel Air Hotel, and some son-of-a-bitch was watering out there—"

"Watering?"

"What?" asked Millie, leaning forward.

"Did you say *watering?*"

"Water!" Millie said emphatically. "And that's *all* I had to drink. A glass of water, and—"

The deposition ended suddenly. "That was it," said Jack, with a grin. "The whole thing was over. Those lawyers just sat there and watched as she ranted and raved about her sobriety. God, she was marvelous!"

Following *Cowboy* Lemmon was cast in two films directed by Richard Quine—*Bell, Book and Candle* and *It Happened to Jane.* Neither of the parts took so much as a cup from the well of talent within Lemmon. His role in *Bell, Book and Candle* was little more than an embroidered bit part in a film spotlighting sexy Kim Novak, who was being curried for stardom by Harry Cohn as a result of his problems with Rita Hayworth.

Novak portrayed a comely witch trying to put the love hex on James Stewart. Lemmon played her brother, a sorcerer, j.g. When Charley Baker saw the film in New York, it appeared to him that Jack had been turned into a toad.

Said Baker, "I called Jack in California and I said, 'Jack—you've been had.' In the film he was not the second lead, he was about the *sixth* lead. I knew how it had happened. Quine is a lovely guy and he and Jack had such a good personal and working relationship. It was all fun and games. Jack would do anything with him. But the studio was using Jack to shore up the film, to enhance the possibility of success.

"I told him that I thought sooner or later he would have to start looking out for Number One. And, to me, Jack was Number One. That's the first time he recognized what I was trying to say—when he saw that film. He said, 'Yes, I really am Number Six or Seven on this totem pole.' "

Baker went on: "Jack loves fun and he loves life. The greatest thing about him is that he is a person first and an actor second. But you can't just run around saying, 'Hey! We're really going to have a ball on this one!'—and that's it."

Lemmon feels he was doing pictures that did not light up the firmament by choice—his own. Many actors at Columbia had little to say about a part or a picture in which they were to appear. But because Cohn liked and respected Jack, he would never order him to appear in a film over Lemmon's strong objection.

"He would never force me," said Jack, "but he did do something else that was marvelous. I hate confrontations and he knew it. Harry would say 'Okay, you don't want to do it? *You* go to the producer, the writer, and the director and tell them you don't want to do it—and *why*.'

"Brother, that was like getting your doctorate. It was very good for me. Harry was being a good papa."

Bell, Book and Candle, Jack says, was the first film where he felt he really didn't know what he was doing. "I don't think I ever found my interpretation of the part. I never had a 'hook' on it; I was just using technique—fishing. I enjoyed doing the film, working with Quine and Kovacs again and, of course, Jim Stewart, who is a fine man and just a master."

It Happened to Jane was, Jack recalls, "a charming picture, made when you could still do charming films. Working with Doris Day was a pleasure. She's very professional, a fine actress. Of course, Quine and Kovacs were in that one, too, so that made it fun.

"We stayed in a two-hundred-year-old house that had an electric piano with earphones, so I could play and not disturb the others who were hard at it in poker and gin games nearly every evening. It was a great time for me; I was back in New England, my marriage was behind me, I was young, and I wasn't concerned about the world around me as I am today. I was like a kid, totally free, flapping his wings."

Whenever Jack got to flapping with a bit too much abandon, a few wing feathers would be snipped by the saucy Felicia, with whom Jack was now having the first of a long-run series of fights that continue to the present. They are battles of considerable ingenuity and sophistication that always keep to carefully charted metes and bounds, eventually arriving at the same terminus: each other's arms. Longtime friends tend to nod off during these skirmishes. They complain the fights are comparable to watching a film loop of a Roadrunner and Coyote cartoon.

Billy Wilder insists Jack and Felicia belong to the "Battle of the Week Club." He believes the fights develop because the straightforward Felicia is not the type of woman who runs off to the bedroom to cry. "Some women," he said with a grin, "are conciliatory. Not so my friend Felicia. It's the knee in the testicles!"

To Jack's amazement, he found the fights exciting. "I discovered," he said, "that I could let it all hang out with her and that's something I never, never could do with another human being. Pow! Let it go! Felicia compelled me to do *that* and still does."

From the beginning there was one unspoken covenant. "There was," said Felicia, "a lot of 'I hate you' or 'I can't stand you' and 'I can't stand it anymore and I'm leaving you' but *never* 'I don't love you.' The love was always there; it was taken for granted."

Robert Mitchum recalls one of the many Jack and Felicia jousts, in which Lemmon turned the event to his economic advantage. "I was giving a party one night at Romanoff's," said Mitchum, "and we had the place decorated in roses—everything from small arrangements on the tables to large pots with rose trees in them. It was a beautiful party, really.

"Jack came with Felicia in his new Thunderbird, that small classic coupe. Well, those two had a scrap and Felicia went home in a cab. Well—don't you know, Jack came to me and told me everything was okay because he would make it up to her in the morning. He said he had wanted to steal a rose tree and there wasn't room in the T-Bird for himself, the rose tree, *and* Felicia. The next week I got a two-hundred-and-fifty-dollar bill for the fucking rosebush! He was telling *me* how clever he was. I'll always believe he picked that fight with her just so he could engineer the theft and have room for the bush."

Lemmon today admits to purloining the bush, but denies that it was premeditated. "I didn't pick a fight for that reason. I was just sitting there; Felicia had gone off and after a while when she didn't return I thought, 'I think I'm alone—she didn't go to the ladies' room and she isn't coming back.' And it was then that I thought, 'God, what a beautiful rose tree.'

"Well, at that time I was dippy about plants; I was a garden nut, so I snitched the tree. I don't remember whether I took it home or gave it to Felicia to make up. But I stole it and took it on the lam in the T-Bird."

In between the fights, Jack was a frequent visitor at Felicia's home, but conducted the romance under Edwardian rules quite foreign to the popular concept of how affairs are handled in Hollywood. If he intended to sleep there, he would park two or three blocks away and walk up—a ruse that may or may not have faked out the neighbors.

"I also thought that Chez, Felicia's mother, might not take too kindly to the idea that I was staying over and the car would have been a dead giveaway."

Felicia corroborates Jack's feeling that he had to keep a low profile around Chez. "My mother didn't want me to get serious about Jack. She was no fan of his; she was rooting for another fellow."

As with any war, there are mementos, rusting relics that attest to moments of glory, high honor, and engagements won and lost. There is one left over from the courtship of Jack and Felicia, and it rests in a frame at their beach home. It is a splintered plywood door panel.

During one of their semischeduled bouts, Felicia repaired to another room and refused to come out. Jack posted himself at the door and whispered, in deference to Chez: "Open up." Silence. "I said open up!" Felicia remained mute. After a dozen increasingly urgent and heated requests, all met by stony quiet, Lemmon delivered a husky ultimatum: "Open the goddamned door or I'll open it!" Silence.

It was more than a sane man could stand. Squaring away, Jack delivered a thundering right cross to the panel, and sent his fist crashing through. Immediately, he regretted the action. Long, jagged splinters protruded, alongside his hand. "*Don't open the door!*" he screamed, even as Felicia, with impeccable timing, yanked the knob.

"After I got my hand back—what was left of it—I should have said 'I'll never play again,' " said Jack. "But I never thought of that." Felicia, taken with the romance of it all, kept the panel, had it framed, and gave it to Jack on their twelfth anniversary.

Later, Jack and Felicia were having dinner at Dominic's, celebrating his healed hand, when they were approached by famed director Billy Wilder. "Can I sit down with you for a minute?"

"Sure," said Jack, who had only a casual acquaintance with Wilder.

"I've got this story," said Wilder, "about two guys who witness the St. Valentine's Day massacre. They're out-of-work musicians, and because the murderers have seen them, they now have to duck and hide. They don't have any money so they join an all-girl orchestra and disguise themselves as women. They're in drag for more than three quarters of the film. Do you want to do it?"

"Yes," said Jack.

"Okay," said the director, rising to leave, "I'll be in touch."

"What do you call it?" Lemmon called after him.

Wilder turned. "I call it *Some Like It Hot.*"

Chapter

XVII

". . . the actor's actor, the divine clown."

—Billy Wilder

SOME INTREPID SOULS are drawn to high-risk adventures like cobra-kissing, sailing out where there be dragons, and making films such as *Some Like It Hot.* The survival rate for these dare-devils is terrible but they press on, lured by challenge and the guerdon of success, which can be extravagant.

Billy Wilder was perfectly aware of the dangers inherent in parading two grown men around in dresses and wigs for the better part of a 120-minute film. The theme was unforgiving, the margin for error negligible. A miscalculation could transform the picture from classical farce to sleazy transvestism.

It was several months before Lemmon was handed the first half of the Wilder–I. A. L. Diamond script. "When I read it," he said, "I fell off the couch in hysterics. It was just bloody brilliant." Jack sensed that he had a tiger by the tail.

"A lot of people thought Billy was crazy to attempt such a film. Friends told me I could be ruined because the audience would think I was faggy or had a yen to be a transvestite. There was no getting around one thing; the picture was a minefield for actors. I finally decided the real trap was to ever *think* of the trap. If one began to worry about that fine line, to fret over audience reaction, it could be disastrous. The only way to play it was to let it all hang out and just go, trusting that Wilder would say, 'Cut,' if it got out of bounds. I saw this character I was to play as a nut from the moon who never really stopped to think once in his life. He didn't act—he reacted—to whatever was happening.

"How else was it possible to justify a guy who, because he's dressed like a woman, delivers a line like: 'If those gangsters come in here and kill us, and we're taken to the morgue dressed like this I'll die of embarrassment!'?

"Now the line isn't that funny unless the character can say it and really *mean* it—because he doesn't *think*. He isn't concerned that he's going to be shot; he's worried he'll be caught in drag.

"Or, how does this guy, if he ever stops to think, get so swept away that he announces to his buddy [Tony Curtis] that he's engaged to Joe E. Brown—and he's all excited about it?"

At first Jack wondered about the wisdom of Wilder. "Each evening Felicia would cue me on my lines, we'd have dinner, and I'd go to bed—somewhere or other. She kept asking me what I thought of Wilder and I told her, 'I guess he's okay.' She's never let me forget that one."

In a short time, Jack was telling an amused Felicia how brilliant Wilder was. In turn, Wilder was steadily becoming more impressed with Lemmon, whom he had selected for the role over several other stars under consideration. He saw in Jack "the actor's actor, the divine clown who could come out and just *do it* and look natural."

Tony Curtis did not adapt readily to the absurdity that was an integral part of *Some Like It Hot*. "When we were testing costumes," said Wilder, "and the boys got into their dresses and wigs, Jack came out of his room floating ten feet high, completely normal and natural. Tony didn't dare to come out, he was so embarrassed by the whole thing. Lemmon had to take him by the hand and drag him out. It was natural to the one; there were inhibitions in the other."

Perhaps what Wilder saw as "natural" is the same trait Freddie Jordan detected in Jack at Andover—the "grace to make a fool of himself" by pretending to be an elephant at a party.

Wilder believes acting comes easily to Lemmon, that it was delivered with him at birth. "He had to be an actor," Wilder said. "I doubt he could have done anything else except play piano in a whorehouse. I've known actors who did not have naturalness—actors such as Gary Cooper and Bill Holden. They were wonderful people, but you could see that they had to shift into a new gear in order to act. It was not easy for them. It was slightly unnatural; there was an element of embarrassment. Not so with Jack."

Lemmon circled his role cautiously, sniffing at the lines, sorting through mannerisms, toying with wigs and makeup. He spent hours with top makeup man Harry Ray, giving him looks he'd worked out, to which Ray matched the makeup. "We would change my lips sometimes, even in the continuation of a scene, making the 'bee sting' a little larger—not enough so the audience could tell, but enough to help on certain looks," said Jack. "Makeup is vital at times in acting; it certainly was for *Some Like It Hot.*"

Those who work and associate with Lemmon will tell you he is a computer bank of visual information. "I can recall going shopping with him," said Ruth Carter, "and being fascinated at the way he studies everything—how a person holds a package, sorts his change—every little detail. You can almost hear the click-click-click as information items are stored away in his brain. Later you may see some of it turn up in a piece of 'business' he does on the screen. He seems to have total recall."

Andy McCullough remembers watching Jack do this kind of data storage at a party. "Lemmon had this guy in a corner and I could tell Jack was 'working' by the way he sat, the way his head was tilted. I went over and listened for a little while and this fellow was talking about his crabgrass and problems at the office. Jack was studying him, using him for his own purposes, picking up on him with an eye as keen as any novelist or portrait painter. The guy was oblivious to what Jack was doing.

"Later, after another party, Jack 'did' the people who'd been there. Not imitations, because imitations are generally caricatures; this was an absolutely dead-level playback of various individuals. He's got an ear like Ring Lardner, a writer's ear. He would do a cliché that someone had used repeatedly, or an affectation of a French phrase. He didn't miss anything."

It was the perceptive Richard Carter who recognized the source of Lemmon's principal mannerisms for the character in *Some Like It Hot.* Watching Jack run through scenes in rehearsal one afternoon, Carter suddenly realized what was happening. Lemmon was playing Millie!

"I didn't know it myself until Dick mentioned it," said Jack. "I guess it was sense memory. I was picking up 'hooks'—her mannerisms, even the wig. I *looked* like my mother. Sometimes when you are faced with a scene in which you must evoke a particular emotion, you can draw from a parallel situation, something you've witnessed or experienced. I seldom do that; it doesn't work too well for me."

Once Lemmon and Curtis had worked up what they felt was the appropriate attire and makeup, they decided what was really needed was a shakedown cruise, a final test. "We agreed," said Jack, "that since it was lunchtime we would, like two ding-dongs, go down to the studio commissary dressed up like broads. One of us, I forget whether it was Tony or me, got the bright idea that a true test would be a visit to the ladies' room. So in we went! I mean, all the way!

"Obviously, all the women were in stalls or this and that; we weren't, you know, peeking or anything. Well, we futzed around in the lounge, pursing our lips and running our fingers over our brows and whatever else we could think of that ladies would do. Do you know, not one of the girls going in or out ever batted an eyeball? They thought we were extras doing a period film on the lot.

"That did it. That gave us the security we needed right there and then. We figured if those women bought it, they'd sure as hell buy it on camera."

The strange new world of womanhood was found to be, in the main, tolerable. There was one miserable exception—high-heeled shoes. Both Tony and Jack suffered constantly from muscle cramps. The studio provided buckets of icewater, lotions, and chamois cloths for them, and the moment Wilder said, 'Cut,' their feet came out of the shoes and into the buckets.

An internationally known female impersonator was brought from Europe to school Tony and Jack in the fine art of being feminine. "One of the most interesting things he taught us," said Jack, "was how to walk like a woman. If you want to look regal and ladylike, he said, you have to stride, crossing one foot in front of the other. It worked amazingly well, but I pointed out that it was about as funny as cholera. I rebelled. I insisted that there had to be an attempt *not* to be good at it.

"The way I saw it, this goof I was playing wouldn't be very proficient at walking in heels. I needed to be barely good enough to look like a clumsy woman. Well, the impersonator gave up in disgust and went back to Europe after three days. He told Wilder that Curtis was fine but Lemmon was totally impossible."

In *Some Like It Hot* Jack got his first, and last, opportunity to work with the fabulous Marilyn Monroe, a girl he found fascinating to watch and impossible to understand. When she saw Lemmon in his female togs Marilyn took a fancy to his dress. When he wasn't around, she took it for her own. The wardrobe department had to make another for Jack.

"Marilyn had a kind of built-in alarm system," Jack said. "It would 'go off' in the middle of a scene if that scene was not right for her, and she would just stop everything. She would stand there with her eyes closed, biting her lip, and kind of wringing her hands until she had it worked out. Now this sounds like selfishness, and I guess it is. But she didn't mean to be selfish—it was the only way she could work. Marilyn didn't give a damn about the director, the other actors, or anything else.

"It would seem that she was doing exactly what she'd done in the take before; but for her, something wasn't clicking quite right. I didn't necessarily approve of that tactic; it was not easy working with her, but it was fascinating. I don't think Marilyn had a great talent—what she had was an ability to use *completely* the talents she did have. Ninety-nine percent of the actors can never pull all the potential, all the talent that they've got out of themselves. I think Marilyn did. She built that into her unique personality and had incredible charisma. There was nobody quite like her; she didn't copy anyone. She was not a great actress, she could—more than anyone I've ever known—just use whatever the hell it was she had fully. She had a good sense of comedy, but she had to bend the character to herself. She knew she was limited and goddamned well knew what was right for Marilyn; she wasn't about to do anything else."

Monroe's unorthodox technique was shrugged off by Jack, but proved unsettling to Curtis, who had more and longer scenes with her. "Tony had one in the third act that ran twelve minutes with Marilyn," said Jack. "When you consider that she had a habit of showing up late, had a tendency to act at instead of with you, and you were never sure of getting through a scene before she stopped it—it's understandable that she drove Curtis a little cuckoo. Fortunately, none of this had a harmful effect on the final result."

Actually, Jack had little time to worry about Marilyn's behavior. He was kept well occupied inventing countermeasures to the maneuverings of the piquant Felicia. At length he detected a flaw. Bright, clever, wily Felicia was a patsy for a put-on. Jack made this buoying discovery one day while they were idly discussing her pet houseplant, Boris, which she kept at the foot of her bed and which, she claimed, "protected" her.

"I'm afraid," said Lemmon gravely, "that you are not taking very good care of Boris."

"What makes you think that?" she asked.

"Just look at that," he said, pointing to a perfectly healthy leaf. "Just what is it you do for Boris?"

"What do you mean, what do I do for him?" asked a now-indignant Felicia. "I feed him. I give him water when he tells me he wants water and I clean his leaves—"

"Aha!" said Jack, triumphantly. "And how do you clean his leaves?"

"I clean him with water and a soft cloth, or sometimes a piece of cotton," she said defensively.

"Just plain water?" Jack asked with knowing concern.

"Yes. Just plain water."

"I can see," he said, with a sigh, "that you don't know about the milk."

"Milk! On a plant?"

Jack shook his head. "Not just any milk. Homogenized milk is wrong, dead wrong. You have to put vitamin A milk on it. Any plant pathologist could have warned you about that. You have to add it because in all of nature only the *Asclepi-adaceae*—you might know it as the common milkweed—makes its own. Water? I can't believe you'd use water! I wish," he said, with funereal finality, "I had known about this sooner."

Having gobbled this yarn down whole, Felicia rushed out in a frantic search for vitamin A milk, gradually discovering that (1) vitamin A milk was no longer being produced; (2) that it was never rubbed on plants by any noninstitutionalized person, and (3) she'd been thoroughly had by her underhanded lover. In the months and years to come, Jack was to pay heavily and often for his folly.

Even while he gloated in chauvinist content, his downfall was being plotted by Richard Quine and Blake Edwards, who had grown weary of hearing about Jack's brand new Thunderbird, which he had received in payment for an appearance on the Ed Sullivan television program. The third day after taking delivery on the car, Jack started to drive out of the studio when he stopped, dismayed at a horrendous sound apparently emanating from the brand new motor of his brand new vehicle.

Sticking to the right lane of the street, Lemmon decided to try and make it to the Ford dealer. At a speed of ten miles an hour he crept, suffering the insults of other enraged drivers and expecting that momentarily a wheel—or worse, the entire motor—would fall off. Inching his way, Jack arrived at the dealer after an hour. He parked and exploded at the hapless service manager, who offered to examine the car at once.

Climbing in, the man started the engine and went ten feet before he stopped, hopped out, and knocked off the right front hubcap. Reaching in, he extracted a variety of large nuts and bolts. He handed them to Jack. "They didn't come with the car, Mr. Lemmon, but that's your problem."

A chastened Lemmon slunk into the driver's seat and pulled away, his mind already at work on bloody revenge. He knew who the culprits were: Quine and Edwards, that's who. He grinned a malevolent grin. Well, they'd picked on the wrong cookie this time. Lemmon knew something about cars and bombs. He determined that the next day he would seek out the local branch of Daddy Jack's joke shop and lay in necessary supplies, including the biggest warhead in the inventory.

With the help of a willing prop man, Jack constructed a device that could be attached to an automobile engine. The design was a work of evil genius; too small to destroy the engine, but big enough so that the owner would certainly believe himself the victim of a Mafia contract. Ready at last, the mad bomber selected the bombee—Blake Edwards.

For a week following the nuts-and-bolts incident, Jack continued to lunch with Quine and Edwards, pretending always that nothing had happened. They were not to enjoy the product of their dastardly act.

Jack had planned the counterattack with cold precision. He would install the infernal device while they were at lunch. He had determined the color, year, and make of Edwards' car, and he had befriended the parking-lot guard, who would now pay no attention to him. One afternoon he skulked out to the lot, hoisted the hood of the automobile, and wired it for sound and fury.

Returning to the commissary, Lemmon waited—and continued to wait until nearly dark. "To my great regret," he said, "I eventually had to depart before Dick and Blake left the studio. Boy, I wanted to be around when that little mother went off. I was tempted to call that night to get a reaction but that would have tipped my hand for sure.

"I was in to work the next day at the crack of dawn. I couldn't wait. When they met me for lunch, they did the same damned thing I'd done. They never said boo. Yet, I knew they suspected me.

"It was killing me that they wouldn't let on; I was just aching to know the details. Four days passed, and still nothing—not one word! Finally, when they were both busy, I dashed out to the lot and raised the hood of Blake's car. The bomb was gone. There were no signs of the blast, which surprised me a little, but I figured it must have worked.

"I had to know, so I gave in and asked: 'Alright, you sonsabitches. You did it, you put the nuts and bolts in my car—now how big was that bomb? I gotta know.' They both looked at me like I was crazy. Now I have seen good actors, and neither of them was that good. I studied them like a hawk but they wouldn't confess.

"Well, the long and short of it is I blew up the wrong car! I hadn't bothered to look up the license plate and they told me I had blasted the engine of a studio executive who Quine said got hysterical what with all the smoke and flames and whatnot. He had the same color and make of car as Blake, unfortunately. Jesus! "

As shooting progressed on *Some Like It Hot* Wilder became ever more impressed with Lemmon's performance. "His unabashed forwardness," said Wilder, "was making that preposterous situation work, elevating, removing the taint of transvestism. Within three to four weeks after the start of production, Diamond and I had decided that this was not to be a one-shot thing with Jack. We wanted to work with him again, and while *Some Like It Hot* was still in the works we got underway with the planning for another one—*The Apartment*."

During this period the alert Lemmon was "picking up" on Wilder, learning much from the brilliant director. "Billy did something very unusual," said Jack. "He kept his former film editor, Doan Harrison, on the set with him as associate producer and never made a shot until they'd both discussed it. As a result, Billy was able to shoot very sparingly, literally cutting the film in the camera and eliminating costly setups that would never be used. Later, Doan would supervise the editing.

"I remember being very impressed when it was pointed out to me that Billy had not used a closeup of me until more than half the picture was done. I hadn't noticed that. Now, when he did go to a closeup, it was of me peering out from the upper berth on a train. I had the makeup on, the wig, and I was wearing a nightie. I had my face cupped in my hands and I was ogling the girls in the orchestra getting ready for bed. It was a dynamite shot and it doubled the impact that ordinarily could be expected. It gained great importance because Billy had played everything loose up to that point. At the same time, it reminded the audience that despite the female get-up, this character was, after all, still a man. When that tight closeup hit the screen it got a roar."

One of the memorable moments in the history of film comedy comes in *Some Like It Hot* when a euphoric Lemmon reveals to Curtis that he's engaged to Brown. "That may well be the best scene I've ever been in," said Jack," and it certainly is one of the most brilliantly written and directed scenes that I've ever seen.

"When we got ready to do it, Billy handed me a set of maracas and I thought he was crazy. I'd already worked out everything at home and I could not imagine what I was supposed to do with those things. As we began rehearsing it hit me what a genius Wilder really was in coming up with those maracas. They served as a perfect—and critical—bridge; a piece of 'business' that would fill the gap between my lines, providing time for audience laughter.

"If Billy hadn't had me dancing around with those things in my 'joy,' most of the dialogue would have been lost, wiped out by laughter. From the moment I said, 'I'm engaged,' the uproar was almost continuous. Every time I'd read a line I'd follow it by waltzing around with those maracas while Tony was looking at me like I'm out of my mind. It was a sensational scene. Virtually every line in it—in the entire film, for that matter—is just sparkling."

Wilder believes *Some Like It Hot* is probably the best film he ever made with Lemmon. "After a certain time," he said, "I guess you are prone to regard your most successful picture as your best. *Some Like It Hot* is kind of regarded as one of the classics of American films. It's strange that after fifteen or twenty years certain pictures remain and get better; while other films, that one might like better, sort of dim; they regress in their importance.

"*Some Like It Hot* sort of snowballed into prominence. Actually, I like certain things in certain pictures. But I must stress that Jack Lemmon is simply incapable of giving a bad performance. He has that marvelous ability to communicate with the audience; it's something you are born with. If an actor doesn't have that, he can't learn it. The audience knows what's going through Jack's mind or soul—and they care."

As the picture neared completion, Jack realized that he was

daily falling more in love with Felicia—a fact that he found exhilarating and nerve-jangling at the same time. He felt very much as if he were riding along with one foot on the accelerator, the other on the brake. While pursuing her relentlessly, he was carefully avoiding any thought of marriage.

"Looking back on it," said Jack, "I think I was afraid of the involvement, the commitment. I know I felt failure from my first marriage, although I didn't totally blame myself. Also, I was so involved with myself and my career that I felt I didn't have the emotional ability to give enough. I didn't worry about the problem of two careers; Felicia was much too level-headed about that."

The reluctance toward marriage was not Jack's alone. Felicia had been married at fifteen and divorced at twenty. The union had produced a daughter, Denise, and a wariness toward rushing into wedlock again.

Chapter XVIII

"The dearest liar—"
—Ruth Carter

SOMEDAY SOMEONE is going to say something bad about Jack Lemmon, and the guy who does it will find himself in a category with whooping crane killers. In a town where cold-decking passes for normal business practice and nobody will read a script unless the writer agrees not to sue if they steal it, Lemmon is accepted on his word. He is Billy Budd in Port Royal.

"Jack is a mixture of artist, movie star, and gentleman," says Andy McCullough, "and the three of them are constantly at war in the community and within him. It is a problem that faces no one else in the industry that I can think of. The big stars are generally studs; they ride motorcycles, they get into fights with people. Most of them are shrewd political operators; they maneuver, they push buttons, test their power. The two stars that I can recall having used this power most often to get their way are widely known as the biggest pricks in Hollywood. Jack could never operate that way; it's not in him."

Jack's deeply imbedded sense of honor, his courtly Old World courtesy, and the elaborate concern he exhibits for people's feelings produce a sense of uneasy protectiveness in his friends and associates. They just know that their sunfish cannot go on forever swimming around among the piranha without being devoured.

Yet he hasn't been devoured. He has prospered amazingly well under the golden-rule banner, to the wonder of those about him. "Saint Jack," Maureen Stapleton calls him. Ruth Carter sees him as "the dearest liar," who will fabricate a cover story when refusing any invitation, even a luncheon with a friend, for fear of hurting his feelings.

"He's a pigeon," says Richard Carter, who sorts through the maze of requests for Jack's time or the use of his name. "Usually, I get a bunch of these things together and go over them with him, because there's no way he can handle them all. But once in a while I'll find he's already committed to something I would have put aside. Somebody will catch him at lunch or at a party and he'll say Yes because it kills him to turn anybody down."

Once he commits himself, Lemmon will be there and on time, barring high water, earthquakes, or plague. Bud Noel recalls that some friends of his, making a trip to California, wanted to meet Jack. "I called Jack," said Bud, "and hell, he insisted on meeting them for dinner. When the time came, there had been a mixup about which hotel they were staying at. Jack spent half the night going from one place to another around Los Angeles trying to locate these people he'd never met simply because they were my friends and he *said* he would. Even after all that, he was still upset and apologetic about missing them. That's the way he is."

Unquestionably there is a tendency among some to take advantage of one such as Lemmon. With the release of *Some Like It Hot* Jack had at last become a star. He knew it was so; the evidence was there in the heightened unctuousness of headwaiters, in the way people nudged each other when he passed, and in the increasing requests for his autograph. Yet the studio seemed not to have noticed. At the pay window, Jack was compensated at a rate not much above that of a journeyman plumber.

While his pictures were beginning to accrue millions at the boxoffice, Lemmon continued to draw between $12,000 and $15,000 per film. The studio heads and his agents seemed content with the inequity, and if it disturbed Jack that the pilot fish grew obese while the whale scrabbled, it was not apparent. He made no complaint.

For one thing, wealth and stardom had never been primary targets for Lemmon. The fun was in the doing, and he was doing the one thing in life he had to do. Meanwhile, youth was on his side; he was footloose and enjoying an enchanting (if sometimes squally) relationship with Felicia. Could any reasonable man, he asked himself, want for more?

In the spring Jack was packed off on a promotion tour for *Some Like It Hot*, a trip that would take him to the East Coast and then on to Europe in the company of Billy Wilder, I. A. L. Diamond, and their wives.

The return to New York was, for Lemmon, like a scene from one of those old show-biz flicks where the local kid makes it big and then comes home. "I'll never forget it," said Jack. "A big party had been planned at the estate of Bill Paley, the head of CBS, and he was going to run the film. All I could think about was the many times I tried so hard to get a job at CBS, when I would lie awake at night and wonder how to get in the door. Now I was going to his home! It was all very exciting."

The first day in town Audrey Wilder called Jack to ask if he'd like to attend a big formal bash that evening, the opening of the new El Morocco. He'd love it, said Jack, but he hadn't brought a tuxedo with him. Audrey said he shouldn't worry because she would call the studio publicist, who would be able to get one over to him.

"It turned out," said Jack, "that the guy who loaned me his tux was about six feet four inches tall, and when I got around to trying on the coat I found that the sleeves came down below my fingers. The shirt collar was a size seventeen. I wore a fourteen and one-half! By the time I got dressed in this tent it was time to go. The only thing I could do was keep my elbows close to my sides and my hands pointed straight ahead at all times! It was ridiculous. I looked like a club featherweight who'd been outfitted at Sa-Ray's. Now, since I wasn't bright enough to rent a tux for the next evening, I went to Paley's in the same outfit!

"Anyway, off we went to this affair at the El Morocco. When we arrived it looked like one of those gaudy Hollywood premieres. There were newsreel cameras, flashbulbs popping, and cops holding the crowd back as all the biggies arrived in their black limousines. And then, there was Lemmon—standing around with his hands raised like he'd been caught in a heist.

"The new El Morocco, as it turned out, was located at Fifty-fourth Street and First Avenue and looked vaguely familiar to me. I had the strangest feeling and I just stood there, trying to figure it out while people were milling around and photographers were saying 'Over here—could we get just one more shot?' Suddenly it hit me and I said, 'My God! It's The Old Knick!' They'd moved the entrance around to the Fifty-fourth Street side.

"I was just rooted there with my arms at half salute as all the memories came washing over me. My first job, Paul and the old movies, Pepe, the crooked projectionist, the floor that slanted, the sawdust and greasy chicken. It was a wild experience and is the principal thing I remember about the evening—that and my tired arms."

For Jack, the trip to Europe was to take on an importance far beyond the promotion of a film and the enhancement of his career. At the conclusion of his publicity chores he would join John Lemmon for a month-long, carefree tour of the Continent.

Father and son had long talked of taking a trip together. Jack had in mind a journey to the Pacific. "When I was a kid," said Jack, "Pop kept telling me about an island that he owned in partnership with four other guys. It was in the Philippines and I kept asking to see it, but he never would go. One day he told me he'd bought the whole thing from the other guys, although he'd never seen it!

"Once when we got to discussing our planned trip, I suggested we go see his island, but he kept hedging. Finally he broke down and told me the truth. He'd had the place investigated and the word came back that at high tide the whole stinking island was submerged. Nobody could live there unless they were on stilts! It was a sandbar.

"So much for the island. We did the European tour, just the two of us, and it was marvelous. It was one of the high points of my life and I thank God that it happened. For the first time I got really close to my father. It was a chance most guys never have, even with a good, solid relationship, to do something with your old man, one-to-one. God, it was wonderful—the memories.

"One night in Venice we were in a small American bar talking with some kids at the next table. They were on vacation from their job with Radio Free Europe. After a while, Pop said it was getting late for an old poop and he was going back to the hotel and bed. So he left and I stayed on to have another drink.

"For some reason I decided I wanted to take a night gondola ride down the canal, even though it was drizzling. One of the girls, an attractive blonde, said she would join me if I could induce a gondolier to take us. Well, the gondolier was a capitalist, not a romantic; he demanded that I lay out a small fortune. The girl could speak a little Italian so we finally haggled him down to triple the going rate and climbed in.

"I told him to take us down to the Bridge of Sighs, and by the time we got near it, the rain was starting to come down. We had just reached the bridge when we saw a second gondola approaching with another couple, but they were nice and cozy under an umbrella. As they passed, the guy just casually tipped his hat and I almost fell out of the boat. It was *my old man*, snuggled up as nice as you please next to a gorgeous little cookie who looked about twenty-one! Oh, he was a ripper! God, we had fun! I was thirty-four years old and just beginning to know my father. I don't believe I began to mature until then; I was a late bloomer."

Returning to California, Jack signed to star in a television play, one of the last of the shows produced for the memorable "Playhouse 90." Director for the script, Bob Joseph's adaptation of Pierre Boulle's novel *Face of a Hero*, was John Frankenheimer.

Jack found the story, that of an ambitious young attorney-general in a southern town, "fascinating but very introspective; one of those pieces that *almost* works—especially for television or film, where you can get in tight for expressions." A little later on, Lemmon was to find out the hard way that it worked not at all on the stage.

The television show did provide Jack with one unforgettable moment that involved a torrential rain, forty extras, and a river—all jammed into a television studio. "This was being done on videotape, not film," said Jack, "and in those days you couldn't stop or edit tape as well, so we would take a fifteen- or twenty-minute segment, start at the top, and go straight through.

"We had a scene in the studio where I pull up in a car and slosh through a foot of water to the river's edge, where there's a big crowd because a girl has been drowned and they think it's murder. Well, we did that scene about three times but something always went wrong; either it was a mechanical problem or the extras weren't doing quite what Frankenheimer wanted. Now John has a temper, and he was back there in the booth on the next stage, screaming. Everyone was worried about all that water in the studio because electrical cables were everywhere. The cameramen were afraid to touch their gear. All hell was breaking loose.

"Finally I heard Frankenheimer hollering: 'I'm telling you people we can only do this scene one more time! There's *got* to be screaming and yelling when the attorney-general shows up—lines like 'Grab that kid' and 'There's been a murder.'

"Well, we started again and we got almost through the scene. Those extras were really letting it out, after John laced into them like that. There was plenty of hubbub, ad-libbing, overlapping lines—the works. Then it happened! Once in a while in a scene like that there will be a split second of pure silence, when no one is saying anything. That's what happened and in that moment of dead air there came a voice from the back of the crowd, loud and clear: 'Mister Lautrec—your bermuda shorts are ready!'

"Well, that did it! I fell into the water. Now Frankenheimer couldn't keep going and just cut the line. In my life I have never seen a director as mad. He came rolling out of that booth with blood in his eye, slogging through water up to his knees and screaming, 'Alright, who did it? Who did it?' We never found out, naturally, because nobody was about to admit to that. Luckily, we did have time enough for another take, which came off okay."

In the wake of *Some Like It Hot*, Jack hit a streak, appearing in a half dozen films in a row that were highly acclaimed or made buckets of money—or both. By 1967 he was the uncontested Number One boxoffice attraction in films. His superb performance in *Some Like It Hot* brought him an Oscar nomination as best actor. The picture won other nominations for art direction, cinematography, direction, writing, and costume design. It took an Oscar in only one category—costume design.

Jack followed the Wilder romp with *The Apartment* and *Wackiest Ship in the Army*, an underrated, off-beat war film. From the beginning *The Apartment* looked like a winner with a script by Wilder and Diamond, direction by Wilder, and a gilt-edged cast: Lemmon, Shirley MacLaine, Fred MacMurray, Ray Walston, Jack Kruschen, and Edie Adams.

Daring for its day, *The Apartment* was a comedy-drama about a junior executive (Lemmon) who finds he can ascend the corporate ladder three rungs at a time simply by lending his apartment key to company bigwigs feverish for a little assignation.

It has been said that Wilder wrote *The Apartment* as a cipher, wisely leaving the characterization to be filled in by Lemmon. Jack saw immediately that the role could be interpreted several ways. Was the guy an opportunist who knew exactly what he was doing? A nice dumb sort who didn't see that he was being used? Or a decent sort whose ambition got the better of him?

"As I saw it," said Jack, "he was ambitious; a nice guy but gullible, easily intimidated, and fast to excuse his behavior. In the end he changes because he faces up to having rationalized his morals. He realizes he's been a dumb kid, he's been had, and that's when he turns in the key. It was interesting that in *Promises, Promises,* the Broadway musical that was taken from *The Apartment,* the character knew precisely what he was up to from the beginning and then later made a decision just not to do it anymore."

In *The Apartment,* as in *Some Like It Hot,* Jack was as much student as star. He was learning from the brilliant, innovative Wilder, learning fast. "Working with Billy I began to understand 'hooks'—those little bits of business that an audience will remember, sometimes long after they've forgotten everything else about the picture.

"The key was a 'hook.' For ten years after that film, people would still come up to me on the street and say, 'Hey, Jack, can I have the key?' Another was where I strained spaghetti, using a tennis racket for a colander. There were some great hooks in *Mister Roberts*—Pulver blowing up the laundry, and his final line: 'What's all this crud about no movie tonight?' * Today, one of the first things I look for in a script is the hook, that little audience-grabber. Remember Joe E. Brown's classic closer in *Some Like It Hot?*—'Nobody's perfect!' Funny thing, over the years many people have come to remember that as my line instead of Brown's, but it was a helluva hook."

One of the funnier moments of *The Apartment* was a Lemmon invention. "In the story," said Jack, "this guy has a bad cold because he can't get into his apartment, which is always occupied by someone else. One of the props I had was a nose spray for the sniffles. I was playing around with it in my dressing room and discovered that if I gave it a sharp squeeze the stuff would squirt ten feet.

"I filled it with milk to make it visible, and when the boss, Fred MacMurray, is chewing out this kid [me], who is very nervous, I used it. I didn't tell anybody, not even Billy, and when Fred said something like, 'Baxter, I hope we're not going to have this problem again,' I said, 'Oh, no sir!' and squeezed in nervous reaction. That milk shot out and sailed right by under MacMurray's nose. He was beautiful; didn't say a word, just gave me a look and went right on with the scene. And Billy left it in (naturally—because he

* Lemmon: "Today, the original line would be used: 'What's all this crap about no movie tonight?' "

always was fast to recognize genius!) With Wilder, like with Ford, the best way is to do it rather than talk about it. If he likes it, he'll use it."

Lemmon is a very professional and cooperative actor, says Wilder, but not unthinking. "He has his own opinions on things, but he's not bull-headed about it. He has often come to me in the morning, very excited, and said, 'I worked on those lines, and wouldn't it be better if . . . ?' I usually just look at him with my jaundiced eye and he'll say, 'Yeah, I didn't like it either!'—and it's forgotten. Now some actors will come to me with an idea and if I turn it down they will do it my way, but try to do it very badly so as to prove to me that they're right. Not so Jack. He's very generous that way. Sometimes he comes up with marvelous things, but at the times that I don't share his enthusiasm he will drop it instantly. He will not stand there with all the lights burning, the extras and electricians waiting, money going down the drain, and argue with me."

The Apartment made it big on Oscar night. Wilder was named best director, and in collaboration with Diamond, won for best story and screenplay. The film won for art direction, film editing, and was named the best picture of the year. Jack was nominated as best actor, but failed to win. He credits the success of the picture to Wilder. "I don't know of any film in which a writer or director (in this case, the same man) so successfully—and brilliantly—blended comedy and drama.

"*The Apartment* contained one of the most demanding scenes I have ever been in—not in the difficulty of the acting, but in the structure of the scene itself, in which my character, Baxter, comes home drunk with a pick-up from a bar who figures she's going to get boffed. He leaves her in the living room and goes to the bedroom to find another girl (Shirley MacLaine) dying, an empty sleeping-pill bottle next to her. Baxter goes back and forth between the kook in the living room, which is all comedy, to Shirley in the bedroom, who is dying—and that ain't funny! Wilder brought that scene off, and believe me, it was a courageous thing to attempt because if it hadn't worked the whole picture would have gone down the tubes."

Twice, now, Jack had failed to win the Oscar as best actor after being nominated. He was beginning to learn a strange fact: you rarely win in a comedy role. It is an absurdity he has come to accept. "There are still idiots in this town," he said, "who think there is some difference between drama and comedy in the sense that drama is *real* acting, while comedy isn't. Of course, that's absolute nonsense. If you talk to anyone who knows anything about this business they will tell you that in general there is no contest; comedy is far more difficult than drama to write, direct, or act successfully. That isn't conjecture; it's an absolute fact.

"There is a wonderful story about the great English character actor Edmund Gwenn that says something, I think, about the business I'm in and about comedy. Gwenn's best friend was George Seaton, who had directed him in *Miracle on 34th Street*, probably the best part in Edmund's illustrious career. Anyway, Seaton, who kind of looked after old Gwenn, finally convinced him to enter the Actor's Home, something Edmund fought even when he was old and sick and in financial straits."

Seaton got word one day that he should come out to the home as soon as possible, because Gwenn couldn't last much longer. When he arrived, he took a chair next to the bed of the old actor and waited. After a long time, Gwenn slowly opened his eyes and recognized his friend. "George," he whispered, "I think I'm going to die."

"Yes," said Seaton, quietly, "I know."

"George, I don't like it. I don't like it a bit. There is no feeling of peace, no feeling of anticipation. George, it's awful. It's frightening and I hate it."

Not knowing what to say, Seaton murmured "Yes, old friend, I guess dying can be very hard."

Gwenn thought about it for a moment and then looked at Seaton. "Yes," he said, "but *not as hard as playing comedy!*"

Those were his last words.

Chapter XIX

"That's no act he's putting on."
—John Knowles

JOE E. BROWN was right. Nobody's perfect, not even the ancients. They were right-on with their calculation that you can't have two mountains without a valley, but in the same breath they warned that a dog was apparently eating the moon—every thirty days.

So it is perhaps forgivable that a group of otherwise terribly bright and talented people could get together and produce one of Broadway's more memorable turkeys. It happened in 1960 and the vehicle was *Face of a Hero*. The star was Jack Lemmon.

In case one is needed, Charley Baker has offered to serve as fall guy. "I was to blame for that one," says Charley, with conviction. "I led Lemmon down the garden path. I had seen Jack in the television version of *Face of a Hero* and he was riveting. I don't think anyone knows more about his potential than I, but he even surprised me on that one; he was so brilliant, so interior. I called him and said I thought he'd accidentally found something that should bring him back to Broadway. Jack said he'd love to do it."

Baker got Bob Joseph to adapt his teleplay to a Broadway play and took it to John Frankenheimer. "I should have suspected a problem when John didn't want to direct it. He was afraid of it, and I thought his fear came from not having directed a Broadway play. It didn't occur to me that he might have spotted some fatal flaws."

Eventually it was agreed that Alexander ("Sandy") Mackendrick would direct. Although Mackendrick's film credentials were excellent (*Sweet Smell of Success, The Ladykillers*), he was shy on stage experience. "I didn't think it mattered," said Baker. "Sandy was brilliant and Joseph had written a scenario play, almost fade-in, fade-out.

"We had a wonderful cast and Jack worked so hard; we couldn't miss. We had investors coming out of the walls and the ladies' groups were calling to arrange theater parties."

Frankenheimer was not alone in sensing trouble with *Face of a Hero* as a Broadway play. Andy McCullough told Jack he didn't think it would work, pointing out that the lead character, the attorney-general (Lemmon) knows the girl's drowning was an accident but is prosecuting an innocent boy for murder. "The trouble," said Andy, "is that the guy never talks to anyone. Unless you invent a character to tell your dread secret to, or do a soliloquy, it isn't going to work on the stage. The audience is going to be wondering what the hell he's thinking about all the time."

Jack knew about the problem because he'd faced it in the television play to some extent. "Obviously," he said, "I didn't think it would be that much more difficult on the stage or I'd never have agreed to do it."

Face of a Hero opened in Philadelphia. "We had gone deeply into the design of the play," said Baker. "It had to be very operative, moving from scene to scene. It was marvelous except that you couldn't *see* it. We opened in total darkness and nobody knew whether that was Jack Lemmon up there. Even if they could have seen him they wouldn't have wanted to, because this wasn't the Lemmon they knew; this was a character full of guilt, soul-searching, not knowing which way to turn."

Reviewers had a field day, handing out unanimously scathing notices. McCullough, who had flown to Philadelphia to see the play, remembers standing in the rain outside the theater following the disastrous opening: "Mackendrick was in a state of shock and Jack had spent a long time over dinner and drinks with him, commiserating, softening the blow. Now, as Jack and I were leaving the theater, three kids came up, wanting his autograph. I told them to blow, but Jack stopped in the rain to sign their books. As we crossed the street I heard one boy say, 'What did you want his autograph for?' The other answered, 'I don't—I can trade it for a Tony Curtis!' Jack loved it. It broke him up."

For two weeks the company worked frantically overhauling the play. "When we opened in Boston," said Baker, "it was tremendously improved, but the reviews were just as bad as they had been in Philadelphia."

Always the optimist, Jack had invited hometown friends to the opening. John Knowles, who by this time was director of the Massachusetts General Hospital, remembers it well: "I was anxious to see Jack in the play. The first time I saw him in a movie I loved him, thought he was terribly funny, but I said, 'God almighty! That's no act he's putting on. Lemmon's playing himself and getting paid for it!'

"Jack called to say the play was opening and wanted my wife and me to come. He said he'd leave a couple of tickets at the boxoffice, and I told him we'd attend if he'd come out to the house later for a little party. He agreed. When I got to the boxoffice the tickets were there and they were wonderful seats. The guy behind the window said, 'That'll be forty dollars, please.' Jesus! *

"We saw the play and I thought he was a fantastic actor. I loved the show. It was a very emotional experience. Afterward we went over to my place in Brookline, where about twenty of us, including Rick Humphrey, raised hell until about four in the morning."

Toughing it out, Lemmon, Baker, and the rest went back to work on the play, desperately trying to patch the leaks before opening in New York. "We were like children trying to create a sand castle," laughed Baker, "and by the time we left Boston we had a much better play."

Felicia and a number of Jack's friends, including Fred Jordan, flew in from California for the curtain raiser on Broadway. "After the show," said Jordan, "we all went to Sardi's, which was the thing to do. There were about fourteen of us, including Jack's mother. As the night wore on, it dwindled down to just Jack, me, and Felicia waiting for the morning papers to hit the streets with the reviews.

"About four o'clock we wandered out and got a paper. The review was bad, really depressing. We walked through Shubert Alley and it was empty; nobody there but the three of us. On a wall Jack spotted a large placard with his picture and the words: Face of a Hero. I'll never forget that. He stopped and said, 'Well,

* Lemmon: "A mistake. Obviously a faulty box-office man!"

there it is, after all these years. Jack Lemmon—trace of a *zero.*' "

Reflecting on the disaster fifteen years after the fact, Baker feels the failure of the play "proves that what you start with is very often what you end up with, although we did make some major improvements in it. I remember my assistant Phyllis Rath said that if the New York critics had been forced to go to the Philadelphia opening and then see it again on Broadway, they would have given it the Pulitzer Prize."

For Jack, the play was not a total loss. "It was a lesson for me," he said. "I learned that failure isn't important because even while you're failing you are learning—and you often learn more from your failures than from your successes; I'm convinced of that. *Face of a Hero* didn't harm me professionally, although a lot of people thought it would. The next morning after we opened there were nine reviews, eight of them stinking! Yet when I came out of my hotel room that day, there were three scripts propped against the door from producers who'd heard we'd flopped and figured I would be available soon. *That's* how much I got hurt."

Those working with Jack on the play came away with renewed respect for him. "Eight times a week for three months," said Baker, "Jack had to get up on that dark stage and play that damned thing, knowing that the people were hating it, hating *him*, because he wasn't doing what they paid their money to see. He never tried to get out of it, never called in with 'theatrical sickness.' That man was up there for every performance!

"When it was finally over, I told him at lunch one day that as his old friend and mentor, I felt I'd really done him in on this one, without having a notion in the world that it would turn out the way it had. He was very kind, said it had been one of the most rewarding experiences of his life. That may have been true; most roles were too easy for him, because Lemmon's facility is simply breathtaking. The ghastly experience of doing something unsuitable and failing made him stretch, become a better actor."

Certainly Lemmon became a more perceptive judge of material and its suitability for him. When he was offered William Gibson's fine play *Two for the See-Saw,* Jack read it, then passed it to McCullough for his opinion. "It's brilliant," said Andy, "a tremendous piece of writing. Do it, do it, do it!"

"No," Jack said, "I've decided not to."

"Why, for God's sake?"

"Because it's the girl's play," Jack answered. "It's great, but the crux of it is the girl's story. I don't want to uproot and go back to New York for a play unless I'm excited about the part—which I'm not. The guy in this play is essentially a straight man for the girl."

"I couldn't see his point," said Andy, "and they finally cast Henry Fonda in the role. When they took the play out of town they then discovered it *was* the girl's play. I hadn't seen it; Fonda, one of the great stage and film actors, hadn't spotted it, but Jack did."

Returning to California, Lemmon settled back into his now familiar pattern of life—the supercharged, on-off relationship with Felicia and a moderate but growing affair with the bottle, an attachment dating from his eighteenth year.

He was especially fond of martinis, which his parents had favored. When pressed to turn in a scientific paper for his chemistry class at Harvard, Lemmon had produced a well-investigated fourteen-page piece on the means by which deceitful barkeeps line their pockets by putting olives in martinis. The practice, he discovered, shorted the customer, since the cheap olive took the place of eight percent of the expensive alcohol.

The paper, "Economic Consequences of C_2H_5OH Displacement by Olea europa in a Mean Martini," brought a passing grade from a dispirited instructor who questioned his "oblique sense of values" but applauded his "obviously thorough and ongoing research."

Although Jack drank no more (and controlled it better) than most in his circle, he was a well-known and juicier target for the inevitable rumors. "A guy came up to me at the studio one morning," said McCullough, "and confided that Jack had to be *carried* out of Scandia restaurant the night before. I told him it was a lie because I'd been with Lemmon. Jack had dinner and two drinks and went home early. We both had to work the next day. But that incident is illustrative of the sort of story you'd hear."

In 1961 Jack was again teamed with Kim Novak, this time in Columbia's *The Notorious Landlady* (released in July 1962), an offbeat comedy-drama set in London but filmed in San Francisco and along the picturesque California coast at Carmel. Among those in the cast were Fred Astaire, Maxwell Reed, Estelle Winwood, and Lionel Jeffries. Director was Richard Quine.

The plot of *Notorious Landlady* was so involved, Jack said he never did understand it. "That thing had so many twists and turns I couldn't follow it. A couple of years ago it came on television and I sat through it again and still couldn't get a handle on it. I delivered lines in that picture with absolute conviction—and I haven't the faintest idea to this day what they meant."

It was the first time Lemmon and Astaire had worked together, although Astaire had met Jack before through their mutual friend, Quine. "Both Jack and Dick liked to shoot pool," said Astaire, "and they'd come up to the house for a game once in awhile. I thought Jack was the funniest man I'd ever seen, in private and on the screen. Yet I'd seen him do some really good heavy drama, too. He struck me as being very nervous—probably because he was trying to do so many things. He's talented in so many ways."

The making of *The Notorious Landlady* was not easy for Jack. His father, not feeling well, had checked in at a hospital. The diagnosis was grim: cancer. Treatments were begun, but from the outset Jack knew there was faint hope.

During filming at Carmel, John Lemmon joined his son. "He was pretty sick," said Jack, "but he still had his sense of humor. Quine gave him a small nonspeaking part in the film and he played it like a trouper."

At the close of production on *Notorious Landlady*, Lemmon was approached by 20th Century-Fox to star in *Days of Wine and Roses* with Lee Remick, to be directed by Blake Edwards. "I was having lunch with my agent, Lenny Hirshan," said Jack, "and it was he who suggested *Roses.* I agreed on the spot and within an hour and a half a deal had been set—or so we thought."

After thinking it over, Jack contacted the producer and said he felt the role should go to his friend from The Old Knick, actor Cliff Robertson, who had done a bang-up job with Piper Laurie in the television version of *Days of Wine and Roses.* However, Robertson had not yet achieved the stardom that would come later, and the studio was adamant. If Lemmon didn't want the part, another star would be selected—but not Robertson. Jack accepted.

The picture ended up being produced by Warner Brothers after 20th, slowly sinking on a gilded $40-million barge called *Cleopatra*, demurred. As an alcoholic public relations man, Lemmon was to give what many in the film business believe was his finest performance ever.

In preparation for their roles, Jack and Lee Remick spent weeks attending Alcoholics Anonymous meetings. "I was greeted very warmly," he said, "which made me a little nervous. They looked like they'd been expecting me! I came away with great respect for those people and that organization."

To get a grasp of the other side of alcoholism, Jack spent several evenings visiting the drunk tank and dry-out rooms at Lincoln Heights jail. "It was frightening, watching those poor souls tortured by delirium tremens. As a result of what I saw we changed several scenes. For instance, we used a dry-out table where you are strapped down, rather than having the guy just wake up in a cell."

Days of Wine and Roses was the culmination of Jack's long search for a great dramatic role. Getting into the character was "a delicious kind of hell" and when he had worked his way deep into the part he "endured the suffering of the damned, as actors often do."

John Lemmon, growing steadily weaker, entered Santa Monica Hospital while Jack was shooting *Roses.* Every day at the close of work, Jack would visit his father, finding him always a little worse. It was a demoralizing experience for him; he felt helpless. "Each day," he recalls, "I had to fight to block my mind to it and try to work."

Before the picture was completed the end came for John. Marge Wickersham, who was there for the final night-long vigil, remembers it as a "terrible ordeal. Jack and my husband Wick took turns going into the room every half hour. Felicia was also with us; she wouldn't leave for a moment. She's made of good stuff, that girl. When there's trouble or a crisis, she's always there."

At Jack's request, Cynthia kept young Chris at her beach home. "I didn't want him to know what was going on," said Jack.

John Lemmon was taken home to Maryland for burial in the family plot. Production on the film was stopped while Jack went back for the funeral. Even that sad time was not without the humor that is so much a part of Lemmon's life—and of us all. "Some find it odd," said Jack, "that I could see anything funny about my father's death; yet there often is a bizarre, comedic side to tragedy. There are some who have an aversion to films that are comedy-drama, as was *The Apartment.* They want drama or comedy, but not both, as in real life."

As Jack was to discover, that same public which cannot comprehend tragicomedy can be viciously insensitive. Soon after arriving in Towson, Maryland, the telephone rang; a call for Jack. Unthinkingly, he accepted it. "Are you Jack Lemmon?" asked a simpering girl.

"Yes."

"Listen," she giggled, "I live here. Can I come over and meet you?"

"Are you aware that I am here to attend my father's funeral?" he asked in disbelief.

"Yeah," she said. "By the way, how do you feel about your father dying?" Jack hung up on her and refused to take any more of the calls which came incessantly during his stay.

Scores of relatives and friends had come to Towson to pay their final respects to the loved and respected John Lemmon. Among them was one of Jack's old acquaintances who approached him within an hour after his arrival. "Listen," he said, "why don't you get out of here for a little while instead of standing around and having to talk about your dad? Believe me, that'll get you way down, boy. Now I know where there's a quiet little bar not far from here. Why don't we slip over there and relax with a drink or two? Besides," he added, "I have something I want to talk to you about."

The plan sounded attractive to Lemmon. Father Jack Lyness, who would officiate at John's funeral services, and whom Jack had known and been very close to since childhood, also urged Jack to get away for an hour and try to relax. "We'll handle things," said Father Jack.

Once in the cocktail lounge, the friend ordered martinis for them. "In fact," he said, "make mine a double." When the drinks came, he leaned over conspiratorily and said, "Jack, I have a little business proposition for you. You are going to make a fortune—"

"I am?"

"—and it's only going to cost you five thousand! You are going to be a multimillionaire!" He took a sip of the martini and continued. "I've got all my money—five thousand dollars—tied up in this thing. We need fifteen thousand and I have one other partner. You will get one-third, because fifteen is all we need to get it off the ground. I am now," he said, voice rising a little, "going to show you what it is."

Reaching into his coat pocket he produced a handful of small brown pills. "You will note," said the friend, "that I am now swallowing one of these pills." He washed it down with the martini. "You see that double martini? Well, I want you to know that I am not the world's greatest drinker. Normally, I would be on my ear from that. However, . . . I may have three, for the simple reason that I *can't* get drunk!

"I could sit here all night drinking those mothers—just as long as I have these little pills, I cannot get drunk! This formula," he said, twirling a pill between thumb and forefinger, "is like instant exploding oxygen! And if you are already tiddly, it sobers you up within twenty minutes! Take it before you drink and you can't get drunk. It is flawless; it is foolproof. It is so good we're running into trouble. We can't get an endorsement from the American Medical Association. We're going to need a little more time and a little more money."

"Why is that?" asked Jack, warily.

"Simple. It will seem as if they are endorsing drinking, and I can understand that; but I'm not telling *them*. Anyway," he said confidently, ordering another double martini, "we'll eventually get their endorsement. We're going to market it anyway." Holding up another pill, he said, "Although I don't need it, I'll just pop another one of these little mommas." He downed the pill and began providing details of the amazing invention.

At the end of forty-five minutes and three double martinis, the conversation ended. Jack said, "He was telling me about the marvelous chemist they had, a druggist back home, when he fell off the stool! I had a terrible time getting him into the car, and all the while I was stuffing him in, he was jabbering away, making absolutely no sense, and trying to find his pocket to give me some of the pills. So help me, for the next three months I kept getting letters from him asking why I hadn't ponied up the five thousand to get in on that tremendous opportunity!"

In Towson, Jack stayed with his father's brother, Vernon, owner and operator of the Vernon C. Lemmon Funeral Home. The family residence was situated above the funeral parlor. John Lemmon's body lay in a room below, awaiting the service scheduled for the following morning.

The family retired shortly after dinner. Unable to sleep, Jack decided at about midnight that he wanted to be alone with his father one last time before the funeral. Clad only in his shorts, he padded downstairs, located a back entrance to the room containing the casket and entered, closing the door behind him.

"I don't know how long I was with him," said Jack, "perhaps a minute. I just stood there thinking, remembering him, us. It was beautiful—one of the—a pure, shining moment in my life. I'm terribly glad it happened; I will never forget it. There was communication, somehow. And I touched him. It was a prayer, I suppose, without being a formal one. Then it was over and I felt very complete, in a way that is difficult to explain.

"Turning, I started to leave—and the door wouldn't open! I discovered that it opened from the other side. I began knocking but nobody could hear me. I was downstairs in the back of the building, while they were in front upstairs. There was another door on the opposite side, but that wouldn't open, either. The only way out was through the front entrance out onto the main street.

"I sat down and started to laugh. Only to Lemmon would this happen! I wouldn't dare put such a scene into a movie; they'd cut it out. Nobody would believe it. After half an hour or so I began to get cold, so I did the New York thing all over again. I marched out the door into the street, past two couples, and up the sidewalk to the front door of the house, where Vernon let me in—with a strange look.

"Funny, when I was in there with Pop, trying to get that door open, it seemed to me—I *swear* I could hear a voice from across that dark room, faint but clear: 'Jackass! You—*jackass*!' "

Chapter

XX

". . . the most in-love idiot . . ."
—*Richard Quine*

IN THE SPRING of 1962 Felicia decided to accept some of the many offers she was receiving to work in New York, and moved into a Greenwich Village apartment owned by actress friend, Edie Adams, who was away at the time.

After a few weeks she found herself enjoying the work and the quickened tempo of life in New York. Jack, on the other hand, was miserable. He began to spend a fortune on long-distance calls. More often than not, Felicia would be out when he called. Jack was afraid she was having too good a time without him.

Late in July Jack called to say he would be coming through New York shortly on his way to Paris to appear in Wilder's new film, *Irma La Douce*. He announced flatly that he was going to see her. Felicia told him that she wouldn't be there; she had accepted a part on the Coast in a production that was about to start shooting.

"My plane literally passed his in the air," Felicia said, "and when he hit New York I was in California."

One evening Felicia came home to find that Jack had been calling for hours. "Call him in New York," said Chez. "He sounds desperate."

Felicia placed the call and found Lemmon very depressed and lonely. During the conversation he mentioned the word "marriage."

"Do you know what you just said?" she asked.

"Yeah, I know what I said. That's the reason I've been calling and calling."

The marriage was held August 15 in Paris with *two* best men—Richard Quine and Billy Wilder—because Jack hadn't the heart to narrow it to one of two of his good friends. "The wedding was more than a little confusing," Felicia said. "You sign a book, the marriage book. French ceremonies are public for foreigners, and most of those attending seemed to be members of the press. The mayor presided, this beautiful-looking old man with white hair and blue eyes. Unfortunately, he was cross-eyed and that's where we had trouble.

"It was a very long ceremony. It had been raining, but as soon as the mayor started talking it was like a fairy-tale. A beam of sunlight came into the room right on us. It was incredible. The ceremony was in French and I kept watching Jack to know when to answer 'Oui.' Jack's French was much better than mine. Well, when he asked Jack the question, he didn't answer. I knew what was happening. Because the mayor was cross-eyed, he seemed to be looking at me; but he was really looking at Jack.

"It was very awkward. Finally Richard and Billy began saying 'Jack! Jack!' thinking he'd gone to sleep or something. I was nudging him and he was nudging me, thinking it was my turn. I thought, 'I've heard of being left at the altar, but my man is here, he's just not going to answer!' Finally, he answered. The next day the English papers were very nasty about it—cracks about the rubber-faced comedian doing it again, at his own wedding."

For the wedding car, Quine made available a white Rolls Royce that had been rented for a picture he was directing. "I wanted to get it painted up with the proper phrases and string some tin cans on the bumper," he said, "but the French had never heard of that custom. I finally got through to them, I thought. When I saw what they'd done, I couldn't believe it. That Rolls looked ready for the Rose Parade, and they'd gotten cans used in those French restaurants—big two-gallon jobs."

Lemmon swears that Quine's tin cans nearly got them shot. "It was during the Algerian problem and there were army guys on the streets. When they heard those cans banging, it must have sounded like another revolution getting underway. They raised their guns and got very excited."

The wedding suite was Felicia's room at the Elysee Park Hotel. "It was the most charming hotel," said Felicia. "Jack decided to have a room across the hall until we were married, then move in with me. Impractical as men are, and not realizing about some things, he would often ask me to be ready to go somewhere within half an hour and I would have just come in out of the rain with my hair a mess. I'd say, 'Sure,' and come out with my hair coiffed. He didn't know I was wearing a 'fall' for those occasions."

To train her new husband for the realities of life, Felicia prepared a surprise the morning after their wedding, when Jack had to rise before dawn for an early-morning scene. "I told him I would go along," she said, "and when the wake-up call came and he went into the next room to answer, I sprang from bed, grabbed my fall and put it on the pillow, and then fixed the covers to look like I was still asleep.

"I hid behind some curtains and waited. He came back in half asleep, leaned over the bed, and said, 'Darling—are you sure you want to get up?' and poked the covers. Well, the whole thing fell apart and he screamed and jumped back! I was guilt-stricken because he was so shocked. He looked as though he were going to pass out."

Jack was even more pathetic following the day's shooting, which called for him to immerse himself in the waters of the Seine. Today's environmentally savvy Lemmon was not so well informed in 1962. Nobody had told him the Seine is not much of an improvement over a sewer. A few drops of the river water reached his mouth and for the succeeding two weeks he endured the pain and inconvenience of acute diarrhea—not an affliction recommended for a honeymooner.

Among the attributes of their accommodations at the Elysee Park was a delightful balcony which became central to a misconception that left even the blasé French speechless with admiration. The Lemmons' balcony was separated by a low wall from that of an adjoining suite occupied by friend Gordon Carroll, a producer for Columbia. Each morning Jack would depart for work before daybreak. Rising at a more civilized hour, Felicia would be joined at breakfast on her balcony by Carroll, who, clad in his robe, would vault the wall.

The venerable waiter who delivered breakfast for the first of these coffee klatches needed no script for amplification. This was not Monsieur Lemmon. Yet he had seen this man each evening with Monsieur and Madame Lemmon at dinner. But of course! He was filled with awe. *Ménage à trois* was a French invention, or at least a vast improvement on a crude Roman version—but never on the honeymoon! *C'est magnifique!* From that moment, American prestige was never higher.

Jack and Felicia do not have a marriage—it is more a notarized affair. They do not follow the established ground rules of wedlock or, for that matter, the guidelines of warfare outlined by the Geneva Convention. They refuse to surrender, take each other prisoner, or reach a truce. "We did make a pact in the beginning," said Jack. "We agreed that there would never be a divorce, no matter what." Adds Felicia: "That does not mean one might not leave the other, and then maybe sneak back and murder him—but no divorce!"

Marriage did not end or attenuate their fights. It did sharpen their dialogue, open exciting new areas of conflict, and, Billy Wilder believes, help them develop a kind of shorthand communication that is a considerable time-saver. "In the beginning of their courtship," he said, "it would take a week for them to have a fight and get back together. Now it's like *Reader's Digest*. The beginning, the culmination, and the making up have been reduced to fifteen minutes."

Nothing worthwhile is ever a base for hostilities. Ask them what they fight about and they are stuck for an answer. "Never," said Felicia, "is it anything of consequence because we usually agree on important matters. We argue about inane things and it gets out of hand; out of context, too.

"Jack argues below the belt, you know. He's getting better about that but he doesn't hold with rules. He gets insulting, and I tell him he argues the way men *think* women argue. That starts the fight and it just builds. He tends to get off of the subject and I'll say, 'You're not arguing the same point anymore and you're insulting me; that proves you've lost the argument.' Well, that infuriates him and—it's endless!"

There are times when the structure of a battle calls for one of them to declare that "I cannot stand it anymore, and I am leaving!" Felicia, when the exit is hers, opts for the local movie house. "I love going to the movies alone. The worst part is going home again with your tail between your legs. I always pretend I've just come back for something if I get caught. But he always knows; he asks, 'Did you enjoy the movie?' "

"When I used to be his neighbor," says Richard Quine, "Jack inevitably showed up at my place when they'd had a fight. Usually about three in the morning I would hear this banging on the door. I'd stumble out in my bathrobe and let him in. He would be mumbling to himself and I'd have to sit down and listen to him rave and carry on. It was never more than fifteen minutes before the phone rang. 'Tell her I'm not here,' he'd say.

"Now, I knew that was absurd because she knew exactly where he was, so I would answer and say, 'Yeah, he says to tell you he's not here.' Lemmon would fume about that but really, that's what he wanted. She would come up to my house and they'd fight a little while and then go home together like Romeo and Juliet. They are absolutely the most in-love idiots I've ever known.

"One night after a preview we all went to La Dolce Vita for dinner and they got into a tiff there. When we left, Jack and I were standing outside talking. They brought his car around and Felicia got in behind the wheel and started the motor. When he heard that, Jack started around the front of the car yelling, 'Hey, c'mon now—I'm gonna drive!' Well, she put it in gear and took off. Now Jack's a pretty agile fellow, but she still goddamned near ran over him! I still don't see how he got out of the way."

"Quine has a director's eye," sniffed Felicia. "I never tried to run him over. *Possibly*—he was in my way."

Jack admires Felicia's ability to maintain her pout. "I blow up—pow!—and then it's over. Farfel [his pet name for her], can nurse it, make it hold up until the next day. It gives her an advantage."

Felicia doesn't feel that being an actress married to an actor, a historically dangerous combination, has been a problem. Appearing in films infrequently, Felicia does not push her career, working only when a part comes along that interests her. Good films and worthwhile roles, she points out, are not that plentiful. Agents sometimes call, breathless over a job offer, but most agents' opinions are subject to a ninety percent discount in Hollywood.

Felicia remembers a call from a subaltern at the William Morris Agency. "I've got this terrific part," he said. "It's perfect for you. Starts shooting tomorrow at Four Star."

"I want to read the script," she said.

"There's no time," he said. "Take my word for it, it's great. There's four guys and only one girl."

"I've seen parts like that with three lines," she said. "I want to read it first."

"Please," he pleaded, "do it! You have my word on it. It's a fabulous part—she's the heroess!"

Felicia could not bear the thought of never acting again. ("If you told me that, I'd fall down in a heap on the floor.") She professes to hate watching herself on the screen. "It is to me," she said, "masochism at its worst level. I find it very painful; I like very few things that I have done and I end up thinking, why the hell am I doing anything? And thank God they pay me for it. Jack, on the other hand is very objective about it; he sees himself as a part of it.

"He wasn't always that way. I can remember when he was doing *Some Like It Hot*, he complained all the way through it that he was in the dark all the time. He would say, 'It doesn't matter what I'm doing, no one will see me—the light's never on me.' "

The Lemmons live in Beverly Hills in a large and gracious home reminiscent of a French vineyard estate. Antiques and artifacts abound; the place is spotless and orderly. Nowhere to be found is a hint of the Lemmon whose room was a "claptrap" as a child. Someone described him as the "only movie star who makes his own bed." Felicia says she's yet to see him make one.

"When we were first married he was very orderly," said Felicia. "If everything was symmetrical, stacked neatly, then he was satisfied. Only lately does he seem to understand that just because everything is in its place, it doesn't mean it's clean. I think that must be a male trait; men are more involved with orderliness while women worry about sanitation. Jack will come home and scream if an ashtray is moved three inches. 'Doesn't the maid have an eye?' he'll ask. 'Does she just clean, and not look at what she's done?' She's disturbed the artistic symmetry of his table!"

Jack's passion for organization includes being prompt. Dinner at seven does not mean dinner at seven-fifteen. Jack consults his watch; Felicia consults her calendar. "She has," insists Jack, "not the faintest conception of time. None. It drives me insane! On top of that she's not consistent—not even consistently late, so that you can plot a fix on her. I've tried to compensate, Lord knows, by saying, 'Okay, we're due there at six o'clock. She's going to plan on being ready by six-thirty and she'll miss that by half an hour. So I'll figure on seven, and I relax. No sooner do I have it analyzed than she'll pop downstairs at five-forty-five and say, 'I'm ready!

"Something is always happening to Farfel three hundred and sixty-five days a year. They are legitimate but they happen only to her. Like some people are accident-prone, she's late-prone. If we're only a little late, her purse will pop open and a ring will get lost in the rug. There's twenty minutes."

Felicia views such precise timing as appropriate for railroad switchmen and astronauts, but not for those attending a Hollywood party. "Living with him is like being in the army," she said. "If there's a party at eight, he wants to actually be there at eight, and everyone knows there is no such thing as being late for a Hollywood party. It's okay as long as he's in his robe, but the second he's dressed—I'm late!"

Except for visiting in the homes of a few close friends, the Lemmons mostly duck the social circuit. Two or three times a week they dine out, usually at one of a half-dozen favorite restaurants. The rest of the time they have dinner at home. "We have our dinner on trays in front of the fireplace in the library," said Jack. "It's more comfortable and less trouble than formal dining."

Jack loves to barbecue. At one time he used to prepare a round meat loaf which he called "the revolutionary cannonball"—a title suggested by a friend's description of the delicacy's general texture and aftereffect. A finicky eater in his youth, Lemmon finally learned to eat salads and lobster at age twenty-one. He cannot abide raw fish or meats of any kind. "If I was thrown into a cell with nothing except raw fish and oysters to eat, it would take a year for me to try them."

Properly "brought up," Lemmon is a man of manners who seldom commits a faux pas—but when he does, it is a major production, magnificently ill-timed. Example: an elegant, exclusive dinner party given by Mrs. Edie Goetz, wife of producer William Goetz, in honor of Mr. and Mrs. Gardner Cowles. Guests included Jack and Felicia, Jack and Mary Benny, and Billy and Audrey Wilder.

Dinner was served at one long table in a room decorated with the works of masters. Jack was seated next to the lovely Mrs. Cowles, who wore a floor-length gown of embroidered white silk with a matching duster which, to Lemmon, appeared to have cost "about a hundred thousand dollars."

Among the courses was red cabbage. In trying to help himself, Jack got the serving spoon caught in a mass of the vegetable and took a huge mound onto his plate. He glanced at Mrs. Cowles, who watched silently. "Growing boy!" he said, grinning sheepishly.

Embarrassed now, Jack determined to show that he was as "Continental" as anybody else there and shifted his fork to the left hand. He would eat European-style. Carefully he sliced his meat at the right of the cabbage on his plate. With new confidence he disdained to shift the fork to his right hand, proceeding instead to push the meat toward the fork with his knife, being, he recalls, "ever so la-de-da."

The meat stubbornly resisted capture by the fork and Lemmon gave the knife a sharp thrust. The blade skipped over the meat and contacted the cabbage, scooping it up and dispatching the entire mass with Peléean force and trajectory at the hapless Mrs. Cowles. One part of the clump, separating during flight, vanished up her sleeve; the other impacted on her person at twelve o'clock high and proceeded thence on a southerly gravity course to her lap.

A cryptlike silence gripped the gathering as Jack pondered his next move, perhaps a turning of the knife on himself in the great Oriental tradition. It was Billy Wilder who broke the awful tension. He said: "Whoops."

Suddenly, with inspired nimbleness, Jack wiggled off the hook. Tapping a water glass for attention, he rose. "I demand," he said, with righteous dignity, "a clean dinner partner." His rally carried the day.

Lemmon is a note-keeper. He carries with him a scrap of paper upon which he jots cryptic messages to himself. It is another aspect of the organized man that he is. Oddly, this tidy pattern breaks down in one area. He is a tool-loser. "I am a do-it-yourselfer—badly. Psychologically I think the exasperation that I have within me arises from the fact that I cannot find tools when I want them. I get consumed with rage because somebody puts them where I can't locate even a screwdriver when I need it. The truth is, I hide them from myself so that I will not louse up the job. I know this is true. It's my safety valve; keeps me from leveling the house.

"Mechanical things don't like me. If I hang a picture, it will crash to the floor six months later. If I buy a Rolls Royce, it won't run. Everybody knows a Rolls is supposed to run. Not for me. And buttons; that's the other thing. I can buy a suit from an emperor's tailor and the buttons will fall off before I can get it back to the house."

Not long ago, Lemmon bought a brand new Rolls Royce—and it ran. For fifteen miles. Poking along behind another car, Jack suddenly realized that the man in front had stopped faster than *he* could. The Rolls now has a new front end.

"I don't know what you must have thought," a flustered Jack told the other driver, "when you saw me coming right up on top of you."

"Nothing much," shrugged the fellow, who'd been watching Lemmon's approach in his rear-view mirror, "I just said to myself, 'Well, I guess I'm going to get hit in the ass by Jack Lemmon.' "

Chapter

XXI

". . . the most generous actor in the world."
—*Carol Matthau*

THE PREVIEW OF *Days of Wine and Roses* established an all-time record for Warner Brothers films. Forty couples got up and walked out in the first three-quarters of an hour. Lemmon, still honeymooning in Paris, got the bleak bulletin from Blake Edwards, who called to tell him the studio was less than enchanted, wanted to make revisions, and was grumbling that it might delay release of the picture.

When Jack returned to California he and Edwards met with Warner Brothers executives who had flown in from New York. "It was a long session," said Jack, "and I gave some performance, telling them that Blake and I believed the film had a good chance of some Academy nominations if it could be released at once. They finally gave in, and later we found out what had happened at the preview. Some ding-dong had run newspaper advertisements without mentioning that the picture was a drama. All the ads said was: Jack Lemmon's Newest Movie. Families came, some with children, expecting to see a comedy, and within the first twenty minutes this raving drunk shows up on the screen. That's when they started to bail out."

The Warner Brothers promotion men saved their drum-and-bugle act for a more likely entry, and *Wine and Roses* opened unostentatiously at the Pix Theater on Hollywood Boulevard. "At least," said Jack, "they did renovate the place first, because the building looked like it was under condemnation." Almost at once the film began to pick up business and eventually became such a success that it turned the old movie house into a first-run operation.

Lemmon's awards prophecy was on the nose. *Days of Wine and Roses* was nominated for Academy Awards in five categories: best actor, best actress, best art direction (black and white), best costume design (black and white), and best song (*Days of Wine and Roses*). Lemmon was nominated for the best-actor award; Lee Remick for best actress. In the end, only one Oscar was awarded—for best song.

Jack's stunning performance erased any doubt that here was one of the premier actors of the world, one capable of spanning the broad gulf between blatant farce and heavy drama with grace and consummate skill. The studios were impressed, but not to the degree that it might modify their dedication to the cash flow. Lemmon was a smash as "the guy next door"; that's what the public adored and that's what it would get. Jack's desire to get out of line and do an off-beat part was seen as a malady common among players, a kind of actors' virus, annoying but short-lived and usually not injurious. It was to be a dozen years and as many films before Jack would again be seen in a major dramatic role.

The years following *Days of Wine and Roses* brought theater audiences the Lemmon they knew and loved in a series of highly successful comedies that were occasionally brilliant, sometimes ordinary, and in one case, wretched.

Under the Yum Yum Tree, released in 1963, was an obvious sex romp about a wolfish apartment house owner bent on seducing one of his tenants (Carol Lynley). Richard Quine had been penciled in to direct but became ill and was replaced by David Swift, who also directed Jack's next film, *Good Neighbor Sam*, a fitting companion piece to *Yum Yum* that had Lemmon pretending to be married to a gorgeous neighbor (Romy Schneider) instead of his own wife. The production was maddeningly average despite the best efforts of Swift and an excellent cast that included Edward G. Robinson, Dorothy Provine, Michael Connors, Neil Hamilton, and Joyce Jameson.

Jack was vaguely discontented with both films before he did them and just plain didn't like them after the fact. "That's certainly no reflection on Swift or anyone else," he said. "In *Under the Yum Yum Tree* I was unhappy with myself *and* the character, a lecherous nut who acted more like a leering kid than a grown man. Both pictures were pure fluff puffs, but the public loved them and they just made sacks of money. Each of those pictures cost approximately one million dollars to make and they grossed ten times that amount."

In the belief that hard work, talent, and success deserve rewards—or perhaps fearing that Jack would have an artistic relapse—the studio awarded him ten percent of the profits from his films. At last Jack was a star to the teller as well as the ticket-taker.

In 1965 Jack teamed again with Richard Quine for *How to Murder Your Wife*, a comedy about a successful cartoonist who gets drunk at a friend's stag party and wakes up married to a beautiful Italian girl (Virna Lisi) who pops out of a cake during the evening's festivities. The bride soon gets the mistaken notion that her husband is out to kill her, not understanding that he acts out each adventure of his cartoon hero, Bash Brannigan, to assure himself that the escapade really could happen.

The picture exposed Lemmon to two of the dangers of film production: high-risk physical stunts—and Italian husbands.

"Virna was a very nice girl," said Jack, "but terribly confused because she spoke no English. She would walk around with this lost look, saying, 'Poor Virna, poor Virna.' She had great difficulty pronouncing her English lines, although they had been translated for her. I soon discovered that she was one fine actress. All her lines for the first half of the film were delivered in Italian, which I do not speak; yet I knew what she was saying! By her gestures, the way she spoke, I knew.

"It was marvelous working with her. I only had one sticky moment: when her husband Franco visited the set. He is a big, handsome fellow, a well-to-do contractor in Italy. I don't think he was really thrilled about his lovely wife going off to Hollywood to make a picture with some nut named Lemmon.

"Anyway, he came over to visit her and arrived on the set at the exact moment we were filming the drunken-party scene, and I think we confirmed any preconceived ideas he may have had about Hollywood. Here was a 'drunken' Lemmon making eyes at his signora who has just surfaced from a layer cake, wearing a bikini. Well, all the guys in the scene were whistling and whooping on cue when off on the side of the set I heard this scream of rage.

"Virna spotted him, and she screamed and ran over to him. Well, the Italian temper was flying! She finally got him to go to her dressing room with her and Quine ordered a thirty-minute break while things cooled down. I had nothing to do so I wandered off toward my own dressing room.

"Now the dressing rooms at Paramount are all alike, little bungalows strung together side by side, each with a front and back door. I don't know if things like this happen to everyone, but they sure happen to Lemmon! By accident I walked into the wrong dressing room, and there was Virna. She was stark naked, standing in front of a full-length mirror fussing with her makeup. Four feet away on a couch sat her husband, looking very unhappy. Naturally I came up with a brilliant line—I said, 'I'm sorry . . . excuse me.'

"He looked at me, then at Virna, and then back at me—and then came off that couch bellowing. I shot out the door and took off like a bird. I ran right off the lot, past the gate and up the street, and didn't stop or look back until I whipped in the back door of Nickodel's restaurant. Luckily, Franco wasn't following me. I don't know what he thought, but I wasn't about to stick around to find out. I couldn't explain it was a mistake—he didn't speak English; I didn't speak Italian. Not that he was in a mood to listen.

"This all happened just before noon and it was about three o'clock before we got him soothed down enough so that we could resume work. Later we became friends and I found him to be a charming guy. Felicia and I visited them at their home in Rome, later on."

Against the dictates of good judgment and the insurance company, movie stars sometimes do scenes that expose them to considerable danger and which should be handled only by professional stuntmen. Stars will take the gamble on occasion because, if it works, the scene will be better. Jack took a calculated chance for such a scene in *How to Murder Your Wife;* it nearly cost him his life.

The script called for the cartoonist (Lemmon) to act out one of the escapades planned for Bash Brannigan—a chase down an ancient, rusting, three-story fire escape. Jack was to race down the first flight of steps, grab a vertical brace and, swinging out and around, head down the second set of stairs.

"My double, Tom Anthony, had run through the scene a couple of times," said Jack, "and it went okay. I did it twice on camera and then we decided to get one more. This time, when I grabbed the pipe and swung, the pipe broke. It happened so fast there was no time to think. There was no fear. I went over head-first into space; there was nothing below except concrete and a pile of old bricks. As I plunged downward I caught a glimpse of a small pipe projecting from the building. As I passed it I threw out my arm and hooked it right at the elbow. It stopped my descent and I just swung there like a pendulum in a grandfather clock.

"Oddly, I didn't feel any pain or shock, and as I dangled there I can remember saying quite calmly: 'It's okay, everybody; don't worry, I'm fine.' I looked down to make sure I would miss the bricks and wouldn't break an ankle or something, and then I just dropped to the ground."

A shaken Quine immediately called a one-hour break, at the end of which Lemmon could not return. He had pulled the muscles in his chest, arm, and shoulder and could no longer raise his arms. After treatment and rest he completed the picture, but in acute pain. "It bothered me for well over a year," he said, "and once in a while, when I would forget and lift my arms too fast in the shower, the pain was like being belted in the chest by a fist."

Two days after wrapping up shooting on *How to Murder Your Wife* Jack started to work on *The Great Race* with Tony Curtis, Natalie Wood, Peter Falk, Ross Martin, and Dorothy Provine. Directed by Blake Edwards, the picture was budgeted at six million and cost twice that figure. "Blake got a little carried away," said Jack, "but I must say he stuck to his guns. At one point the studio banned him from the lot for two days to make him shape up, but Warner Brothers gave up because it was costing them even more with everybody sitting around doing nothing. The film has grossed approximately twenty-six million dollars to date and still hasn't broken even. It will have to take in thirty million before it starts to show a profit."

Lemmon found several things about Peter Falk that were both stimulating and disconcerting. Among them was a tendency to ad-lib. "You were never sure," said Jack, "whether you were really doing a scene or not, but it sure as hell kept you on your toes." Another nettling aspect of Falk was his ability to shoot a great game of pool. His envious fellow performers, Lemmon among them, despaired of ever humbling him. Then providence guided a visitor to the set.

Advised that a well-known pool champion had dropped by to watch a movie being made, "Lemmon's losers" soon reached an agreement with the pro and he was introduced to Falk as "Doctor Brown, a Cleveland dentist who shoots a fair game." In a trice a match was set.

"It was lovely," a grinning Jack said. "He destroyed Peter! They played two games and it was the same story both times. Peter would break, run a few balls, and then that was the end of it; Doctor Brown would wipe him out. I think the final scores were one-fifty ten and one-fifty twelve—in favor of Doctor Brown. Falk never said a word; he just stood there kind of sweating, and with his face a little pallid. The only thing moving on him was that one eye, watching the balls drop in. When it was mercifully ended, Falk quietly put his cue away. He'd just been worked over by an artist and he knew it. He said: 'I'll tell ya, Doc, if you fill teeth like you fill them pockets, you're one hell of a dentist.'"

The Great Race was released in 1966 but it was of secondary importance to Jack; Felicia upstaged the picture by giving birth to a beautiful daughter, Courtney Noel, on January 7. She is absolutely the apple of Jack's eye. "He's so crazy about babies it's ridiculous," says Felicia. "He watches baby food commercials on TV the way some men watch football games or X-rated movies. He just drools; he'd have a dozen children if he had his way."

Lemmon was next matched with Walter Matthau for Billy Wilder's *The Fortune Cookie*, a pungent comedy about a Television cameraman who gets knocked down at a football game, then feigns injury to collect damages. For Matthau, a top stage actor for years, it was a break—his first chance at the right role in a major film. He made the most of it, receiving an Oscar (for supporting actor) for his flawless portrait of a shyster lawyer. It gave him a leg up on stardom and made him a close friend to Jack—as close as one is likely to get.

As mentioned previously, Lemmon arouses in his friends a protective instinct, a desire to screen him from pain, evil, even inconvenience. This impulse appears especially strong in Matthau who, when discussing Jack for publication, is courteous, friendly, and nearly opaque. From a man of immense depth and intelligence you extract name, rank, serial number. It is an experience not unlike going to the library for *The History of the Decline and Fall of the Roman Empire* and coming home with the catalog card.

Not so taciturn is Carol Matthau, Walter's pretty and charming wife, who talks candidly of the Lemmon–Matthau relationship and of her own friendship with Felicia, which is as strong as that of the men. Carol says, without equivocation, that Jack "sprung" the film career of her husband.

"When Walter accepted the part Wilder offered him in *The Fortune Cookie,* he did so without having seen the script, which had not been finished. Walter believed he was getting a part in a Lemmon film where Jack would, of course, have the starring role. When the script arrived, Walter discovered that he had a wonderful part compared to Jack, who had to play nearly the entire picture in a brace, confined to a wheel chair."

Lemmon was delighted at the chance to work with Matthau. "I had tremendous respect for him," he said. "He had great talent and we all knew it. Wilder wanted him for *The Seven-Year Itch* back in the fifties but the studio said he was too unknown. So it was a case of just not getting the right part or he would have been a star long before he was. Wilder wrote the part in *Fortune Cookie* especially for Walter; I knew it was *the* part, but I didn't give a damn. I felt my function in that piece was to be the maypole and let the other actors run around me. Anyway, I'll play straight man to him anytime."

The obvious inequality of the parts did disturb Matthau, who called Jack after reading the script. "Why," he asked Lemmon, "are you doing this when you are the star? It's obvious that I have far the better part."

"Don't you think," replied Jack, "that it's about time?"

To the Matthaus, Lemmon is "the most generous actor in the world." Says Carol: "One thinks of actors as being so narcissist; they are frightened and therefore selfish and all those things. But not Jack; he just isn't."

Before *The Fortune Cookie* could be completed Matthau suffered a severe heart attack, which Carol played down as best she could to the studio and to Walter's friends and co-workers. "I lied to everyone," she said. "At first I told them it was indigestion, that we were taking him to the hospital for tests. Then I said it wasn't a serious heart attack and that all he needed was a little rest. I was stalling and trying to find something each day that was good to tell Walter. I bought seven weeks of time that way.

"I would talk to Jack every evening; talk in circles, delaying. I didn't know then what it meant to hold up film productions—the cost and such—or I might not have done what I did. One evening I was talking with Jack and not telling him the truth, and just before I hung up he said: 'Carol, there's something I want you to know. You never have to level with me.'

"That was such a beautiful thing to do at such a terrible time. It let me off the hook; it was the most graceful, generous gesture."

Carol and Felicia are the ultimate in constant companions. They spend such massive blocks of time talking to each other that Billy Wilder calls them "the pixilated sisters." He is baffled at what they find to discuss at such length and with such frequency. "My wife and I," said Wilder, "dropped in at a beach restaurant one evening at eight o'clock to have dinner and were told we had just missed Mrs. Lemmon and Mrs. Matthau. I asked if they had been there for dinner and was told No, they'd been there for lunch. The girls had spent eight hours talking!"

The talking doesn't bother Jack, who often joins them at lunch. "He calls us his 'concubines,' " said Carol. "I'm his Number One concubine and Armen Bagdasarian is his Number Two. I'm his *real* love, you see. Felicia is just a front! Jack is adorable about it all; we take him shopping and to lunch and he sits there very patiently while we chatter."

It may pain the girls to find out that Jack's real loves are golf and fishing. When he can find an available few hours Lemmon heads for the links. Freddie Jordan, one of a handful of Jack's golfing buddies, remembers playing as many as forty-five holes with Lemmon in one day. "Jack has tremendous energy," said Jordan, "and he requires very little sleep. We'd often play one of the public courses. Here's this movie star out there hitting them with all the other folks. He's very 'down home'; there's nothing of the snob about him.

"What impressed me was his indifference to the fact that he sometimes looks like a terrible hacker. I've seen him blow eleven strokes on one green before a national television audience, but never lose that grace. He reminded me of Charlie Chaplin in *The Gold Rush*, eating his shoe, but with great dignity. Jack has learned a lot about the game in the last few years, and he's a good golfer now. If he had more time to play, he could be very good."

Since his teenage years at Wolfboro Jack has been an ardent fisherman. As soon as his son Chris was old enough, Jack took him along on his fishing expeditions. Gordon Stulberg, vice-president of Columbia Pictures and later president of 20th Century-Fox (now in private law practice), was a companion on several fishing trips with Lemmon, and remembers him as "absolutely the most uncomplaining human being in the world. I've never heard him say 'Ouch,' even on a pack-horse trip over a twelve-thousand-foot mountain range in Wyoming. He's an unbelievably equitable guy on an outing.

"On that Wyoming trip we were on the horses all day, getting into camp at about eleven at night. We fell into an exhausted sleep and once something woke me at about four in the morning. It was still dark, just getting that first gray hint of dawn, but Jack was not in his sleeping bag. I got up and stumbled around until I found a path down to the lake. About twenty feet from the water I noticed a red glow up ahead and thought it might be a firefly, but the biggest goddamn firefly you ever saw.

"As my eyes became accustomed to the light I realized it was Lemmon, smoking a cigar and casting a line—fishing for trout! After that eight-hour pack and three hours' sleep, he'd gotten up in the dark and freezing cold, got his tackle together—God knows how—and was out there all alone, fishing. Very much one with himself. It's one of the images of him I will always have."

Even on the wilderness fishing jaunts Jack was not always able to find solitude. On one trip to Henry's Lake, Idaho, the local townspeople found out Lemmon was on hand and came to visit at the ranch house where he and Stulberg were staying. "The first evening we arrived," Stulberg said, "the place was full of people. It was very lively until after midnight."

Stulberg was awakened about two in the morning by a noise and climbed down from the loft where he was sleeping to check it out. He found Jack sitting alone in the kitchen, oiling his reel. "He was like that on every trip," said Stulberg. "He loved to fish so much he could never get to sleep the first night."

At three in the morning, still in the kitchen, they heard a knock on the door. Opening it, Stulberg was confronted by a tall farm boy. "I hated to knock at this hour," the boy apologized, "but I heard that Jack Lemmon was going to be here."

"That's Jack," said Stulberg, pointing to Lemmon.

"I'm sure sorry to bother you, Mr. Lemmon," he said, "but I live in Idaho Falls—that's a hundred miles south of here—and when I heard you were going to be at Henry's Lake I got on my motorbike and took off lickety-split. About halfway up here, going through Saint Anthony's, I hit the brakes and flipped over onto the concrete. I broke my leg, and it's taken this long to get it set at the hospital and have a cast put on. My friend drove me up here in his truck. What I was wondering—I would sure be obliged if you would autograph my cast."

Said Stulberg: "While we sat there with our mouths open, this kid clumped across the room and stuck his leg up on the desk; Jack asked, 'Where do I sign?' We sat up the rest of the night after that."

Jack's relationship with Chris was, to Stulberg, the one disturbing element in their otherwise idyllic trips. "Whatever the compulsion," Stulberg said, "and you never know what makes people tick, Jack had an obsessive feeling about the boy at that time—absolutely obsessive. Chris was spoiled beyond peradventure; yet he had some of Jack in him. There were times when I wanted to *kill* Chris—not because of anything he did to me but because of his demands on Jack or Jack's responsiveness to Chris' whims. It was so apparent on those trips: Chris' slightest wish was Jack's command."

Whatever the reason for Jack's obsequience toward his son, it failed predictably as a tactic (if, indeed, it was intended as such) to deliver Chris from the problems that beset a significant percentage of young people in the sixties. Chris, who readily admits to having been a "spoiled, miserable kid," had sampled marijuana in his early teens and by fifteen was experimenting with LSD. Neither Jack nor Cynthia were aware of his drug use.

After finishing grade school in Santa Monica, where he'd lived with his mother, Chris moved to Florida. Cynthia, who had divorced Cliff Robertson, later remarried—this time to Miami businessman Robert D. McDougal III. It was in Miami that word got to Cynthia about Chris' use of LSD.

"Well," said Chris, "my mother went berserk, thinking I was going crazy, and she called my father who, I must say, handled it brilliantly. He got me on the phone and asked straight out, 'Hey, Chris, have you been taking LSD?' There was a long pause. I couldn't lie because his approach was so honest. I said, 'Well, yeah—kind of.' He said, 'How can you "kind of" take LSD?' and then the fireworks started! We talked for hours and when it was over, we were both in tears. After that I always felt free to talk with him about any problem."

There were to be problems aplenty to talk about. Chris was enrolled in a liberal private high school in beautiful Sedona, Arizona, near Flagstaff. Like his father before him, he was interested in music. His grades were dominated by the fourth and sixth letters of the alphabet.

With a week to go before graduation from the eleventh grade, Chris and several friends were ejected from their dormitory for "being a little sauced and having too good a time." They promptly stole two school buses, bought some beer, and decamped on a tour of Arizona. The carefree caravan was apprehended by police near Jerome, Arizona, and returned to Sedona. Chris was given a failing mark for the eleventh grade, kicked out of school, and told to be off campus by sundown.

Walter Matthau's son David, who also attended the school, reached Jack by telephone and told him what had happened. Chris finally made contact with his father from a pay phone at the Phoenix airport. "I was absolutely scared stiff," he said. "I called collect and when my pop said, 'Okay,' to the charges, that did it. I was in tears before I even said 'Hello.' Dad said, 'Chris, it's okay.' Without me even telling him, he understood that I'd made a very bad judgment and he forgave me. I decided to go back to Mom in Florida, which was a mistake, because I was running away."

Chris' first day at the high school in Coral Gables was a shock to him. "At the school in Arizona," he said, "we were allowed to smoke, call the teachers by their first names, and if we walked into class half an hour late—well, that was okay, because you could still get in a lot of learning in the half-hour that was left.

"When I came to class at Coral Gables I had a cigarette in my hand and I was fifteen minutes late. I went over to the teacher and said, 'Good morning, Betty, my name is Chris Lemmon and I'm looking forward to being in your class.' Well, she sent me straight down the hall to the principal because I'd been smoking, been late, and had addressed her by her first name—all of which were against their rules. Well, I rebelled, and in trying to live by *my* rules I screwed myself up and had to take the twelfth grade over at another high school in Florida."

After studying music for a brief time at the University of Miami, Chris returned to California with vague ideas of a "hippie kind of life where I could be free, have my own pad, and play around with the girls."

Felicia recalls how Chris broached that subject one afternoon at their beach home, when she and Jack had been nudging him about his plans. Chris outlined his idea, which centered around "taking a year off to just relax."

"From what?" exploded Jack, who'd finally reached his limit. He then proceeded to inform his son that he could either enter college, seriously, or get out and take a job, even if it was pumping gas.

"Chris looked stricken at the idea of pumping gas," laughed Felicia, "and he enrolled at college. I was very proud of Jack for putting it to him like that."

Chris, who is now majoring in music at California Institute of the Arts, is thoroughly grateful. "Thank God my dad took another chance on me.

"Boy, for about three weeks there before I decided to go to college, Dad and Felicia really laid into me! I dreaded to see them because I knew what they had to say and I didn't want to hear it. Fortunately for me, I had to hear it sooner or later.

"As far as my relationship with Felicia goes—I love her. I can only think of a couple of times when I didn't love her. At first it bothered me because she was my stepmother and yet acted very much like my real mother. I couldn't understand why she did that, why she cared, and how dare she take such liberties! The other thing that bothered me was that she was right! Every time she threw something in my face she pegged it on the nose. She got me, clean as a whistle! I seldom even had room for argument.

"There have been times when I really didn't like Felicia. I sometimes wished she would go away or that she'd never married my father. On the other hand, he has a happiness with her I don't think he could find with anyone else."

The fishing trips with Chris continue. Each fall Jack and his son fly to Alaska to a favorite spot, where they rendezvous with several of Jack's old friends. "I hope these yearly trips give Chris something of what I felt when I finally toured Europe with my dad," said Jack.

Looking back on it all, Lemmon, like most parents, is not sure that he has been a good father. "I don't keep saying that I should have spent more time with Chris or that I wish I'd done something or other; I don't have concrete regrets. I just don't know how effective my efforts have been. I *think* I've been a pretty good father, but I don't *know*.

"If I had it to do over and knew what I know now, I might be more strict. There's a point at which reasoning and patience seem to have no effect. Chris finally got interested in music, so now he seems to be coming along okay; but for awhile there it was like talking to a wall of granite. Courtney has some of the same traits. I'm telling you, I can talk until I turn blue and it doesn't faze her. I guess I'm just echoing most parents."

There are times when films, like children, will not do what you want them to do, no matter how hard you work at it. *Luv,* taken from a hit play by Murray Schisgal, was released by Columbia in August 1967 and to this day nobody is sure why. *Luv* starred Lemmon with Peter Falk and Elaine May, and according to Stulberg, it was "a disaster from the day it started shooting. For some reason the roles were switched, and Falk was playing the part Jack should have had, thereby killing off any chance the picture might have had for a commercial success."

Jack was worried about the film, but followed the Cagney philosophy of steaming ahead doing the best possible job, even in a losing cause. Andy McCullough, with the detachment of the onlooker, was characteristically blunt. "Junk the movie," he said to Jack. "It's going to be an absolute disaster. Just scrap it. I saw the play, I know the way it has to be handled. The set has no style, Falk is wrong for the part, Elaine is wrong, and you are wrong. Get them to wrap it now and not release it. It's appalling."

Luv became one of those Hollywood oddities—the picture that gets produced despite the fact that everyone agrees it is certain to bomb. It did.

Fortunately, Lemmon, like the World War I pilots, climbed out of the wreck and went right back up again—this time in a story that worked: Neil Simon's Broadway smash, *The Odd Couple*, the tale of two divorced men trying to live together. Teamed with Jack in the film was Walter Matthau, who had starred as Oscar in the stage version. The director was Gene Saks.

The Odd Couple was the reverse of *Luv*. From the beginning it had the smell of success and was finished, without rushing, a week ahead of schedule. "We zipped right through without a problem," said Jack, "and everybody was sick when it was over because we'd been having such a good time making it."

The picture finished, Jack marked time, playing golf and puttering around the house while waiting for the July release of *Odd Couple* and for arrangements to be completed for his next film, *The April Fools*, in which his leading lady would be the French beauty, Catherine Deneuve.

One Sunday morning Jack watched a ball game prior to picking up Millie, who was to spend the day with him and Felicia. After two telephone calls and no answer, Felicia told Jack she was worried about his mother. "I was beginning to get a little edgy myself," he said, "although if she was sleeping, the phone wouldn't wake her. Millie was too deaf."

Frightened now, Jack drove to his mother's apartment house and pounded on her door. No answer. "I ran downstairs," he said, "and borrowed a hammer from the landlady. She didn't have a key because Millie wouldn't give her one either. She was so damned independent!"

With the hammer, Jack smashed the window, yanked out several louvers, and crawled through. Millie was lying on the bed, motionless. "It was obvious—it isn't very pleasant—Millie was gone. She was lying there, all dressed up like she was going to a party. That would be her way.

"I covered her with a blanket and called Farfel and the doctor. It was the end of a free spirit."

The funeral for Millie was held in Towson, Maryland, at the Vernon C. Lemmon Funeral Home. Jack, Felicia, and Richard Carter attended, along with a huge number of her friends and relatives. "It became more like an old-fashioned wake," said Richard. "We were all gathered in the house there and all of a sudden the wine and booze began to flow and the stories were going around. I remember I was over in a corner with Felicia and we commented that this is the way Millie would have wanted it. Boy, would she have loved being there! "

Chapter XXII

"Who the hell is this Chicken Little?"
—*Television executive*

THE PUBLIC LIKES to pigeonhole its actors. Raquel Welch is a sex symbol; John Wayne, a big tough guy; and Lemmon, a likable, tragicomic character heading north in a southbound world. In Jack's case the myth cracked in 1969 when he suddenly turned up on television breathing fire in a hard-nosed documentary called *The Slow Guillotine*—a film that booted the nation headlong into the environmental revolution of the seventies.

This writer had a piece of that action, and the telling of the story necessitates a short detour into first-person narrative.

One miracle of *Guillotine*, other than its effect on those who viewed it, was that it got on television at all. Those engaged in the film business will tell you that any important picture is the product of strife brought to fruition in spite of, rather than because of, those who run the studios.

That pattern held for *Guillotine*, a straight-on, toe-trodding exposé of our crumbling environment. From its inception, the project was buffeted by all the familiar corporate nonsense: petty jealousies, nickel-and-dime intrigue, and the fears generated by any work of truth. The result of such intramural bickering often affects a production either through semantic surgery or cancellation. Through a process of guile, gall, and gamble, *Guillotine* eventually came to the tube without a single word or frame being cut or diluted.

The project began in 1968 when KNBC-TV, the NBC-owned station in Los Angeles, agreed to let me write and produce the documentary. The program department was not thrilled with the idea, inasmuch as I had been the station's publicist and had little experience with documentaries. Besides, the idea was controversial and likely to ruffle feathers in industry and government, the source of profit on one hand and the station license on the other.

As filming progressed and the story came into focus, I foresaw that my leaders might soon become a good deal more nervous. Some data we'd gathered were highly unsettling. For a better feel of the material, I spliced the film and interviews together and screened it. Artsy-craftsy it wasn't; a selection of uninspiring scenes interspersed with two dozen "talking head" interviews, mostly with scientists.

Yet, without sound effects, without music, without narration, what came off the screen was mind-boggling. In separate, unconnected statements, the men of science had reached an unanimous conclusion: ecological disaster was both probable and imminent.

Strong stuff. I had little confidence that a flat-out, take-a-stand documentary could be finessed past the bureaucracy, but the urgency of the story made it worth the trying. Such an approach was a major departure from the standard information film, and new furrows would have to be plowed. I decided to lace the narration with humor, irony, satire. If it worked, the film would be a sensation. If it bombed, it would be no worse than the product the public normally saw.

A special narrator would be required—someone who could command an audience and hold it through some rather grim statistics, who could deliver the message with class and spirit. A movie star would be just the ticket, providing I could find one with courage, a nagging sense of social responsibility—and a willingness to work for scale. My budget allowed $300 for a narrator.

By sheer good luck I happened to interview a man concerned about the unwholesome effect of airborne pollutants on the human respiratory system, a pediatrician named Dr. Arthur Grossman. When I'd finished the interview with Dr. Grossman we sat chatting while the camera crew packed our gear. It was then the doctor dropped a line that was to change the nation's thinking—and my life. "I treat Jack Lemmon's kids," he said casually, "have you talked with him? He's interested in this subject." My pulse jumped. I'd been a Lemmon fan since he'd dazzled me with his performance in *It Should Happen to You.* The perfect narrator! Lemmon could recite the ingredients in a frankfurter and it would sound like a lift from Rostand. I leaned on the Doc and he promised to contact Jack for me.

Two days later I heard from Richard Carter, who'd heard from Felicia, who had gotten the message from Dr. Grossman. Carter said he'd taken the matter up with Jack, who was interested but who would have to see a script first.

I wrote the narration script but took the precaution of drafting a closing monologue that had the unmistakable aftertaste of vanilla. I remember thinking how well the monologue went when you read it to the tune of "Good Ship Lollipop." Still, it would do the trick for my fidgety friends at KNBC. It was soothing. Nobody could turn it down. I would, of course, write the *real* closer later. It was trickery vile, but a necessary evil in the cause of right.

The script was accepted with relief and the next day they were after me to pick one of the local newsmen to do the narration. They were stout fellows, all, and capable at laying on the evening events, but they weren't up to what I had in mind. "No need," I lied, "I've already reached an agreement with Jack Lemmon to narrate." The program executive blanched. "Do you realize," he gasped, "that you have committed this station to a very major star?" Said I: "It is a very major story." I figured it would be, too—if Lemmon ever agreed to do it.

That evening my film editor, Jim Puente, who looked upon me with the respect Indians used to accord the daft, gathered up our bits and pieces of film and interviews and we went to Ryder Sound Studio in Hollywood to show Jack Lemmon our goods.

When we walked in and I saw him sitting there big as life, puffing away on a $1.50 Havana, it hit me suddenly—the awful things I'd done. My bravado all ran out on the floor. What crust to offer a great star a script written by a novice at his kitchen table and dealing with a subject that might well bring the man undeserved grief. What's more, a small voice needled, if he tells you to get lost, your head will roll like a dropped orange tomorrow morning. If there had been a gracious way to do it, I'd have bolted. There wasn't and I didn't.

I handed him the script and mumbled that it didn't have a closer because I hadn't thought of one yet. I sat next to him in sweaty agony while all my great film, which now took on the grainy look of Aunt Agatha's anniversary footage, rolled through the projector. Afterward, Jack silently studied the script, leafing through it with what I thought was undue speed. One of his agents drifted over. He had the look of a man who wanted no part of either a prophet or a loss and he was in danger of getting both. He leaned over and whispered to Jack that his participation in this thing could disparage giant advertisers, and in all likelihood, dry up the source of free cars for use in his movies.

Lemmon pondered that angle for a moment, then shifted the cigar to the corner of his mouth. A small gleam came into his eye. "Fuck 'em!" he said. "Let's do it!"

That was on a Thursday evening. I scheduled Lemmon's narration filming for the following Saturday morning at the California Museum of Science and Industry where Director Bill McCann blocked off a whole wing and allowed us to use the automotive exhibit for a set.

On Friday I stayed all night at KNBC and rewrote the closing monologue, removing vanilla and putting in all the hundred-proof stuff I could manufacture. In the next room, friend and newsman Charles (Chuck) Parker, who'd been standing in for me in the press department while I played producer, was putting the words on cue cards. At dawn I dropped copies of the new ending on the desks of my bosses and split for the museum. By the time anybody got around to reading the "revised" edition, the filming would be over.

Director Gary Markas and I agreed that it would require a good deal more temerity than either of us could work up to consider "directing" Lemmon. I told him to put Jack on his marks and drop the reins. He could run his own race.

Lemmon's first move was to wave off the cue cards Parker was holding for him. "You don't get eye movement that way," he said matter-of-factly. As we watched popeyed in disbelief Jack would glance briefly at the script and then do the scenes from memory, letter for comma. Rarely was more than one take required. I could not believe what I was hearing. Lemmon, with a lifted eyebrow here, a shrugged shoulder there, was taking what I now perceived to be my 29-cent lines and giving me back $2.50 and change. He was showing the rookies how it's done in the big leagues.

Finally, we shot the closing statement. I handed the new pages to Jack, who read them quickly and then glanced up at me with a dropped-eyelid look that said he understood precisely what I was up to. He handed the script back, stepped in front of the camera, and carefully placed the stub of his cigar on a nearby railing. "Okay," he said. "anytime you're ready, C. B."

The final lines he delivered went like this:

Now we have shown you tonight how your resources are being plundered—year after year after year, and this while the government talks of studies to determine "criteria" and "levels of tolerance."

Science keeps trying to devise a tree that will grow in polluted air. Now for crying out loud, why do we have to put up with that? And meanwhile, back at the factory, industry pleads for tolerance because purification equipment costs money.

Well, it's enough!

Now write to your congressman, the governor or the mayor—and don't ask. You *demand* action! Tell them what you saw on this program and if you get a form letter back, send a copy to his political opponent and keep one for yourself. You should know his name on election day.

And if *you* don't take over, pollution *will;* because at this point it looks very much like Chicken Little was right!

There was silence for a moment after he finished. Then something happened that I'd never witnessed before. That tough NBC news crew broke into spontaneous applause. It was over, finished at last. Jack shrugged into his topcoat and as he headed for the door, turned. "It's great stuff guys," he said, "but it'll never get on the air."

Monday morning a program executive stomped into my office, eyes bulging, brandishing a copy of the script. "Who the hell," he stormed, "is this Chicken Little?" I knew then that I'd done the right thing.

The show went on the air in May in the late afternoon slot on Saturday, a time people use for buying prefried chicken and waiting for the movie to come on. It didn't matter. By the time *The Slow Guillotine* was still a couple of minutes away from the closing theme the NBC switchboard in Burbank was jammed, the two operators on duty working feverishly. They handled 138 calls in minutes, while hundreds of others gave up trying to get through. The next morning wires and letters began arriving. *The Slow Guillotine* and Jack Lemmon had scored the mightiest audience impact in KNBC's twenty-year history of broadcasting.

Lemmon's office was swamped with mail—more letters than for any film he'd ever made. They were not the customary fan communiqués. The writers didn't tell him he was cute or ask for an autographed photograph. They applauded his gutsy stand and said they were writing to their elected representatives.

One viewer said he hadn't been to a movie since *The Wizard of Oz* but would pay hard-ticket prices to see every film Lemmon made in the future. Lawyers, doctors, scientists, politicians, teachers, students, housewives—they all wrote, not just to Lemmon and NBC, but to their congressmen. California senator Alan Cranston reported a deluge of mail, usually demanding a personal letter, not the form type.

Those who dared send form letters found such mail showing up in the hands of their political opponent, as suggested in the *Guillotine*. It was tough mail, ordering action, not words. Politicians began to act.

Truth had shocked an apathetic public into action. One woman wrote that she dragged her husband dripping from the shower to exclaim: "Look! Look, honey! They're telling the truth on television!"

Lemmon's narration had been so convincing many viewers believed the whole program had been "extemporaneous." Some complained that the program was too short, that it should have lasted an hour. The film *was* an hour in length; Jack had simply mesmerized his audience.

Critics hailed *Guillotine* and talked of a new Lemmon who "lashed out angrily" at polluters and a do-nothing government in his "fiery" closing statement. It was not a new Lemmon; it was another facet of the same man that nobody really knew.

The film became perhaps the most honored locally-produced program in television history, receiving seven major awards, including two Emmys from the National Academy of TV Arts and Sciences, and the prestigious Alfred I. duPont–Columbia University broadcast journalism award for investigative reporting.

The top brass at NBC refused to put *Guillotine* on the network, though Jack had made it clear he would waive any and all fees. In the long run, it made little difference. The program appeared on all five NBC-owned stations and on many other outlets that requested it.

I resigned from the KNBC staff shortly after finishing the film but continued producing under contract for another year, turning out two more environmental films with Lemmon and one with Eddie Albert. The films enjoyed heavy audience response and won another Emmy. More important, they were a major force in pushing the government to pass new laws and enforce those already on the books.

In the struggle of its birth, *The Slow Guillotine* whipped up little-league animosities that were a long time dying. The big, golden national Emmy won by the show resides in the trophy case in KNBC's lobby. But until 1974, when the *Los Angeles Times* took note of it, the trophy was turned backwards so that none might read the inscription and discover what program had been so honored.

Chapter XXIII

"Jack will take it."
—*Marlon Brando*

AT SOME NEBULOUS POINT during the past decade Jack Lemmon became a superstar. It is an intangible. When an actor tops the summit he isn't notified by registered mail. There's no card for the wallet, no item in *Daily Variety*. He just *knows*, somehow, and so does his public.

Superstardom is a title that puzzles. "There was a time," said Fred Astaire, "when those who became successful were called stars. Then that wasn't enough; they decided some were 'superstars.' I keep wondering when that will not be enough, when we have to have 'super-superstars' and so on."

The title carries with it all the familiar ingredients necessary to turn a nice guy into an insufferable son of a bitch: power, fame, glory, money—and the serious attention of nearly every female he meets. Lemmon watchers saw no discernible change in Jack, whose style of living, disposition, and hat size remained constant.

That a superstar manages to cope with his status is something to marvel about. In his natural habitat (Beverly Hills, Hollywood) it's easier; the public is used to dining at a table next to Walter Matthau or Gregory Peck. You wait for a street light to change and don't think much about the fact that Glenn Ford is standing there waiting too. Get a few miles away and it's something else.

Moving with Lemmon through an airport in a town like Sacramento is an education. He moves quickly, head down, with a slightly bow-legged walk, like a cowboy who spent his early years as a sailor. There is method in his moves; his public reacts when he's ten feet past them, too late to corner him for an autograph. You can hear whispered remarks trailing him, like sound behind a jet: "That's Jack Lemmon!"

When trapped, as he once was at a political function, Jack shows incredible patience. A photographer on the scene watched in awe as Lemmon stood for two hours having his picture taken with back-slapping legislators and giggling secretaries, the only outward sign of stress being quarts of perspiration. "Jesus Christ!" said the photographer. "How the hell does he stand it? He's just as nice as when we started."

Lemmon acknowledges that some people seem to expect movie stars to be different, and "not in a very nice way. Sometimes I'll meet someone and we'll be talking and suddenly they'll say, 'Gee, you're really nice. You act just like you do in the movies.' They're surprised that I don't act like a jerk; they expect actors to be testy, remote, and stuck-up. I don't want them to think that about me, personally, or as a member of my profession."

Lemmon is instantly likable, on screen and off. Just as one senses that it would be safe to pet a collie but not a doberman, you feel that it would be okay to speak to Jack, to seek his autograph. He is approachable, the other side of the coin from a Brando. Walk the street with Marlon and people leave you alone. In a restaurant, he eats in peace. His public keeps its distance.

Because of the closeness between Jack and his fans he is a target for the hustle. Recently, in the cocktail lounge of the Century Plaza Hotel in Los Angeles, he received a note penciled on a cocktail napkin. It was from a mother-daughter hooker team, a brassy, platinum-wigged pair seated ten feet away. Said the note: "Dear Mr. Lemon [*sic*]—My daughter would like to get in the movies. She has great potential.—Her mother."

On another occasion Jack was handed a tab belonging to two women in a booth across the Room. They had told the waitress that "Jack Lemmon is paying for our drinks." Jack, who'd never seen them in his life, paid. It was easier. The girls would brag the next day that Lemmon bought drinks for them the night before, and start one more rumor. If he failed to pay, a scene would be likely, with a juicier rumor to follow.

Jack believes many people have the wrong idea of success. "They equate it with money or fame and they think it ends your problems. It doesn't; they just change. You get new problems just as important and sometimes more so. A few years ago I read a headline: SUCCESSFUL RAILROAD TYCOON KILLS SELF. Well, he wasn't successful or he wouldn't have committed suicide. The guy was miserable, unhappy because he probably hated what he was doing. Because he was a tycoon didn't necessarily mean he was a success. That was somebody else's opinion of him, not his own—and it's your opinion of yourself that really counts.

"A man who sweeps streets," Jack went on, "can be a success *if* he loves what he's doing and does it as well as he possibly can. He doesn't have to be the best, any more than I have to be the best actor.

"There's another thing I hope to God my son learns, and that is that failure is not important. It's fear of failure that we should worry about; that's what keeps us from trying something new, stretching ourselves. We learn from failure."

Lemmon uses Laurence Olivier as the supreme example of how to run a career. "Olivier is not a rich man, but nobody in this profession commands more respect. When he does a Polaroid commercial I applaud, just as I do when Hank Fonda comes on television selling film. I think that's terrific. They do it so they may do the other things—the projects that pay little or nothing.

"Olivier dropped everything to run the National Theater. I'm sure that didn't pay him a fortune, but the money wasn't as important as his work. And Fonda will do a play with no guarantee that he'll make anything out of it. I admire them for that."

Jack's close friends are quick to point out that while he may admire Olivier and Fonda, Lemmon does not follow in their footsteps. "When," asked one, impatiently, "is Jack going to get on with it? I know it's hard to find good parts, but here's one of the great actors of our time doing stuff that doesn't require half of what he's got to give!"

A scan of Lemmon's career over the past few years lends some credence to the complaint. He rose to eminence in a series of pictures that, with a couple of notable exceptions, belong in the little-note-nor-long-remember category.

The April Fools, released by National General in the summer of

1969, couldn't surmount its schizoid nature despite the best efforts of Jack, Catherine Deneuve, and a supporting cast that included Myrna Loy, Charles Boyer, and Peter Lawford. Directed by Stuart Rosenberg, the film yawed, seemingly unsure whether it was to be a comedy or drama. In the end, it became neither.

Neil Simon's trapped-in-Gotham comedy, *The Out of Towners*, offered a classic display of Lemmon timing and an impressive performance by Sandy Dennis, but it suffered from one-note pacing that kept the film from achieving its obvious potential.

Despite a good script based on James Thurber material and top-drawer performances by Lemmon and Barbara Harris, *The War Between Men and Women* (National General, 1972) was not a winner. *Daily Variety* whooped it up as "a first-rate comedy peopled by some delicious humans," and predicted a "wide general response in theatrical release." They were wrong.

Critics were in general agreement that Billy Wilder's comedy *Avanti!* had only one flaw; it was too much of a good thing, needing only to be turned over to a merciless film editor with orders to bring it back thirty minutes shorter. The picture teamed Jack with Juliet Mills in the tale of a Baltimore businessman who falls for the daughter of his late father's mistress.

Among other funny scenes, *Avanti!* offered Lemmon and Mills in the first nude appearance either had made before the camera. The bit in the buff was all for laughs, Jack not being Burt Reynolds and Juliet having been force-fed until she was thirty pounds overweight. One New York critic couldn't resist smirking that Lemmon's bare bottom looked like a "pink prune."

Juliet was more gracious. "If one must do a nude scene, Jack Lemmon is the perfect partner. I think he was more nervous than I, but he was acting funny to help me through it." The scene was shot in the Bay of Naples with the stars perched on a rock swarming with tiny marine animals. "I was more concerned about *them* than my nudity," said Juliet. "Those little beasts kept biting my ass with their nippers. But how could anyone be nervous after Jack Lemmon sits down next to them, naked, and whispers: 'Now's your chance to sneak a peek at stiffy!' "

As do most actors, Lemmon had always wanted to direct a film. His chance came in 1971 with *Kotch*, a picture that would mark Richard Carter's first outing as a producer. Getting the production off the runway had been a two-year ordeal for Richard who, after optioning the Katharine Topkins novel and commissioning John Paxton (*Cross Fire*, *The Wild One*, *On the Beach*) to write the screenplay, ran head-on into the traditional resistance to excellence that permeates the studios.

Studios that backed Frank Sinatra in *The Kissing Bandit* and Vaughn Monroe in *Singing Six-guns* showed no interest in an old man who helps a teenage girl in trouble. Not unless it had a "Lolita" angle to give it a little extra zip. Unimpressed with that idea and as determined as ever, Carter kept plugging.

"I sent a copy of the script to Jack," said Richard, "more as a courtesy than anything else, just to let him know what I was moonlighting on. A couple of weeks later he called, wanting to talk to me about *Kotch*. My first thought was, 'Oh, my God, he wants to play it!' I wondered how the hell we would ever make him look like a seventy-six-year-old guy. At the same time I was thinking of what he could bring to that part with his great sense of timing.

"I went to Jack's house to talk about it. I had a list of names, directors I was thinking about. Jack saw it and asked, 'Can you put me on that list—down about fifteenth from the top?' I just looked at him. I hadn't even thought about Jack as director. I said 'We got a deal.' "

Fredric March was approached to star as the lead character, Joseph P. Kotcher. He accepted and the package was complete. And a very attractive package it was. One by one every studio in town passed on it. "We had a couple of nibbles," said Richard, "but they wanted us to get another star, someone who was a bigger draw at the moment."

Richard reckoned *Kotch* was dead in the water, but the following day Jack received a call from Walter Matthau. "If you haven't cast that part of the old man yet," he said, "would you tell them about me? I'd like to do it."

"I almost fell over," said Jack. "Richard and I had discussed Walter as Kotcher, and even though I felt he could play anything, thought he might be too young for the part, and might not want to do it."

After huddling with Richard and John Paxton Jack called Walter. "Terrific," he said, "we're all set."

"In that case," said Matthau, "I guess I'd better read the script." He had agreed to play Kotcher without having glanced at the screenplay, solely on the recommendation of his wife.

"It was a lucky happening," said Jack, "because Carol had sworn she would never again voice an opinion about something Walter was planning to do. This was because she once advised him he'd be out of his mind to do *The Odd Couple*, which she thought was the worst piece of junk she'd ever read. She didn't ever want to be that wrong again. When she read *Kotch* she was so taken with it she got Walter up at five in the morning to tell him 'You have got to play this part. Call them today.'

"Walter's reaction was simple. He figured if Carol had been that far off about *The Odd Couple*, as bright as she is, it sure wasn't going to happen twice. He knew she'd never dare open her mouth unless she was really convinced this time."

The project was finally underwritten by ABC Pictures for a gaunt budget of $1.6 million. Carter, in keeping with the tenor of the enterprise, formed the Kotch Company, a division of Frugal Films, Ltd., complete with stationery that looked as though it had been gathered up after a longshoremen's picnic.

Friends and relatives were pressed into duty as members of the production crew. Felicia took a part in the film playing the old man's daughter-in-law. Ruth Carter, who had been working on the project with Richard all along, was now on the production staff. "I couldn't believe we were finally going," she said. "I'd been worrying about finding an older man to play Kotcher for so long that when Richard came home and said, 'Walter's going to play it,' I said, 'Walter *Pidgeon*?' "

Lemmon approached directing the way he attacks every project—full bore, burying himself in the task. He did his homework on *Kotch*, selecting his cameraman (Dick Kline) and film editor (Ralph Winters) well in advance of the production start date. "They were nice guys who would work with me, not against me," said Jack, "and tops in their field. Before filming we put in some long sessions and as a result we had no real problems when we started shooting."

Alan ("Boomie") DeWitt, actor, director, and associate in Lemmon's company, was concerned when Jack took the *Kotch* assignment. "With my 'director's ego,' " said Boomie, "I figured I'd better be there when they were shooting. If he needed any help or had any questions, I could hold his hand. From the moment Jack started he was totally secure as a director, as knowledgeable as someone who'd been doing it for twenty years. He never asked me a thing; didn't need to. He knew that camera almost as well as the cameraman. I had been directing for a long time, yet Jack knew things that I didn't."

Directing a picture was a valuable experience for Jack, one that "can help make you a better actor, accentuating the necessity to view the whole rather than your part in it; concentrate on 'what should I do, not what can I do.' There's a big difference."

Carter's stubborn faith in *Kotch* was rewarded when the picture received an ovation at its sneak preview in San Diego. Later, the Academy members would nominate it for the Oscar in four categories: best actor, best sound, best film editing, and best music (Marvin Hamlisch's song, "Life Is What You Make It").

It's not easy for a major film star to break out of the commercial compound and flex his creative muscles by appearing in a stage play (or directing). If he tries he will be descended upon at once by his agents, who come in perspiring haste, armed with a see-through plastic folder of reasons why he cannot commit this heresy. Their reasons for not doing a play have the aesthetic merits of a belch: rehearsals tie up the star for weeks at the pay of a meter-reader. A flop leaves him with empty pockets and a bad press. Should (God forbid!) the play hit big, he's trapped for a minimum run of months which might net a couple of hundred thousand dollars.

This preamble out of the way, the agents loosen their Pucci cravats and lay on the clincher. During the time their client is futzing around with the thesps they could hustle the network biggies for a quickie TV epic and rake in a pile or land their boy a feature flick for a gunnysack of the long green. For talent reps, ten percent of the sack is where it's at. If Michelangelo had signed with a hot agency he could have stopped mucking around with ceiling frescoes and made some heavy bread dashing off soup ads.

Usually the agents prevail; that's what they do best—but not always. Lemmon returned to the stage twice after *Face of a Hero*. In 1969 he scored a triumph in Robert E. Sherwood's *Idiot's Delight*, a story set in the Swiss Alps, where a grab-bag assortment of characters are assembled at a hotel during a time when the world is on the verge of war. First staged in 1936 when Hitler was strutting his intentions, Sherwood's work was awarded the Pulitzer Prize.

The play, which starred Rosemary Harris with Jack, was mounted impressively at the Ahmanson Theater in Los Angeles and was warmly applauded by reviewers. The loudest raves went to Lemmon for his superb portrayal of Harry Van, the piano-playing song-and-dance man. Without his standout performance, some reported, the thirties' work might not have held up so well.

In 1974 the Mark Taper Forum in Los Angeles was the site of a glittering revival of Sean O'Casey's famed tragicomedy *Juno and the Paycock.* Starring in the play, which had been originally staged at the Abbey Theatre in 1924, were Walter Matthau, Lemmon, and Maureen Stapleton. The story of poverty-ridden Irish tenement dwellers helplessly buffeted by a senseless civil war, was loaded with such Hollywood star power that critics lay in wait to clobber it as a "vanity production."

At the helm was veteran film director George Seaton. Matthau was cast as "Captain" Jack Boyle, the vain peacock (paycock) of a husband to long-suffering, down-to-earth Juno (Stapleton). Lemmon appeared as Joxer Daly, Boyle's conniving, mooching pub pal.

The play generated interesting, paradoxical reviews. Some critics passed it off as an ego trip for show-biz celebrities and an affront to O'Casey's good name. Most admitted with relief that *Juno* had been superbly handled by stars doing their level best to put on stage what O'Casey had written. A couple of "critics" verified a suspicion long held by the criticized by piecing together their reviews from the program notes, having obviously never heard of either the play *or* O'Casey.

With the release of *Save the Tiger* by Paramount in 1973 it was obvious that Lemmon had at last found a part with the stuff from which Oscars are made. The off-beat script, about a dress manufacturer who can't reconcile modern business "ethics" with the idealism of his youth, was the first for writer Steve Shagan, who'd previously turned out Tarzan episodes for television. The theme intrigued Jack. He saw in the protagonist, Harry, a dramatic role of substance; a ticket to the roller coaster instead of the fun house.

The studios kept to their pattern, wanting no part of a downbeat, message picture. Paramount finally agreed to underwrite the film, but at a one-million-dollar budget, not much above that allocated for a television movie. In order that the picture could be made at all, Jack waived his fee, working instead for minimum scale: $165 per week, plus a percentage of the gross. The film was planned and shot in sequence on location in Los Angeles by director John Avildsen.

Even as *Tiger* was being filmed there was talk that Lemmon might at last be in line for his long-overdue Oscar for "best actor." When the picture was released, critics lined up on Jack's side, with columnist Joyce Haber leading the pack by conducting screenings for Academy members at her home. Jack was, in due course, nominated.

As Oscar night approached, Las Vegas odds-makers had Lemmon listed as a strong favorite to take the award. Jack told close friends that he believed his chances looked good. But they had looked good three times before. Among the nominees for "best actor" was the winner from the year before, Marlon Brando, who had followed his *Godfather* stint with a scorching performance in *Last Tango in Paris.*

Two days prior to the awards ceremony, this writer whiled away the afternoon with Marlon in the bedroom of his Mulholland Drive home in Beverly Hills, where the great actor was holed up with a case of the sniffles. The talk ranged from the best methods for constructing mud fences to problems of the environment, to the Oscars. Did Marlon think he had a good shot at one this time?

"No," he said, "I think Jack will take it." He yawned and stretched, then added with a lazy grin: "Anyway, they're still mad at me from last year."

Jack was no longer so confident. He was the talk of the town now for quite another performance, his "speech" at a gala affair honoring James Cagney. Lemmon, who was due in surgery for correction of a hernia the next morning, had been taking pills prescribed by his doctor and foolishly sipping on wine at the same time. By the time he stepped before the microphone to pay tribute to his old C.O. from the U.S.S. *Reluctant*, his carefully thought-out statement had eluded him. Jack rambled, stalled, rambled some more—unable to make sense and unwilling to give up.

Suddenly, up from the audience popped writer-director Sam Peckinpah to yell at Jack to get the hell off the stage and sit down. Peckinpah, who'd "had a few" himself, was ejected from the hall and Lemmon returned to his table and a boiling-mad Felicia.

"I was very upset," she said, "because he'd had several glasses of wine on top of the medicine. He was a mess. When he got to the table he leaned over and whispered, 'How was I?' and I said, 'Terrible, but we'll talk about it later.'

"Well, I'd said the wrong thing because he knew he was terrible. He began to get mad and at one point I just got up, took a half-full glass of water, and poured it on his head. He said later that he saw pictures of it with captions that said I'd *flung* it at him. As I remember, I *tipped* it with great sophistication. Either way it was deserved."

Richard Quine credits Peckinpah with "saving Jack's ass, because Sam was so much worse, everybody tended to forget about Lemmon.

"When I got to Jack's table the place had pretty well emptied. There were a lot of reporters and photographers around. I sat down and Jack laughingly buried his head on my shoulder like a little boy. Later, that picture appeared in a London paper.

"The next morning Jack called me and asked: 'Rich, did I screw it up last night?' I said, 'Buddy, you came as close as you're ever going to get.' " (While in the hospital Jack received a bundle of roses with a note of apology from Peckinpah. Jack answered the note and a lively correspondence ensued. The men, who never had met, became friends.)

Lemmon was up early on the big day. This writer called him at ten o'clock to wish him luck. "Hi ya, Slick!" he said, cheerily. "I was gonna call you as soon as I'd finished throwing up!" He was in the company of the *Los Angeles Times*' Chuck Powers, who took note of the line for his day-with-the-Oscar-favorite feature.

Fidgety, Jack made, and then cancelled, a golf date. He had lunch at The Daisy, where one of the menu items (sliced apples and cheese) is named after him. Carter, Powers, and supporting-actor nominee Jason Miller (*The Exorcist*) joined him. "We all had a little wine," said Carter, "except Jack. He had an iced coffee." Following lunch, Jack got a haircut he didn't need, just to kill time.

As the ceremonies that evening got underway the butterflies ceased their pylon-racing in Lemmon's stomach. Surrounded by the pomp and glamor of Hollywood's big event, he was remembering other times, when landing a no-salary job at The Old Knick had been almost as important as an Oscar nomination. He wished John and Millie could be with him.

Then he stopped remembering. Liza Minnelli, last year's winner as "best actress," was opening an envelope. A thousand years or so later she said the long-awaited words: "Jack Lemmon—for *Save the Tiger!*" It was magic time. Cohn's "Harvard man" had become the first actor in history to win an Oscar in both supporting- and best-actor categories.

His acceptance speech was simple and brief. He noted that some found fault with the awards system. He conceded that there were imperfections, but made it clear that as far as Lemmon was concerned the Oscar was "one hell of an honor" and he was thrilled to accept it. His thrill was shared by countless fans who felt it was recognition long past due.

When the numbing joy of victory subsided, Jack had gained a

new perspective on awards. "I began to understand that no trophy is more important than the body acceptance by the public for what you've done. Nothing can replace that moment when someone stops, not to say, 'Gee, you're Jack Lemmon,' but to tell you of the pleasure your work has brought them and their family. Another very meaningful thing is when a colleague you respect comments on your work. I will forever remember Alec Guinness slipping a letter to me at a party, shortly after my not getting the Oscar for *Some Like It Hot*, with instructions to read it later. When I opened it at home, I found four handwritten pages that talked of awards and what they mean, along with his thoughts on the work I'd done. I sat there and cried."

Jack feels, as do many actors, that the Academy Awards system can never be entirely equitable: "Nomination is one thing—and I think we should look upon that as an honor equal to winning the Oscar—but then we have to choose one of five nominees as the best. That's impossible, really, because each part offers different problems. The only sure way to know who deserved an award would be to see all five in the same role.

"The finest acting," said Jack, "looks the simplest. A great actor can make a tough part look easy—and be overlooked because of it. And it's hard to know where the director left off and the actor took over in a scene; it's such a combination of efforts.

"I'm sure anyone who has ever received the Oscar will tell you there were many others who also deserved to, but didn't. For example, Eddie Albert was simply brilliant in *The Heartbreak Kid.* I don't see how anyone could have handled that role better. He was nominated, but didn't walk away with the statue.

"Sometimes an actor or actress can give a standout performance and the Oscar will go to someone else for an equally fine job, but perhaps in a film that got more recognition."

During 1974 Jack was approached about directing the film version of Jason Miller's prize-winning play, *That Championship Season.* The project never came to fruition but it did provide a memorable moment during a luncheon meeting between Lemmon and Miller at the Hideaway Restaurant in the Beverly Wilshire Hotel.

Miller had just asked Jack how he thought James Cagney would be in the role of the coach when an earthquake struck, rattling and bouncing the bottles and glasses on their table. It was Miller's first experience with this California phenomenon and he reacted by clutching the table and waiting it out, white-faced and silent.

Jack saw in the situation the perfect set-up for a one-liner, and when the room stopped moving he delivered it. "*That*," he told the shaken Miller, "is how I think James Cagney would be!"

Following *Save the Tiger* Lemmon appeared with Walter Matthau in another Billy Wilder production, *The Front Page*, an adaptation of Ben Hecht and Charles MacArthur's classic comedy about newspaper reporters in Chicago during the 1920s. The film turned out not so classic, with critical reaction a mixed bag of huzzahs and ho-hums.

Jack at last got the opportunity to work with his favorite actress, Anne Bancroft, in Neil Simon's *The Prisoner of Second Avenue*, under director Melvin Frank. It had long been Frank's desire to work with the pair. "I'd been trying to do a film with Lemmon for years," he said, "but for one reason or another we never got together. I think Jack is one of the two great actors I've seen develop in my years in the business; the other is Brando. And I have always admired Bancroft; she's a great actress."

Anne Bancroft found Lemmon "just the nicest man I've ever worked with; nice to a point where he's *crazy*. I'll tell you about an incident that explains what I mean. We had a scene in *Prisoner* where he had to carry a shovel in—a very close two-shot favoring me. I played that scene with tears in my eyes because Jack had accidentally hit me in the shin with that shovel. The director saw something was wrong so he stopped everything. I had a big bump on my leg, but it was Friday and over the weekend I fixed it up. When we came back on Monday the first scene was a retake of the shovel thing.

"Well," she continued, "Jack brought the shovel in and I anticipated getting hit again. He is so full of energy, you're sure he's not noticing; but he never touched me. The take was fine, but Jack limped away. To avoid hurting me, he had cut himself. He was bleeding and we had to bandage his leg; his wound was much worse than mine. He is so kind he hurt himself rather than injure someone else. That's a little crazy! It's the *nicest* crazy I know, and I know a lot of crazy people."

Critical reactions to *Prisoner* varied but were polarized, either adoring or hostile. *The New Yorker*'s Pauline Kael mounted a scathing attack, announcing that "a Jack Lemmon picture has become something to dread." She nailed Simon's script as "degradation humor" and "in context, mercilessly unfunny." Mel Frank got his lumps for directing in "his usual sagging, fifties style . . ." Only Bancroft escaped her wrath. Kael's critique triggered a rare (and perhaps significant) display of anger in Lemmon, who feels there are two unforgivable sins a "critic" can commit. One is to criticize an actor, writer, or director on a personal level. The other is to overlook the vast difference between forming an opinion and being opinionated.

"Actually," said Jack, "I guess I'm upset at myself for even being bothered. Maybe Frederick the Great had the right approach when he said, 'I go through my appointed daily stage, and I care not for the curs who bark at me along the road.'

"First of all, in judging a film it's never easy to determine who should get credit or be faulted, because a movie represents the combined efforts of so many people. The problem is compounded because so few critics have any firsthand knowledge of the film-making process. Some argue that it isn't necessary; that a critic should just walk into a theater like the average person and form an opinion. That's false. The critic is supposed to be the expert; he places himself above the public by advising that public on the quality of films.

"Good critics," Jack continued, "are often tough, but they are demanding because they're trying to improve the quality of the product, and I'm all for that. Still, I don't think all the critics combined can kill a film if the public wants to see it. Word of mouth remains the key to success for any picture."

Lemmon believes critics deserve to be commended for their role in boosting good films that have little money behind them. "By pounding away, they can push these pictures over the top, and they've done this time and again.

"There are many good critics across the country—far too many to list; but I will say that on the West Coast I don't think anyone can beat Charles Champlin of the *Los Angeles Times*. I've gotten some pretty bad reviews along with the good ones from Chuck, but he's always been honest and constructive, as has Arthur Knight, another fine critic. I get the feeling these men love film, which is the most important necessity. They've remained close to the motion picture business for years and they've learned their craft."

At least one member of the Lemmon family has had no trouble at all with the critics. Nine-year-old Courtney made her show business debut in 1974 as the voice of Virginia for ABC's animated special for children, "Yes, Virginia, There Is a Santa Claus." The show received an Emmy. "Forty-eight years it took me," said her proud papa, "and she wins the first time out!"

The Emmy awards telecast was still on when Courtney placed a call to classmate Jackie Falk (daughter of Peter Falk, who moments earlier had received an Emmy for his work in "Columbo").

Jack, who eavesdropped, related Courtney's end of the conversation:

"Hello—Jackie? [Pause.] He did?—me too! [Pause.] So whatcha doin'?"

So much for all that Hollywood jazz.

Chapter XXIV

"Today is not yesterday."
—*Thomas Carlyle*

IT IS ALTOGETHER POSSIBLE that this, the final chapter, should be the first, for the Lemmon of yesterday is fast becoming unrecognizable in the Lemmon of today.

Jack passed the half-century mark of his life on February 8, 1975. Shortly thereafter he abruptly stopped drinking—a decision that has the look of permanency. He will tell you that this landmark event had to do with his health; that alcohol was beginning to have physical effects, such as lowering his energy level. It is more than that; much more. The *old* Lemmon drank.

Those close to Jack can perceive the changes; bits and pieces of the old flaking away like the ablative material of a rocket nose cone under the heat of reentry. Deep within Lemmon a wrenching, soul-searing metamorphosis appears to be underway. What it portends no one, probably not even Jack, can say.

There are signs. The man used to "submarine" a lot. That's what Richard and Ruth Carter called it. You'd be talking with Jack and suddenly realize that he was no longer with you. He was looking at you, but his mind had risen and, hand-in-hand with his soul, had gone off to a better place where they could be alone.

Jack doesn't submarine anymore.

Victoria Brooks, Jack's secretary, thinks he has "the saddest eyes I've ever seen." It is an apt observation and one made many times by many people. A pervasive sadness has always been there in Lemmon (see childhood photo) and more than that—agony. The face can be comic but the eyes seldom stop playing tragedy.

That veil of misery shows signs of lifting at last. This writer's wife, Veda, always found Jack's nervousness catching. "Now I don't feel that," she says. "He's calmer and there's a deeper sincerity, even when he frowns. Somehow he seems more serious—but as dear and sweet as ever."

Superstars are not just people, they are almost institutions. When they make decisions or undergo change, the waves spread and touch many. There are people and businesses who will find the new Lemmon unsettling. There was a time when Jack was a patsy for the panhandlers, corporate or individual. Not so, these days.

Sorting through the usual weekly pile of demands for his time and money the other day, he came across a request that he fly to New York and help anoint some functionary at a testimonial dinner. The letter, perhaps from past experience, had the tone of a demand. "You will be expected to speak for twenty minutes," it informed him.

"That," snapped Lemmon, "is a bunch of crap! " He ripped the letter in two, crumpled it in a ball, and sailed it toward the wastebasket. A few months earlier he might have caught the plane.

Even now the word has gone forth about this unfamiliar being that used to be "good old Jack." The inevitable division is beginning among his friends and associates. On the one side is a delighted cheering section; on the other, the puzzled and frightened. At a recent meeting an old friend commented over cocktails that he "liked the old Lemmon better, my drinking buddy."

Jack has surveyed his future and decided he wants to do what he's always done, only better. Better. That could be interesting. It is not difficult to imagine a scenario where the agents and studio moguls have gathered once again to chart Jack's destiny and select which lucrative laugher he is to film next. The decision may be a painful one for them. Lemmon might practice a little proctology with their program. One thing does seem certain. Molding the man will not be so easy in the future. There's more steel in the alloy.

Jack's reformation appears to be very much one of his own making. Perhaps there was no other way. Billy Wilder sensed that it would be so, as he points up in a story he finds analogous to Lemmon. It is a true story about the greatest clown of Europe, who visited a psychiatrist because he had been in a deep depression for a long time.

After several sessions the psychiatrist said: "Your problem is that you have been living too much within yourself. You must go out, see the other side of life; not just that gray little world you've built for yourself. Enjoy yourself! Listen to music. Go see Grok!"

Said the great clown, sadly: "Doctor, I *am* Grok."

This writer had concocted an impressive closer for this book. It was a suggestion for Jack's epitaph. Along with the words about his acting and good deeds would have been the mention that here was a man who made it to the top in the most competitive business in the world—and never stepped on anything but a stage to get there.

That line wouldn't work now; it falls short. But perhaps a better one is in the wings. They might be able to set down that he finally saved the tiger.

Index